ANALYSING POWER I ̗ JE

Analysing Power in Language introduces students to a range of analytical techniques for the critical study of texts. Each section of the book provides an in-depth presentation of a different method of analysis with worked examples and texts for students to analyse and discuss. Answer keys are also provided for the analyses.

Taking text analysis as the first step in discourse analysis, *Analysing Power in Language*:

- explores the relationship between the goals of discourse, the social positions of the speakers, the contexts in which they are produced, the audience for which they are intended and the language features chosen
- presents a powerful approach to text analysis that reveals the links between language usage and a community's assumptions, convictions, and understandings
- identifies a range of power types, appropriate to different contexts
- explains and illustrates a social approach to text analysis with important linguistic concepts woven in seamlessly with examples of discourse
- offers concrete guidance in text and discourse analysis with carefully crafted examples and fully illustrated explanations.

Incisive and thought-provoking yet also accessible, *Analysing Power in Language* is essential reading for advanced undergraduate, postgraduate and research students studying discourse analysis.

Tom Bartlett is Senior Lecturer in Language and Communication at Cardiff University, UK.

Praise for this book

'A rare gem indeed: an accessible introduction to Systemic Functional Linguistics, built on solid theoretical foundations, and yet giving hands-on advice on practical text analysis. Written in a clear and engaging style, the book builds a bridge from text to discourse, and shows readers how to cross it.'

Gerlinde Mautner, *Vienna University of Economics and Business, Austria*

'Tom Bartlett's book is a terrific new "how-to" guide for apprentice discourse analysts. While ambitious in its coverage of linguistic concepts, it remains grounded through diverse and useful exercises for students needing to move from text analysis to the interpretation of the "magical properties" of language in social context.'

Annabelle Lukin, *Macquarie University, Australia*

'Through an exploration of the contexts and wordings of the speeches of contemporary political, religious and cultural figures, and others, Bartlett presents an accessible framework for text analysis that leads to a critical analysis of discourses of power. His explanations and exercises are engaging and thought-provoking with helpful suggestions for exploring the background of the texts analysed and further reading.'

Sheena Gardner, *Coventry University, UK*

'This book is an engaging, comprehensive and much-needed bridge between the analysis of the specific language used in texts and an understanding of their effects within the historical, cultural and social contexts in which they were produced. Tom Bartlett uses his well-practiced expertise in analysing text as "gateways" to discourse to breathe life into linguistic analysis, drawing on many examples of real texts and incorporating exercises to scaffold readers into in-depth methods of text and discourse analysis. It is certain to become a treasured textbook for anyone teaching courses in rhetoric, discourse analysis, language studies or communication, and a highly welcome read for those wanting a greater understanding of the relationship between language and power.'

Anne McCabe, *Saint Louis University, Madrid, Spain*

ANALYSING POWER IN LANGUAGE

A practical guide

Tom Bartlett

Routledge
Taylor & Francis Group

LONDON AND NEW YORK

First published 2014
by Routledge
2 Park Square, Milton Park, Abingdon, Oxon OX14 4RN

and by Routledge
711 Third Avenue, New York, NY 10017

Routledge is an imprint of the Taylor & Francis Group, an informa business

British Library Cataloguing in Publication Data
A catalogue record for this book is available from the British Library

Library of Congress Cataloguing in Publication Data
Bartlett, Tom, 1962-
    Analysing power in language : a practical guide / Tom Bartlett.
        pages cm.
    1. Discourse analysis—Social aspects. 2. Power (Social sciences) 3. Sociolinguistics. I. Title.
    P302.84.B37 2014
    401'.41—dc23
    2013025389

ISBN: 978–0–415–66631–2 (hbk)
ISBN: 978–0–415–66630–5 (pbk)
ISBN: 978–1–315–85193–8 (ebk)

Typeset in Bembo
by Swales & Willis Ltd, Exeter, Devon

For Mary, Sadie and Jamie
And the random fits o' daffin' –
The finest of discourse types.

CONTENTS

LISTS OF FIGURES AND TABLES

Figures

Tables

ACKNOWLEDGMENTS

Martin Luther King Jr's *I have a Dream* speech is copyright material and is reprinted by arrangement with The Heirs to the Estate of Martin Luther King Jr., c/o Writers House as agent for the proprietor New York, NY. ©1963 Dr Martin Luther King Jr. ©1991 Coretta Scott King

Lord Coe's address to the IOC is reprinted by arrangement with the British Olympic Association and Lord Coe.

The extracts from Cardiff University regulations and the Head of School's Welcome are copyright of Cardiff University and are reprinted with permission of Cardiff University and the Head of the School of English, Communication and Philosophy.

All other texts and extracts are either the author's own data or in the public domain.

Many thanks to former students Millie Davies and Abby Jones, who brought the Chavs and Lord Coe texts to my attention.

And, lastly, many thanks to the communities of the North Rupununi Savannahs of Guyana and, in particular, to Uncle Henry, Walter, Nicholas, Gordon and Sara (as they are called in this book).

TRANSCRIPTION CONVENTIONS

W: Now [what X was saying **Eu**: [You gotta	overlapping speech
=	no perceptible pause between words
(xxx)	unclear speech (roughly one x per syllable)
(shortfall here)	best guess
(?how it is)	more tentative guess
[…]	data omitted
((noise of flipchart))	transcriber's comment
Eu: This what we don't understand. *<<rustling of papers>>*	action contemporaneous with stretch of speech
<u>far</u>	greater stress than expected
…/(p)	short pause in speech (roughly, up to 2s)
(11s)	timed pause in speech
↑	higher than expected pitch
↓	lower than expected pitch
VANESSA	louder than normal
°here and leave this one°	quieter than normal
°°either way°°	far quieter than normal
<that is why the action>	faster than normal
>the current fix <	slower than normal
lo:gging	lengthening of vowel
hello	said laughing

A NOTE ON THE PRESENTATION OF TEXTS

Some of the texts in this book are presented just as they come without being divided into clauses or other units. When referring to particular parts of these texts I shall therefore talk about "line numbers".

However, where necessary or useful I have divided texts into clauses. This means that main clauses, subordinate clauses and finite projected clauses are on separate lines and have their own numbers. When referring to particular parts of these texts I shall therefore talk about "clause numbers".

When individual clauses are taken from a text in order to illustrate a grammatical point I will number them in sequence with other examples. The only exception to this is the Martin Luther King text where the repeated analysis of a couple of stretches of text would have made it confusing if I had numbered them differently each time.

1

TEXTS AS GATEWAYS TO DISCOURSE ANALYSIS

1.1 Introduction

Language – squiggles on paper or disturbances of the airwaves – can move us, a remarkable idea captured by the Portuguese writer José Saramago in his novel *Blindness*:

> *The doctor's wife has nerves of steel, and yet the doctor's wife is reduced to tears because of a personal pronoun, an adverb, a verb, an adjective, mere grammatical categories …*

The idea that grammar has such magical properties may come as a surprise to some, but it is an idea that has been around for a long time. Historically, the word "glamour" is a variant of the word "grammar", with the current meaning reallocating the magical powers of grammar to the enchantment that comes with style and physical beauty. Times and tastes may change, but one goal of this book is to convince you that grammar is still magical and glamorous!

As well as casting emotive spells, language can be used to achieve more concrete goals, as when a priest or government official pronounces a couple man and wife, or when a judge sentences a prisoner to ten years' hard labour. The power to reduce someone to tears and the power to sentence someone to jail are both pretty impressive attributes – but can we say, in either case, that the words used are in themselves *powerful*? Would they have achieved the same effect if they had been uttered by someone else? Or to someone else? Or in a different setting?

Utterances such as "I pronounce you man and wife" were labelled *performatives* by the philosopher J. L. Austin (1962) because the very act of saying the words performs the social act they describe – but only under certain conditions. Austin called these *felicity conditions*, in contrast to the *truth conditions* that determine if an utterance can be considered to be factually *correct* or not. Austin argued that it might be possible to determine the factual truth of utterances such as "The King of France is Bald" (though philosophers found this a trickier problem than you might have imagined!), but that it does not make sense to say that "I pronounce you man and wife" is either true or false. Rather, it makes sense to discuss the conditions necessary in order for this utterance to perform the act the speaker claims to be performing. In this instance, the speaker must have the officially sanctioned *authority* (either religious or secular) to marry couples and the couple must both want and be eligible to be married (to each other!). A more complicated case would be that of promises: does saying "I promise to do it" count as a promise, with no conditions attached? What if the speaker had their fingers crossed behind their back? What if they are not in a position to carry out the promise? And what if the hearer doesn't want the action to be carried out? And what about the exact *wording*: what if they had just said "I will do that"? Does that count as a promise? Children seem to have different rules from their parents on this point.

And what of the emotive power of language? Would everyone have been moved in the same way by the words heard by Saramago's doctor's wife? Well, for a start, they would have to speak the same language (though the sound of language can often be enough to arouse emotions, as with Jamie Lee Curtis's amorous response to John Cleese's Russian in *A Fish Called Wanda*). This may seem a bit obvious, so consider instead the question of the appropriate *style* of language and, for example, the different effect of colloquial or official language in getting an audience on your side. Which one is more effective will depend on a variety of factors and, in particular, the nature of the *audience*. The point I am making here is that *all* language use is performative (Baumann and Briggs 1990), and that the effect of the performance does not reside in the language used alone but is the result of a range of social and cultural factors *with which the language used makes connections*. In other words, it is perhaps better to think of power as being realised *through* language rather than as residing *in* language. This means that we need to look at more than language itself in order to discuss its powerful effects, to consider what it is that is being performed and whether the performance is successful (powerful) or not. However, as linguists our starting point is the language used, and in this book I will set out various means for analysing and describing language in such a way as to open it up to wider questions about the social and cultural factors that influence the effect it can have. Just what was it about that particular adverb that might have moved the doctor's wife? And why might a personal pronoun produce such an effect? Most likely, none of the words would have had much effect on their own, but the way they were woven together in a particular context did. When words (spoken or written) are woven together in meaningful ways we refer to *texts* – which has the same roots as the word "textile", from the Latin word for "to weave". Words gather meaning from the company they keep and the patterns they enter into, and the meanings they accumulate relate to their speakers and their hearers in different ways. But we cannot tell from the *texts* alone how they will be received any more than we can tell whether "I pronounce you man and wife" is a legally binding utterance without knowing more about the conditions in which the utterance was produced. Conversely, we would not be able to talk about that particular context without an understanding of the words that are spoken, their meanings and their histories, their "social life". Taking language and context together we talk about *discourse*,[1] and the study of situated language use is called *discourse analysis*. Texts are the records of spoken or written language and are, from the linguist's point of view, a gateways into discourse analysis.

As you can see from the above passages, I am generating as many questions as answers, and this will be the pattern for the remainder of the book. However, as the subtitle of the book is "a practical guide", asking questions without suggesting how they can be answered – or at least approached – would be more than a little unfair; so, in the chapters that follow, I will set out fairly concrete methods for a detailed analysis of text as text and for opening up gateways to discourse analysis. At the heart of the descriptive method I'll set out in the book is a theory of grammar known as Systemic Functional Linguistics (SFL). There are several reasons for this, the most important of which is that SFL has been developed as an "appliable linguistics". You'll most likely have to add the word "appliable" to your spell-checker, or your computer will keep changing it to "applicable" when you're not looking. This is because the term "appliable linguistics" was coined by Michael Halliday, the originator of SFL, to make a distinction between a general theory of linguistic description that can be applied within a huge variety of situations – that is, an *appliable* theory – and a method of description that is *applicable* to, or suitable in, certain restricted cases. In other words, SFL has been specifically developed as a means of describing language as a system for making social meanings, a social semiotic, so that linguistic, or textual, description based on it should be able to open texts up to discourse analysis. So, from the perspective of this book, while I will set out one particular approach to discourse analysis, the descriptive skills you develop can be applied within a wide range of discourse analytical traditions, each with their own goals and agendas. For the texts that we will look at in detail in the chapters that follow I will at times provide analyses from my own fieldwork where I have gone beyond the text to try and answer the wider questions it provokes; at others I can only suggest the sort of questions that are brought to light by a detailed analysis of the text, questions that you as researchers would be expected to tackle in order to make sense of the text as the trace of discourse.

1.2 Grammar, text, context and discourse

In the opening paragraph of this chapter I gushed at the magical properties of language as "squiggles on paper or disturbances of the airwaves", as if that was all there was to language. While acoustic and graphic patterns are language in its most physical form, what they are doing is providing the platform for the more abstract properties of language. The quote from Saramago captures the next level, the "grammatical categories" that the squiggles and waves represent. I would add "lexical categories" here, as grammar and lexis work together at this level, as *lexicogrammar* (words in bold italics appear in the glossary on pages 184–190 of this book). In technical terms we can say that acoustic or graphic signals *realise* lexicogrammatical categories. But, of course, Saramago is being a little disingenuous: it is not these categories that move the doctor's wife to tears (except in the classroom, perhaps), but the meanings they make when spoken or written, the *semantics*. This provides us with the next level of abstraction, the meaning lexicogrammatical categories make when they are strung together in utterances. In technical terms, the lexicogrammar realises the semantics of an utterance. And, at the risk of moving you to tears, there is one further level of linguistic abstraction: the way in which the semantics of utterances work together to realise *contexts* (or interact with them, depending on your view).

Above, I talked about the important distinction between a text as a piece of language in isolation and discourse as the production and uptake of text in a social context. I also said that the goal of this book is to enable you to produce detailed textual analyses, but that these were to be seen as gateways to discourse analysis, as questions in need of answers rather than as answers themselves. The focus of this book, then, is on the interface between lexicogrammar and semantics, how words and grammar create the meaning of *utterances*, and the interface between semantics and context, how the meanings of texts contribute to social meanings, but it also goes beyond that in suggesting how the textual analyses produced can serve as the basis for discourse analysis, the analysis of text in action in specific situations. In Fairclough's (2001) terms, this means moving from an objective description of the language of texts, through an interpretation of its meaning as utterances in context, and on to possible explanations of why the text was produced when it was and what its effect might have been. This represents a move from objective to subjective accounts of language use, as interpretations and explanations are the products of individuals and can be hotly disputed. However, if we can base these interpretations on an objective description of the language, then we have more solid foundations on which to build our discussions. This means that we need a way of describing words and sentences – lexis and grammar – that is objective on the one hand yet provides a platform on which to build our interpretations and explanations on the other.

1.3 Different perspectives on grammar

In general there are three main approaches to grammar.[2] The "traditional" or *prescriptive* approach, something you were maybe taught at school and which is the basis of many self-help books, is the idea of "good grammar" as "speaking correctly". Within this approach, you are told to never split infinitives and that a preposition is something you never end a sentence with. However, these rules are based on how others want us to speak rather than what we actually do in real life. Speaking in ways that others approve of is an important consideration, as there are consequences to whether we are perceived of as speaking properly or not. It is also useful, in discourse analysis, to know whether the utterances being analysed are "standard English" or not. But in such cases we would want to consider what sort of language was being used and to consider why – just saying that it is "wrong" is a bit limited!

Descriptive approaches to grammar focus instead, as the name suggests, on describing the rules that underlie what people actually say. So, in these terms, examples 1 to 3 would be "grammatical" while example 4 would not be, as it is not the product of anyone's grammar (as far as I know):

1. I ain't got no money.
2. Me and her went down the shops.
3. See the footie last night?
4. Mat cat sat the the on.

Within descriptive grammar there is a further distinction between formal and functional approaches. Formal approaches are not so much interested in the meaning of different sentences as in describing the (subconscious) rules that determine whether a sentence is well-formed or not. So, from a formal perspective, example 4 is ill-formed as the rules of English are such that the determiner "the" can only occur before a noun (such as "cat" or "mat") or an adjective and a noun together (as in "the ugly cat"). In contrast, sentence 2 is well-formed, as "me" can be the subject of a sentence if there is another subject along with it (because this is what people do), although this would be considered "bad grammar" in a prescriptive approach.

Despite their differences, formal approaches and prescriptive approaches are alike in seeing grammar as a set of rules for making well-formed sentences – they just differ on their criteria for what counts as well-formed. Formal approaches to grammar stop at the lexicogrammar, the way nouns, adjectives and verbs can be strung together. Words and sentences are concrete aspects of language. In contrast, the perspective we will be using in this book is a *functional* approach,[3] which sees grammar as a **meaning potential** (Halliday 1978:39), as a set of options for expressing ourselves in different ways that has developed to meet our expanding communicative needs as we have developed as a species. In these terms, language is a social act, the making of contexts, with the more concrete levels of semantics, lexicogrammar and phonology/graphology at the service of this primary function. From this perspective, when we are putting sentences together we can "choose"[4] to talk about a particular animal, a cat, for example, if this serves our communicative purpose; if we do, we then have further choices as to whether we want to describe it – as "ugly", perhaps – and how we want to single it out – as "that ugly cat", "my ugly cat" or "the ugly cat", for example. The choices we make will determine how the sentence looks. So, while formal approaches look just at the ordering possibilities, the functional approach we will adopt highlights the functions of the words, both the similarities in function of the words "the", "that" and "my" (indicating *which* cat) and the difference in meaning between them. From the functional perspective the possibility of having an isolated "the" without a noun does not arise, as using "the" is a functional choice we are only faced with once we have already made the choice to talk about something. So, while the functional approach is still concerned with well-formed sentences, it goes beyond the formal approach in providing descriptions of text that relate to the *communicative functions* of the choices made and in allowing us to contrast the choices made with those which were available but which were not taken up. These are very important advantages if we want to use our textual descriptions as the basis of interpretation and explanation as part of discourse analysis, as I hope will become clear as we progress through the book.

1.4 Three areas of meaning potential

Another important distinction in the SFL view of language, and one that has shaped the organisation of this book, is that there are three different types of meaning in language, a distinction that applies both to the semantics of utterances and to the "meaning" of lexicogrammatical categories. It also has important repercussions when discussing context. Though this is a complex concept, it can be illustrated fairly simply with the following examples:

5. The cat sat on the mat.
6. Did the cat sit on the mat?
7. The mat was sat on by the cat.

As you can see, all three examples refer to the same activity in the real world, they therefore realise the same *experiential* meaning. This could be summed up as the cat being an Actor (the performer of an action); the action being SIT; and "on the mat" telling us where (called a Circumstance of location). This experiential meaning of the clause as a whole (semantics) is realised through particular aspects of the lexicogrammar: through the meanings of the various individual words; through the word order; through the combination of the preposition "on" with the *nominal group* "the mat" to mark the location; and in example 7 through the preposition BY telling us who or what is the Actor.

However, while the experiential semantics is the same as example 5, in example 6, we have a question instead of a statement, as marked by the word order of "did" before "the cat". This signals that rather than telling we are asking, an aspect of *interpersonal* meaning. So, we have a second type of meaning which is realised by specific features of the lexicogrammar.

In example 7, we have the same experiential meaning (more or less, but I'll gloss over that just now ...) and the same interpersonal meaning as example 5, but we have placed "the mat" at the beginning of the clause.[5] It's hard to see the purpose of this by looking at a single sentence as variation of this kind is normally dependent on the surrounding sentences, or *cotext*:

8. The dog sat on the table but the cat sat on the mat.
9. My mum was very proud of her new floor coverings until the mat was sat on by the cat.[6]

We can see that placing "the mat" at the beginning of the **subordinate clause** in example 9 links it to the category of "floor coverings", and for that reason we refer to variation such as this as **textual** meaning, where the semantics of the text as a coherent unit is facilitated by features of the lexicogrammar (word order in this case).

So, we can say that clauses realise three types of meaning, the experiential, the interpersonal and the textual, each with their own special areas of the lexicogrammar. Halliday (see Halliday and Matthiessen 2004:29–31) refers to these areas of meaning as **metafunctions**. Metalanguage is language about language (for example, words such as noun, verb and clause), so metafunctions are the functions of functions, capturing the idea that while different elements of lexicogrammar and semantics all have their own specific function these can be grouped together into the three broader categories of experiential, interpersonal and textual meaning.

Moving from clauses to texts and contexts, the distinction between the three metafunctions has important repercussions as, in general, the experiential meanings in a text serve to delineate the **field** of discourse (what's being done or talked about); the interpersonal meanings bring out the **tenor** of discourse (the relations between the speakers or their attitudes to the subject matter); and the textual meanings work together to establish the **mode** of discourse (the type of text we are dealing with). Later we will look at each of the metafunctions in turn, describing how the lexicogrammar realises different types of meaning, how these meanings **construe** different aspects of the context, and the social implications of doing this.

One important note before we move on: while the metafunctions are more or less independent of each other in that the choices in one are not theoretically constrained by choices in either of the others, this does not mean to say that they do not act independently in discourse. Quite the contrary, as we shall see, as it is the combination of the three types of meaning that define context-making as a social activity.

So, enough theory – let's look at some text and generate some questions!

Exercise 1.1

Read through Text 1.1 and make rough notes about the language using your own terms. A major aim of this course is to introduce you to technical terms to refer more specifically to the thoughts you may already have about the features of different texts and to provide you with a systematic means of bringing these ideas together, but for now a few different ideas in your own terms will do!

Once you have discussed your ideas in groups or in class, answer the more specific questions that follow:

Text 1.1 Part 1

1 The most pressing question we now face, we might well say,
2 is who and where we are as a society.
3 Bonds have been broken,
4 trust abused and lost.
5 Whether it's an urban rioter mindlessly burning down a small shop that serves his community
6 or a speculator turning his back on the question of who bears the ultimate cost for his
7 acquisitive adventures in the virtual reality of today's financial world,
8 the picture is of atoms spinning apart in the dark.

Questions

1. What do you think of the style of the extract in general?
2. Do you think the extract comes from a text that was (i) written to be read privately; (ii) spontaneous spoken speech; or (iii) written to be read aloud? What is the basis of your judgement?
3. Would you say the text presents a positive, negative of neutral picture of society? Again, what is the basis of your judgement?
4. Who do you think might be the author of the text and what do you think their goal is?

Now look at the how the text continues (see page 182) and follow the link to the video clip, then discuss questions 5 to 16:

5. Were you surprised by the speaker and the occasion? How does this knowledge fit in with your earlier ideas?
6. What is the background to this text?
7. What position does the speaker adopt with respect to:

   (i) the background as subject matter?
   (ii) his listeners?

8. Why do you think that the speaker refers to both rioters and bankers in the text?
9. What effect do the speaker's clothing, the procession and the setting have on the text?
10. How does the speaker's *status* affect the text?
11. What *role* is the speaker taking on as part of his status?
12. Is this a role that has always been seen as appropriate to someone of the speaker's status?
13. What audience(s) is the speaker addressing?
14. Will his various audiences respond to his words and his status in the same way?
15. Through this text, do you think the speaker has a single goal or several?
16. How does the speaker achieve an idea of continuity or *cohesion* across the two parts of the text?

There are no hard and fast answers to questions such as these, but as the purpose of this chapter is to introduce you to some core themes and concepts in discourse analysis, I will suggest a few possible answers that should give you food for thought. These are in the Appendix. In later exercises I will provide keys at the back of the book when you are asked to do a linguistic analysis, but I will leave the discussions to you.

1.5 Key concepts 1

As I stated above, the point of the above exercise was not to provide any definitive analysis of the text, but to raise interesting questions that will be taken up in the remainder of the book and to introduce some core concepts. Brief definitions are given for many of these terms in the glossary, but it will be useful to recap them in some detail here before moving on.

Text refers to a single coherent stretch of language, whether originally written or spoken. It is possible to analyse texts without reference to extratextual information, purely on the basis of the meanings of the words used and the structures and patterns in which they occur. Words and sentence structures together are referred to as the **lexicogrammar**. We can use the term textual patterns to refer to the relations between sections of a text larger than a clause.

Cotext refers to parts of a text that appear alongside particular words or sections that we are discussing and which might affect the meaning or interpretation of these. For example, the second section of this extract provides cotext that changes our understanding of the first section.

Context refers to how a situation is defined by the conjunction of experiential, interpersonal and textual meanings. This is a tricky concept that will be developed throughout the book. It is important to distinguish context, cotext and environment (below), and different authors use these terms differently. Many authors use context to refer, more or less, to what we will call environment, and some use the term context as a synonym for cotext.

Environment refers, in this book, to any non-textual background to a text that is in any way relevant to that text. This is a very broad and often vague category that can cover a range of features from those "close" to the text, such as the pomp and ceremony surrounding the Archbishop's sermon, for example, and the identity of the speaker, to those that are less immediate, such as the social background to the text and the changing role of the Church of England in social life. One purpose of this first exercise was to show how important environmental features are in providing (or suggesting) a fuller interpretation of a text as a social act. A major goal of the rest of this book is to provide a systematic way of considering the relationship between text, context and environment.

As we have seen, **meaning** is also a slippery concept that means a variety of things. At one level we can talk of the meaning of words as we find them in dictionaries and, a little more problematically, of the meaning of particular grammatical structures (as in the difference between *the dog bit the postman* and *the postman* *bit the dog*). We can refer to these as text-based meanings as they can (generally) be read off the text in isolation. However, we can also talk about the meaning of a text or parts of a text in terms of its purpose or effect. This is something that requires some extratextual information and I'll refer to this in the book as social meaning. The slipperiness of meaning as a concept can be illustrated by its different meanings in the phrases *What does this word mean?*, *His words meant a lot to me* and *What did he mean to do?* These three meanings are of course tied up together (that's why English uses the same word!) and one of the aims of this book is to investigate these interconnections.

Behind all these ideas, and the focus of this chapter, is the distinction between text and **discourse**. While text refers to the words produced, so that two people on different occasions can produce the same text and a text can be removed from its context, discourse refers to the situated production of texts, their use on a particular occasion in a particular context. Unlike texts, then, discourses cannot be repeated. A good discussion of the difference between text and discourse is provided by Widdowson (2004:1–16), while the following quote from Blommaert[7] (2005:3) provides a useful definition of discourse:

> Discourse … comprises all forms of meaningful semiotic human activity seen in connection with social, cultural, and historical patterns and developments of use.

Semiotic activity is using signs or symbols and can be used to refer to various ways of making meaning, but in this book we will look only at language. There are many good books on **multimodal** meaning that look at how pictures and sounds, for example, work in conjunction with text, but such considerations are beyond the scope of the present book, though many of the ideas developed here will be useful in multimodal analysis. Kress and Van Leeuwen (2001), in particular, has developed a descriptive framework for multimodal analysis that is based on the same general categories we will use later to analyse texts.

To sum up, the purpose of this book is to provide you with the skills to undertake the detailed analysis of whole texts … and to see limitations of such analysis and suggest ways of turning your textual analyses into **discourse analysis**. In this next section I will provide a heuristic model for the analysis of text as discourse. The term "heuristic" means that the model is not intended to be an exact representation of reality but rather a quick and dirty sketch that suggests relationships between text and society and forces us to think about these. As such, it is not suggested that the approach I'll set out is by any means exhaustive nor the only way to move from text to discourse. I'll refer to this model, or parts of it, throughout the book, and discuss how different features of language can be considered more fully through consideration of the model. You should also bear the model in mind as you are reading through the book, and particularly when you are attempting the discussion questions in the exercises.

1.6 Positioning

Looking back at Text 1.1 we can say that the Archbishop was taking up a ***position***, or a number of positions, though his sermon, and that this position made sense against the ***storyline*** of current events in the UK at the time of speaking. And once his sermon was broadcast, his position became part of that storyline as it continued to develop. This three-way relationship between acts (in our case discourse acts), positions and storyline is the basis of the branch of social psychology known as Positioning Theory (Harré and van Langenhove 1999) and is captured in Figure 1.1.

There is a problem with this model, however, if we are interested in looking at how taking up discourse positions can be effective or powerful, as the model appears to give speakers free rein in adopting whatever position seems most advantageous to them against the evolving storyline. As a model of discourse in action the positioning triangle masks three assumptions. The first of these is that the speaker is entitled to take up the position they do, or are seen to be entitled to in the eyes of their audience. Clearly the position taken up in Text 1.1 is effective because of the speaker; it would not have had quite the same effect if I had got up and said it or Richard Dawkins had. Following Bourdieu's (1977) economic analogy, we can talk about a speaker's status as their ***cultural capital*** and say that, in the right context, this endows their words with a ***symbolic capital*** beyond the value of their content alone. The second assumption, hinted at above, is that the speaker has control over the right type of language (referred to as the ***code***) for taking up the desired position in the current context. This is why I speak differently when ordering a pint of beer and when giving a lecture. The third assumption is that the same discourse act will carry the same value before any audience (or on any ***marketplace***, to continue with Bourdieu's economic terms). As was suggested in the analysis of the Archbishop's sermon, different audiences may have taken his speech in a variety of different ways. In sum we can say that while a speaker's positioning does not translate automatically into *power* as the ability to get things done, it may always be a latent attribute of different speakers, power can only be realised in practice (that is, an effective position taken up) if the speaker has the appropriate cultural capital within the specific marketplace and competence within the appropriate code, constraints which were missing in the original positioning triangle. We can therefore impose a second triangle of cultural capital, code and marketplace over the original positioning triangle to model these constraints within a *Positioning Star of David* (see Figure 1.2; see also Bartlett 2008, 2009, 2012a).

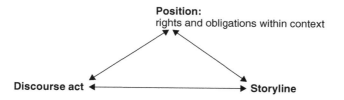

FIGURE 1.1   Positioning Triangle, adapted from Harré and van Langenhove (1999)

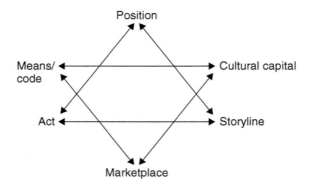

FIGURE 1.2   Positioning Star of David

While in general terms the variables of cultural capital, marketplace and code can be said to place constraints on the positions open to different speakers, from an alternative perspective they can be viewed as offering opportunities (though not without constraints). For example, if I want a bit more prestige at a party, I can change the topic of conversation to something I know about; or if a politician wants to show they are down to earth, then they can change their style of language to a local dialect, if they have the correct roots.

As I said above, the Positioning Star of David is a heuristic model, a way of thinking about the **constraints and affordances** of language as discourse. As such I will make reference to it as appropriate throughout the book, but I am not going to base every bit of analysis on every feature of the model. Sometimes a little focus is better. To finish this introductory chapter let's look at another text and discuss the textual features it exhibits, using the Positioning Star of David as a prompt where helpful.

Exercise 1.2

Text 1.2 is the conclusion of one of Winston Churchill's most famous wartime speeches. Read up as much as you can about this speech, about Churchill, and about the period in which the speech was made. Then discuss the questions that follow.

Text 1.2 Churchill's "On the beaches" speech

1 Turning once again, and this time more generally, to the question of invasion, I would
2 observe that there has never been a period in all these long centuries of which we
3 boast when an absolute guarantee against invasion, still less against serious raids, could
4 have been given to our people. In the days of Napoleon, of which I was speaking
5 just now, the same wind which would have carried his transports across the Channel

6 might have driven away the blockading fleet. There was always the chance, and it is
7 that chance which has excited and befooled the imaginations of many Continental
8 tyrants. Many are the tales that are told. We are assured that novel methods will be
9 adopted, and when we see the originality of malice, the ingenuity of aggression,
10 which our enemy displays, we may certainly prepare ourselves for every kind of
11 novel stratagem and every kind of brutal and treacherous manœuvre. I think that no
12 idea is so outlandish that it should not be considered and viewed with a searching, but
13 at the same time, I hope, with a steady eye. We must never forget the solid assurances
14 of sea power and those which belong to air power if it can be locally exercised.
15   I have, myself, full confidence that if all do their duty, if nothing is neglected, and if
16 the best arrangements are made, as they are being made, we shall prove ourselves once
17 more able to defend our island home, to ride out the storm of war, and to outlive the
18 menace of tyranny, if necessary for years, if necessary alone. At any rate, that is what we
19 are going to try to do. That is the resolve of His Majesty's Government – every man of
20 them. That is the will of Parliament and the nation. The British Empire and the French
21 Republic, linked together in their cause and in their need, will defend to the death their
22 native soil, aiding each other like good comrades to the utmost of their strength.
23   Even though large tracts of Europe and many old and famous States have fallen
24 or may fall into the grip of the Gestapo and all the odious apparatus of Nazi rule, we
25 shall not flag or fail. We shall go on to the end. We shall fight in France, we shall
26 fight on the seas and oceans, we shall fight with growing confidence and growing
27 strength in the air, we shall defend our island, whatever the cost may be. We shall
28 fight on the beaches, we shall fight on the landing grounds, we shall fight in the
29 fields and in the streets, we shall fight in the hills; we shall never surrender, and if,
30 which I do not for a moment believe, this island or a large part of it were subjugated
31 and starving, then our Empire beyond the seas, armed and guarded by the British
32 Fleet, would carry on the struggle, until, in God's good time, the New World, with
    all its power and might, steps forth to the rescue and the liberation of the old.

Questions

1. What is the topic of the text? Is there one main topic? If there is more than one
    topic, is one topic more prominent than others, and how are the other topics
    related and how are they introduced in a coherent fashion?
2. Would you describe the text as neutral or emotive? On what evidence? What
    different types of emotion are invoked? Do they relate to different subtopics
    and/or appeal to different groups of people?
3. Who does Churchill refer to when he says "we" (or "us", or "our" or "ours")?
    Is this always the same group of people? Does it always include his audience? Is
    it always clear exactly who is being referred to? What is the effect of referring
    to a group of people as "we"? Who is in opposition to this "we" at each point?
    And what groups are referred to as "they" (or "them" or "their" or "theirs")?
4. When does Churchill refers to himself (as "I" or "me" or "my" or "mine")
    rather than "we"? Is this done at strategic points? What is the effect?

5. How strongly does Churchill make his various statements? Does he make use of *hedges* to downplay some of his comments and *intensifiers* to strengthen others?
6. Churchill uses several different timeframes in this extract. How are these connected (logically and linguistically) and what is the effect of this?
7. How would you describe the type of language Churchill uses in terms of formality?
8. In what way is this text a *performance*?
9. How important is Churchill's *status* as Prime Minister at the time in producing this performance? How would you describe the *position* or *stance* that Churchill takes in this text? Would such a position be open to other speakers? Would the effect of these words have been the same from different performers?
10. How important is the political climate in which the speech was made in *legitimating* Churchill's position? Does it rely for its effect on the *audience* sharing certain views and opinions? What are these?
11. It is said that just after he finished this speech, Churchill muttered to a colleague, "And we'll fight them with the butt ends of broken beer bottles because that's bloody well all we've got!" What do these words tell us about the speech as a performance and Churchill as a performer?
12. What would it mean to say this speech was *effective* or *powerful*? How would it be possible to measure this success? Are there other ways available to us today for judging the effect of this speech that were not available at the time?
13. Could Churchill have made an entirely different type of speech at this point? What sort of speech?
14. Do you think the status and roles of the Prime Minister today are the same as in Churchill's day? Would the Prime Minister, or leader in your country, today make such a speech "in the same way"?
15. Is there anything else of interest in the speech (in this extract or elsewhere) that you would like to comment on or ask questions about?

There are plenty of questions here, hopefully provoking much discussion and generating many new questions! And for each question it would be possible to write a whole essay, focusing on a particular aspect of Churchill's rhetoric. Such an approach is sometimes referred to as *cherry picking*, as it is said that discourse analysts of different political persuasions can pick and choose what they want to look at in a text in order to support their own preconceived agendas – what Widdowson (2004) calls their *pretexts*. While such a state of affairs is almost unavoidable, the goal of this book is to provide a means of analysis that brings together a variety of different aspects of the speech and to consider how they work together to create a text and how they function as discourse within the wider context. In this way the method could be called a form of *mesoanalysis*, a middleground between the *microanalysis* of some theoretical linguistic research and the *macroanalysis* of some socially-grounded approaches. To finish this chapter, let me draw on literature once again, and Borges's short story *On Exactitude in Science*. In this tale a mapmaker becomes progressively obsessed with making his *mappa mundi*, or map of the world, ever more detailed and accurate. Eventually, he produces a full-scale replica of the world with every fold and contour, every mountain and river so accurately reproduced that it is impossible to distinguish the original from the copy. The map is perfect – and utterly useless. And just as maps are not countries but abstract representations of those features that are considered relevant at a particular scale and for a particular purpose, so linguistic descriptions are abstract representations of real-time language designed to capture certain features at a particular scale. You choose the scale to suit your purpose. If we get too bogged down in the nitty-gritty of the texts we lose sight of their purpose as social acts; but if we only focus on the texts as social acts without considering how they have been put together, then I think we lose sight of what makes them text, what makes them language. The mesolevel of description I introduce here, will, I hope, be a good starting point both for those who want to sharpen their focus and for those who want to expand it.

Notes

1   This term is unfortunately used in many related ways. For the purpose of this book, "discourse" means something along the lines of "contextualised language use". For a discussion of the difference between text and discourse see Widdowson 2004.
2   Halliday (2002:384–417) refers to the study of grammar as an academic discipline as "grammatics". The relationship between grammar and grammatics is the same as that between language and linguistics.
3   There are various functional approaches to grammar, many of which can be used in discourse analysis. I am using the Hallidayan approach here, but this does not mean to say other methods could not be used to answer the same questions that we will ask of texts.
4   This does not necessarily imply a conscious choice.
5   This brings to mind the old joke: What's the difference between a cat and a sentence? A cat has claws at the end of its paws and a sentence has a pause at the end of the clause… .
6   This example hints at the differences in experiential meaning I skated over as, unlike examples 5 and 6, it suggests that the mat has been affected in some way.
7   This book is particularly recommended, but don't be fooled by its title, it is a very complex book and not really an "introduction" at all!

2

PLOUGHING A FIELD (OR TWO)

2.1 Introduction

In this chapter and the following we will look at how speakers *construe a field of discourse*. The field of discourse refers to the topic of discussion or to any activity, such as booking a holiday or playing bridge, that is being carried out at least in part through language; construing a field refers to the ways in which our choices in language work together to interconnect a range of people, things and events as a coherent and recognisable whole within the activity or topic. The concept of construal is very important in discourse analysis; it suggests that there will be individual differences in representing or acting out the same event but without suggesting that any particular version of events is closer to the truth than any other or that any of the speakers is going out of their way to misrepresent a topic or to waylay an activity. In terms of activities, you may have a situation where different participants have different understandings of what is expected of them within a given situation, so that one may be attempting to construe the event as a business meeting, for example, while the other may be attempting to construe it as a social event. Similarly, when two people reconstrue a past event they may produce very different pictures as each will remember different people and activities as being particularly salient. They will in all likelihood structure their construal around these people and activities to produce very different yet equally true versions. Similarly, when discussing abstract topics, different speakers will centre their construals around different aspects, yet each will feel that they are providing an accurate picture. Construal is rather more than representation, therefore, as representation implies capturing a pre-existing reality, whereas the concept of construal captures the idea that this reality is created afresh in the act of discourse itself – different aspects of the event are "made relevant" (Hasan 2009:177) according to the present communicative needs and purposes of each speaker. These purposes are not necessarily either conscious or strategic, but whether they are or not, they offer interesting insights into how different social actors position themselves and others either as actors within a particular setting or as providers of information and audiences. Or, as we shall see, as both actors and informers simultaneously.

The analysis of fields of discourse will be spread over two chapters. In this chapter we'll look at the ways in which speakers establish and develop a field of discourse in general terms, and in Chapter 3 we'll look more specifically at how speakers construe different participants' involvement in the activities being represented or carried out. This will involve a relatively in-depth account of the *transitivity* system in English.

The presentation in this chapter will be in two parts. In Section 2.1 we'll discuss in more detail the idea that the field of discourse can refer to either a topic of discussion or ongoing activity, or to both at once, and consider the difference between *immediate* and *displaced* contexts and the degree to which these contexts are defined by language.

In Section 2.2 we'll revisit the metaphor of a text as a weaving together of individual strands into a single piece and we'll look at those linguistic devices which serve to hold the fabric together and those that develop the distinctive patterning.

In each section I'll work through some examples and suggest how the analyses can be used as the basis for discussing the text as discourse, though this will always involve drawing upon our knowledge (or construal!) of extralinguistic features of the environment. These range from the immediate setting through the participants' backstories and credentials and onto the broader sociopolitical background against which the immediate event is taking place. As will be the case throughout the book, worked examples will be mixed with exercises and further topics for discussion.

2.2 Immediate and displaced fields

In the opening chapter I discussed the importance of distinguishing the *environment* in which discourse takes place (what is already there, including speakers' semiotic histories and salient material features of the setting) and the *context* that is created – construed – from the environment by the discourse itself. This can be most clearly exemplified in terms of the field of discourse, though it is equally as important when discussing the tenor, as we shall see in Chapter 4. As suggested above, there are in general two types of field, or rather two extreme types and a variety of ways of mixing these. The most obvious of the two extremes is when the people and events being talked about are within the speakers' *immediate environment* and have a direct role in the activity they are currently engaged in. A good example of this would be the talk between learner and instructor in a driving lesson as in this situation the talk is almost exclusively concerned with the lesson itself (McCarthy, 2000) but constitutes only part of the activity, as the lesson also necessarily includes material actions. The other extreme is when the subject matter of the talk relates to events that are *displaced* from the immediate environment and the material activity in which the speakers are involved. Hasan gives a straightforward example where a couple are doing the washing up while discussing politics. In this case the field (or at least the field of discourse) is politics, not washing up. The couple, however, may from time to time refer to their current activity, in which case the field changes to "washing up". Things can be more complicated, however. Let's take the example of a history lesson. Here the teacher may start off by giving an account of some battle from history. The battle itself is then the field of discourse, and is clearly displaced in time and space from the physical setting of the classroom and the current activities of the teacher and students. At another level, however, the teacher's recounting of the battle is clearly a part of the overall activity of "giving a lesson". In such contexts the talk may move from *displaced* to *immediate* events as the teacher interrupts the narrative to address members of the class directly, perhaps to instruct them in the relevance of the story or to give some instruction or other. Note that this is different from the washing up example as the change in topic in that case represents a shift in activities (or a shift in attention between two simultaneous activities) while in the history lesson the narrative and the instruction both form subfields as integral parts of the wider activity of "giving a history lesson".

In this chapter we'll see how language is used to construe both immediate and displaced fields and some of the different ways in which they can combine. Starting with displaced fields, Text 2.1 shows just how far removed the field of discourse can be from the environment in which it occurs:

Text 2.1

Once upon a time in the middle of winter, when the snow was falling softly, a queen sat at a window sewing. The frame of the window was made of coal-black ebony. And whilst she was sewing and looking out of the window at the snow, she pricked her finger with the needle. Three drops of blood fell upon the snow. The red made a pretty pattern upon the white snow, and she thought to herself, "I wish I had a child as white as snow, as red as blood, and as black as ebony."

Soon after her wish came true and she had a little daughter, with skin as white as snow, with lips as red as blood, and with hair as black as ebony. The Queen called her daughter Snow White. But not long after the child was born, the Queen died.

A year passed and the King married another wife who was as beautiful as she was proud and haughty. She could not bear that anyone else should surpass her in beauty. She had a wonderful mirror which she used to look in, saying:

"Mirror, mirror, on the wall,
Who is the fairest one of all?"

And the looking-glass would answer:

"Thou, my Queen, art the fairest of all!"
Then the Queen was satisfied, because the mirror always spoke the truth.

But Snow White fast growing to be a beautiful child. In time she grew to be as beautiful as the sunshine in the morning, even more beautiful than the Queen herself. And the day came when the Queen asked her mirror:

"Mirror, mirror, on the wall,
Who is the fairest one of all?"

And this time the mirror answered:

"Thou art fairer than all but one:
The beautiful Snow White, as fair as the Sun."

This shocked the Queen to her heart. She turned green with envy and her heart turned black with hatred. From that time on, whenever she looked at Snow White, her heart heaved in her breast, she hated Snow White so much.

Envy, pride and hate ate at in her heart like weed amongst the flowers, so that she knew no peace. So she called a huntsman, and said, "Take Snow White away into the forest, for I no longer want to see her. Kill her, and bring me back her heart as proof of the deed." The huntsman, a kind and simple man, obeyed, and took her away. But when he had drawn his knife, and was about to pierce Snow White's innocent heart, she started to cry, saying:

"Oh, kind huntsman, let me live and I will run away into the wild forest. I promise I shall never come home again."

I'm sure you will have recognised this as the beginning of Grimm's classic fairy tale Snow White and the Seven Dwarfs (the Brothers Grimm were renowned linguists, by the way) and that you can imagine a likely environment for the telling of the tale as a child's bedside with a parent telling the story, yet the field that is being construed is far removed from this environment in almost every respect. This is highlighted from the beginning: the displacement from the here and now is a crucial feature of fairy tales, with the temporal reference to "once upon a time". This is the standard opening to fairy tales and it places the events which will transpire in a far off but unspecific time. While the time reference is not specifically stated as being distant, I think it is fair to say that it is implied; the phrase "long, long ago" could safely be added to the text while "a few years ago" could not! Similarly, the tale takes place far from the bedroom in which it is being recounted, in a palace, no less, and once again we would not have been surprised to hear the distance emphasised through the stock phrase "far, far away". The opening of the tale thus establishes that both the temporal and spatial settings of the field of discourse are very different from the environment in which it is taking place.

Within the spatiotemporal setting of the fairy tale we are introduced to a range of participants, events and themes as further salient elements of the field that is being construed. The participants are, firstly, the queen, the king, and their daughter, then the king's second wife and her talking mirror – another feature showing the distance between the environment and the context, this time in terms of possible worlds and what can take place in them (see Chapter 3 on processes and participants). After this, the huntsman is introduced and the location moves to the "wild forest". We therefore have three different settings, the good queen in her palace, the evil queen in her room and the huntsman in the forest, all of which form part of a larger magical field of far away and long ago. Within each of these settings different events take place and different, but overlapping, themes are developed, themes which will be crucial to the story: in the good queen's palace we have beauty, life and death; in the evil queen's room, vanity, fear, envy and hate; and in the forest, fear, violence and, as it turns out, the compassion of everyday folk.

This simple analysis brings out several important points:

- the field of discourse can be far removed from the environment in which it takes place temporally, spatially and even in terms of possible worlds;
- the field of discourse includes participants, their actions and the settings in which they occur;
- different subfields can combine to create an overarching field;
- as a text progresses from one subfield to the next a level of continuity is maintained in terms of participants and/or themes.

Focusing on the first of these points, we can say that, in this example, the text is *constitutive* of the field: that is, the places, characters and events described are all created by the text itself, and are not copresent in the environment. Conversely, we could say that those present in the environment are not construed as relevant to the text. But this is not entirely true. Consider again the opening line, "Once upon a time". This is a stock phrase that signals that the speaker is about to tell a fairy tale and so sets up the participants in the environment as teller and hearer of a particular type of narrative and, in so doing, also sets up a certain relationship between them. This can be seen, therefore, as an implicit reference to the people in the environment and to the form of text that is going to be produced. As was suggested above in relation to the history lesson, and as we shall explore further below, texts that are in the main constitutive of the field of discourse often contain references to the act of speaking or telling and even those that do not can still be interpreted in terms of the social role they fulfil in the "here and now" and the relationships they set up (another type of construal) between the speaker and hearer. In the case of a fairy tale that relationship is typically between young child and parent or teacher, and in those cases where it is not the resonances of this typical relationship will be in some way meaningful. In other words, *a field is never wholly constitutive as the creation of a constitutive field is a real-time act in itself.*

Let's now turn to the opposite extreme where text and actions work together to carry out an activity that is wholly or mostly construed as taking place within the immediate environment:

Text 2.2 (from Ventola 1983)

A: Travel agent, female, 30–40 years
C: Customer, male, 18–25 years

(The customer enters and walks up to the counter; the assistant interrupts her work and starts serving the customer)

A   1   Can I help you?
C   2   Yes
     3   I'm after uh … a quote on a trip to Cairns … student concession
A   4   High school or tertiary?
C   5   Tertiary
A   6   Tertiary to Cairns
     (2s *A* looks up the price)
     7   One forty-three sixty one way
     8   Just double that for the return
     9   Two eighty-seven and twenty
     (1s)
C   10   Say two twenty?
     11   yeah
     (2s)
C   12   Okay
A   13   Okay?
C   14   Thanks a lot
A   15   Thank you
     16   Bye-bye.

From the language of Text 2.2 we can easily recognise the activity that is taking place as a service encounter in a travel agent's. This context is not entirely construed by the language, however, as it also requires both the appropriate setting and various material actions from the participants. Most obviously, the encounter takes place in a travel agent's shop and if it did not we would have to consider it a highly marked variation of the activity! In this setting the two participants have different roles to fill: the travel agent herself and her customer, or potential customer. The travel agent's role is to attend to the customer's needs, and this is signalled at the outset both through her interrupting her current activity (a material action) and her addressing the customer (a linguistic action). Further linguistic signals of the activity as a service encounter are the customer's statement of his needs (3), the discussion of prices (7–11), and the closing sequence of turns that first confirm that the encounter has been successful (12–15) and provide leave-taking (16). The exact nature of the service encounter is signalled by the lexis involved: "quote on a trip … student concession" (3), "tertiary to Cairns" (6), "one-way" (7) and "return" (8). A further material aspect of the encounter is the travel agent finding the required information (between 6 and 7). We can see then that in this short text there is only a single context construed, a particular type of service encounter. Naturally enough, this is the immediate context, as borne out by the high use of "you" and "I", referents to the immediate participants. There are different roles entailed by this context – how "you" and "I" relate to each other – and we shall look at how these are construed in Chapter 4. We can also see how the language in Text 2.2 is *ancillary* to other actions, working together with the material actions that are also an essential part of the encounter. In other words, the language is not entirely constitutive of the context.

The essential elements of encounters such as this, material and linguistic, generally take place in a strict order – thanking followed by leave-taking followed by the giving of information and then the travel agent's offer to help just wouldn't work! Activity structures such as this are called *generic structures* (Halliday and Hasan, 1985, Chapter 4; Martin, 1992, Chapter 7) and are the object of much research, though fixed routines such as this are not the focus of this book. Beyond the essential elements of generic structure for different activities there are also usually optional elements, often side routines not directly concerned with the activity to hand. For example, it would not have been surprising to have seen the travel agent and customer exchange some small talk, most likely at the beginning of the encounter or before the closure and the leave-taking. One likely topic would be the weather or recent events in the participants' lives, depending both on how well they knew each other and the nature of the service encounter. The speakers would therefore be construing displaced contexts alongside the immediate context of the service encounter. The exact function of such social talk within transactions is an area of much discussion. In early discourse analysis it was largely considered as incidental, but most would now agree that it at the very least serves a function in "oiling the wheels" of the transactional talk. For example, McCarthy (2000:101) provides the following extract from a driving lesson, a type of service encounter that is characterised by an almost total focus on the immediate activity, as opposed to, say, visits to the hairdresser's, where small talk abounds:

Text 2.3

```
 1  I   It's a nice day now actually [isn't?
 2  L                                [Oh it's beautiful yeah
 3  (2s)
 4  L   Makes you full of the joys of spring doesn't it?
 5  I   It does yeah.
 6  L   I um walk through Merrion Square usually in the mornings
 7      [I: Right] so you can tell the progress every morning
 8      [I: Yeah] cos er you've got the crocuses out last week
 9      [I: Oh of course yes] and you've got the trees budding
10      [I: yeah] the cherry blossom
11  I   Oh yeah it's a nice time of the year.
12  L   Oh yeah it's great.
13  I   Back down to third again.
```

McCarthy describes how social talk like this generally occurs only on long clear stretches of road where there are no manoeuvres to be made by the learner and that they thus serve to fill in awkward silences. This example is rather different from the case of the couple talking about politics while doing the washing-up, however. In that case the washing-up talk interrupted the political talk, whereas in the driving lesson, the social talk plays a function within the activity as a whole as it helps to set up a more informal relationship between learner and instructor, a relationship that should facilitate the lesson as the immediate activity[1]. In technical terms we can say that the small talk serves to **recalibrate** the interpersonal relationship between the driver and instructor. So, just as we saw above that there is an immediate dimension to displaced texts, we can see that there are also often stretches of displaced talk playing an important role in events that are primarily centred on the here and now. There is therefore very often a degree of fuzziness or overlap between contexts in which language plays an ancillary or a constitutive role, and in categorising the activity as a whole we have to consider what the primary purpose of the talk is.

The driving lesson provided us with an example of an activity in which language essentially plays an ancillary role in construing the immediate context while displaced, linguistically constituted contexts may serve subsidiary functions within that activity. Let's now look at an example of the opposite case, where the focus of the activity is largely displaced talk but where language is also used in ancillary fashion to order the immediate setting and facilitate the focal activity. The following text comes from my fieldwork in Guyana where I was looking at discourse on sustainable social development between an international development organisation, Iwokrama[2], and the local largely Makushi Amerindian communities. Bartlett 2012a is a book-length discussion of the interactions between the two groups and I shall be drawing on examples from this fieldwork throughout this book. In Text 2.4 Sara[3], a professional development worker with Iwokrama, is setting up a discussion of local resource management and establishing Walter, a prominent local figure, as the chair for this discussion. See p. xi for transcription conventions:

Text 2.4

1 S: The second thing is is whether or not we want to continue with drinking water,
2   (xxxxxxx). Now (xxxxx) topic of discussion, where do we go from here. (xxx).
3   What=what is, what kind of thing you've put together so ↑far and what is the
4   future ... next steps of activity. (xx) remember, this is just the beginning, it's a (?step)
5   assessment. Of (x) developing a management plan ... erm, what does T- ... what
6   does T- want to do ... and to what extent would you like to ... continue to have
7   Iwokrama involved in ... in ... in facilitating it. And in ... in building capacity
8   to to (xx). ((data omitted))
9 S: Okay, so you're prepared to finish off the water. [Okay.]
10 W: [I feel] the whole point
11   (xxxx).
12   ((unclear background discussion))
13 S: I wish ... I was hoping that maybe you could (xx) do it (to the other xx room).
14   Just kind of get one person to do what er ... what ... er er I was hoping (?to be)
15   facilitator and one (person xx) to do the planning (xxxxx). Yeah?

16 W: Okay.
17 S: Right, Walter, you in shape for this?
18 W: A'right.
19 S: (Or we could) try …
20 W: (xxxxx).
21 S: (xx) did you want (xxx). So we need … two other people … Vanessa … Nicholas …
22 W: VANESSA! COME NOW! °(xxxx)°.
23   ((shuffling)) (12s)
24   Come here and do some writing.
25   (9s)
26 S: Here, Vanessa, (you could do with this pen).
27   ((mumbling)) (50s)
28   So …

As with Texts 2.2 and 2.3, we can recognise the context of Text 2.4 from the language alone (Hasan, 1995:228) as a consultative meeting, or even more specifically, a consultative meeting on development planning. In practice, however, this context is only partly construed through language. Significant non-linguistic features that contribute to construing the context from the environment are purely material, such as the arrangement of the seating (demarcating the chair from the audience); the positioning and movement of people within this space (signalling a shift in roles); and the use of the flipchart to take notes. Some of these features may be "silent", though they should be noted somewhere in a good transcription (see line 22), others may be alluded to in the text, made salient through the language. This is particularly the case here as Text 2.3 comes from the beginning of the meeting and as a result the language is overtly directed at organising the agenda (1–11), the physical setting (12) and the roles to be played (13–27) rather than to the discussions which are the purpose of the meeting. Or rather, these physical features are not relevant to the content of the discussion, but they are important to the way the discussion is carried out. This stretch of text is therefore quite explicitly ancillary, but it should be remembered that even the language of the discussions that follows, while constitutive of displaced contexts, is also ancillary to the non-linguistic features described in making this event a meeting.

A related point to note is the high frequency of first and second pronouns (I, WE, YOU) in Text 2.3. In this way the speaker and audience are construing themselves as part of the context, a further indication that this section of the text is largely ancillary. As suggested above, the use of I and YOU often relates to the roles within a particular activity. Whereas I described the roles in Text 2.2 as being *entailed* by its purpose as a service encounter, in Text 2.4 we see that these roles, rather than being naturally entailed, are being specifically allocated by Sara (we'll look at this in more detail in Chapter 4). In doing so Sara makes her position as the organiser of the event clear and, as we shall see later, this is going to have an effect on the functioning of the central focus of the activity, which is the discussion of a management plan and Walter's role in leading this. In contrast to the driving lesson, then, where we saw displaced contexts being introduced to oil the wheels of the immediate activity through the recalibration of personal relations, we see here how Sara's handling of the immediate activities that establish the background of the planning meeting can also serve to recalibrate interpersonal relations and how this could have an effect on the later discussion, which is the main purpose of the event.

So far we have seen cases where the immediate context and displaced contexts can be fairly clearly distinguished even though one may be playing some part in the functioning of the other. And in both the washing-up example and the driving lesson we see how the topics of the parallel contexts, even though they are prompted in some way by the immediate surroundings, remain largely tangential to the immediate activity. In the following examples, the immediate and displaced contexts are more directly aligned and we will see how the distinction between the immediate and the displaced is not in fact always so clear cut. We will also see from these two texts how it is not only personal relations that can be recalibrated, but also the storyline against which the discourse is unfolding, which will have implications for the positioning and power of the various speakers.

In the first example Sara is explaining the concept of Sustainable Utilisation Areas (SUAs, areas of the forest where the resources can be exploited in a sustainable fashion, as opposed to Wilderness Preserves, which are not to be exploited):

Text 2.5

1 Sam just asked me if I could tell you a little more about the SUA process, how it's working.
2 I'm not with – in Iwokrama the person in the department who's managing the whole SUA.
3 The process is (xxxx xxxxxx),
4 and they have come up with a system where they meet ...
5 they have created a team,
6 and on that team you have the four NRDDB representatives,
7 and there are two representatives from the gov-, from the Guyana Forestry Commission,
8 which is a government agency,
9 Guyana Environmental Protection Agency has representatives there
10 and it's all listed in there.
11 So, the idea was, what they thought they could do was bring together communities, these government representatives, Iwokrama, to sit down and think about what would be the best way to plan the area, to plan the businesses that they would develop in the area, the management of the land in terms of SUA.
12 The thinking behind it is that these people would meet quarterly,
13 that's (xxxx) the couple of months in between,
14 and what they would do is sit down and talk about how the process is going

15 and they could share what are their concerns and what they think should happen.

16 So from the community perspective the idea was that the NRDDB representatives would be able to bring to the meeting what they think are important for their villages.

17 Because, remember, the SUA is really Iwokrama developing businesses in the preserve.

18 And those businesses are going to operating, it's –

19 one possible business is logging;

20 a second is ecotourism;

21 a third is harvesting things like nibbi and cassava, for selling,

22 they call it non-timber forest products.

23 And so the idea was: How could this affect the communities?

24 How could the communities become involved,

25 the community can benefit, from what was being preserved?

26 What we have discussed so far at Iwokrama is whether it will be possible to, for, in between those meetings, when the NRDDB reps meet that there's a smaller meeting just with the communities.

In this text we see that Sara's introduction (1–2) plays an ancillary role in establishing the context, along with key features of the environment, in that it relates directly to the present activity of the meeting itself, signalling Sara's role as a giver of information in the setting of the meeting. This is a common strategy at the beginning of speeches or presentations, as we shall see. From then on the text plays a largely constitutive role in describing the meetings that have previously taken place and the potential business opportunities of the SUAs. Sara's discussion of the first of these topics, previous meetings, clearly construes a displaced context in that it is being entirely recreated through her talk. As the current activity within the meeting is a discussion of the SUAs, however, this talk can also be considered as ancillary to the construal of the event as a meeting. This brings home a general point that when the immediate activity relies heavily on the talk between interactants, as with a discussion or a meeting, the borderline between constitutive and ancillary language is often a fuzzy one. And this line becomes fuzzier with regard to Sara's talk about potential business opportunities, which are to some degree displaced yet directly involve the communities, representatives of whom are copresent and to whom Sara makes direct reference. We shall return to this point later.

A further point of interest in Sara's talk is that even when the text is essentially constitutive she throws out the occasional reference of its purpose within the immediate event, reminding her audience of the ancillary function of this constitutive talk. For example, in clauses 11, 16 and 23 Sara uses the phrase "the idea was" and in clause 12 "the thinking behind it is". In this way Sara signals the relevance of these displaced events to the immediate activity as an explanation of SUA processes. An even clearer reference to the immediate activity comes in clause 17 where Sara directly addresses her audience, asking them to "remember" what the SUA signifies.

Let's now look at Text 2.6, from shortly after Text 2.5 in the same meeting, in which Uncle4 Henry, a local community elder, takes up the task of explaining SUAs:

Text 2.6

1 Mister Chairman, I would now like to ask a question and then make some comments,
2 because it seems that (xxxx xxxxx).
3 Now, I would want to ask the question:
4 How many of you here understand the interpretation of SU – Sustainable Utilisation ... Area?
5 How do you interpret it?
6 What do you think it really means?
7 Because that the core of what we are discussing.
8 D'you all understand it?
9 Many of you don't understand,
10 it mean that you wouldn't grasp readily what this meeting is all about.
11 Now the meeting that ... the meeting we attended with this group of all the representatives from various organisations:
12 We sat down there to discuss (relatively commonplace) intuitions,
13 but we discussed the Sustainable Utilisation Area in depth.
14 The Wilderness Preserve is another area,
15 that is where the zoning is important.
16 And to mark that place, zone, to identify the Sustainable Utilisation Area, here is where your knowledge – all of us knowledge comes into play.
17 Because we are the people who are familiar with that forest,
18 we are people closest to the forest more than anybody else who live outside,
19 because it's, we have a way of life that's part of it,
20 and we are the ones to give an advice.
21 And we should take it in that vein.
22 Because whenever you're down,
23 whoever comes (from there) will return,
24 we remain here.
25 And whatever is built or constructed, whatever it is,
26 we will remain.
27 Of course some of it is (not).
28 But then we're working to defend it,
29 because all of us, you know, worry.
30 Now, the Sustainable Utilisation Area mean the area which you can use natural resources there in a sustainable way.
31 You keep it ... not going down,
32 But if possible you keep it increasing
33 so that those things, whatever it may be, whether it be vine, medicinal plants, frogs, centipedes, snakes, fishes, baboon, or what-you-call- it,

34 it must remain there
35 and you must not be de-, de-, depleted.
36 So that our generation that (xxxx) to keep it.
37 You take out
38 but then you must help to have that recycling going on
39 so that the reproduction of the resources going on.
40 Whatever you do for reforestation,
41 planting seedlings should grow up.
42 If you find a special medicinal plant.
43 Because
44 if you find –
45 obviously if you find a very valuable medicinal plant, which can cure some
    diseases, you'll have it in that.
46 Which means if you go and take out that natural resource you have there,
47 you're going to be depleting (established connexion).

In Uncle Henry's contribution we see that the first ten lines are devoted to establishing his role as a giver of information in the current activity (as with Sara, above) and making clear the relevance of the displaced talk that follows to the current meeting as he questions the level of knowledge on the topic of those copresent. This talk in this section is clearly, then, ancillary to non-linguistic features in establishing the context of the meeting. This section is therefore similar in function to the opening lines of Text 2.5, above. Yet even in the displaced talk that follows we see how Uncle Henry continuously emphasises the involvement of those present in the SUA process, a tactic Sara uses only in passing. We also see Uncle Henry addressing his audience directly, as WE (17–29) or YOU (30–47); instructing his listeners on the significance of their actions (40–47); and telling them how they should behave (34, 35, 38). In this way, while Uncle Henry's text is constitutive to the extent that it reconstructs the content of former meetings (directly referenced in 12 and 13), he uses this as a prompt to advise and instruct his audience, which are ancillary acts in the context of the meeting. The significance of Uncle Henry's shift from WE to YOU will be discussed in Chapter 7, where we will look at these two texts in more depth.

Another notable distinction between Text 2.5 and 2.6, and one we will return to in Chapter 7, is that Sara and Uncle Henry construe their fields very differently, even though both are describing the same concept, the SUAs. Sara refers predominantly to meetings, organisations and business opportunities. Uncle Henry, however, while touching on these issues, focuses more on the community, their way of life and their relationship with the forest. We can also refer to this as a recalibration, this time of the field of discourse or storyline rather than of the interpersonal relations construed. A central point of this book is to show how these two aspects of discourse work in tandem, as shifts in field, both immediate and displaced, can entail or facilitate shifts in interpersonal relationships, while shifts in interpersonal relations can lend weight to shifts in the field of discourse. These are all aspects of positioning and power. Let's now look in more detail at how the immediate context and shifting displaced contexts and interpersonal relationships can be used together to good effect in discourse5.

Exercise 2.1

Text 2.7 is Seb Coe's address to the International Olympic Committee as part of London's successful bid to host the 2012 Olympic Games. Various commentators have credited both Coe's involvement in general and this address in particular as having been instrumental in London winning the bid, so it is a text that is well worth analysing as it is generally perceived to have realised a successful piece of discourse.

Read through the text and then answer the questions that follow.

Text 2.7

1 I stand here today because of the inspiration of the Olympic Movement.
2 When I was 12, about the same age as Amber,
3 I was marched into a large school hall with my classmates.
4 We sat in front of an ancient, black and white TV
5 and watched grainy pictures from the Mexico Olympic Games.
6 Two athletes from our home town were competing.
7 John Sherwood won a bronze medal in the 400m hurdles.
8 His wife Sheila just narrowly missed gold in the long jump.
9 That day a window to a new world opened for me.
10 By the time I was back in my classroom,
11 I knew
12 what I wanted to do
13 and what I wanted to be.
14 The following week I stood in line for hours at my local track just to catch a glimpse of the medals the Sherwoods had brought home.
15 It didn't stop there.
16 Two days later I joined their club.
17 Two years later Sheila gave me my first pair of racing spikes.
18 35 years on, I stand before you with those memories still fresh. Still inspired by this great Movement.
19 My journey here to Singapore started in that school hall
20 and continues today in wonder and in gratitude. Gratitude that those flickering images of the Sherwoods, and Wolde, Gammoudi, Doubell and Hines drew me to a life in that most potent celebration of humanity Olympic sport.
21 And that gratitude drives me and my team to do whatever we can to inspire young people to choose sport.
22 Whoever they are,
23 wherever they live

24 and whatever they believe.

25 Today that task is so much harder.

26 Today's children live in a world of conflicting messages and competing distractions.

27 Their landscape is cluttered.

28 Their path to Olympic sport is often obscured.

29 But it's a world we must understand and must respond to.

30 My heroes were Olympians.

31 My children's heroes change by the month.

32 And they are the lucky ones.

33 Millions more face the obstacle of limited resources and the resulting lack of guiding role models.

34 In my travels over the last two years, speaking with many of you, I've had many conversations about how we meet this challenge.

35 And I've been reassured

36 and I've been uplifted

37 we share a common goal for the future of sport.

38 No group of leaders does more than you to engage the hearts and minds of young people.

39 But every year the challenge of bringing them to Olympic sport becomes tougher.

40 The choice of Host City is the most powerful means you have to meet this challenge.

41 But it takes more than 17 days of superb Olympic competition.

42 It takes a broader vision. And the global voice to communicate that vision over the full four years of the Olympiad.

43 Today in Britain's fourth bid in recent years we offer London's vision of inspiration and legacy.

44 Choose London today

45 and you send a clear message to the youth of the world:

46 more than ever, the Olympic Games are for you.

47 Mr President, Members of the IOC: Some might say

48 that your decision today is between five similar bids.

49 That would be to undervalue the opportunity before you.

50 In the past, you have made bold decisions: decisions which have taken the Movement forward in new and exciting directions.

51 Your decision today is critical.

52 It is a decision about which bid offers the vision and sporting legacy to best promote the Olympic cause.

53 It is a decision about which city will help us show a new generation why sport matters. In a world of many distractions, why Olympic sport matters. And in the 21st century why the Olympic Ideals still matter so much.

54 On behalf of the youth of today, the athletes of tomorrow and the Olympians of the future, we humbly submit the bid of London 2012.

55 Mr President, that concludes our presentation.

56 Thank you.

(Source: www.london2012.com/documents/
locog-publications/singapore-presentation-speeches.pdf)

Questions

A. Language features

1. Identify those stretches of the text that are (a) primarily constitutive of the field; (b) primarily ancillary to non-linguistic features of the address as an event.
2. How many different subfields did you identify within the constituted fields?
3. Is there an overarching field that unites these subfields?
4. What themes are developed in the text, and do they relate to specific subfields?
5. List the linguistic features that led to your answers in 1 and 2.
6. Discuss how the constitutive features also play an ancillary role within the address as an event.
7. Discuss the use of personal pronouns.

B. Social features

Before answering these questions you should read up on Sebastian Coe and his career as an athlete and a politician and his role in London's bid for the 2012 Olympic Games. You should also do some research into the Olympic Games and the way in which the host city is decided, particularly with reference to the growing emphasis on the "legacy" of the Games. Having a background knowledge of these areas will help you to move from analysing the text as text and on to its analysis as discourse.

1. Discuss the storyline of Coe's speech and the different roles Coe construes for himself.
2. Discuss how these different roles contribute to Coe's overall "position" within the presentation.
3. In what ways do you think Coe's history as an Olympic gold medallist affects his status as a bidder – even though, or because, he never mentions this?
4. In what ways is Coe's speech designed for the specific audience?
5. To take your situated analysis further you could have a look at the other speeches at www.london2012.com/documents/locog-publications/singa-pore-presentation-speeches.pdf and discuss any connections you see between the texts, taking into consideration the different authors and their different roles and cultural capitals.

2.3 Cohesion, continuity of reference and motifs

I said above that the two principal ways in which a text holds together are by: (i) maintaining a continuity of *reference*: that is, repeatedly referring to the same people and things, though maybe using different terms to refer to them; and (ii) by maintaining and expanding certain themes or topics – or *motifs* as I shall call them here, as theme and topic have specific meaning in linguistics. Motifs can range from types of people, participants or activities to ways of evaluating people and what they do (see Chapter 4).

2.3.1 Reference

Continuity of reference is very often realised by pronouns. As these function to signal that the speaker expects the hearer[6] to be able to identify who or what is being referred to (the *referent*) without the need to identify them explicitly, pronouns often refer to the last mentioned person or thing, though they are also commonly used in spoken language to refer to someone or something that is in the same environment and that can be identified with a nod of the head or by pointing. When there has been a gap between mentions of a specific referent the speaker will often use a nominal group beginning with THE as this allows hearers to simultaneously identify the referent in some way and to signal that the speaker expects that the hearers should be able to *recover* the referent from the previous talk by means of the identification given. When the hearer is not expected to be able to identify the referent, on first mention for example, the speaker will signal this through a nominal group which describes the referent and which includes an *indefinite article*, A or AN for single things and SOME for more than one thing.

Sometimes identification is assumed to be possible because of shared common knowledge of the world or because the referent is in the same immediate environment rather than because of any previous mention. Very occasionally the referent can be only be identified from further identification that occurs a little later, as in "He's a strange man, my brother". There are technical terms for these different types of reference. *Anaphoric reference* is when the referent can be recovered from a previous mention; *cataphoric reference* is when we have to wait a little to discover who is being referred to. Anaphoric reference and cataphoric reference are both examples of *endophoric* (or text-internal) reference; *exophoric reference*, on the other hand, is when we can work it out from the immediate environment; and *homophoric reference* is when shared knowledge is sufficient, as in "I've left my wallet in the kitchen" or "The Prime Minister made a terrible gaffe yesterday". Homophoric reference can therefore be a good way of presupposing or construing a sense of shared knowledge and beliefs, and this is an important part of positioning speaker and audience within the wider environment, often in opposition to an outside group.

Another way to signal that identity can be recovered is through the use of names and titles, as in "Lord Coe". Titles can be used either when the speaker believes they share common knowledge with the hearer, and so can be used for a first mention, or when the referent was previously mentioned, perhaps by some other means.

Sometimes reference is used to help identify a different person of thing, as in "his brother is a strange man". Here the *possessive adjective* "his" helps us identify a new participant (the brother) by connecting them to someone who we are already talking about (him). Alternatively, when talking about two examples of the same thing we can use *possessive pronouns*, which stand on their own, as with "mine" in "his car is older than mine". In these ways there is both continuity and change of reference, an important device for allowing speakers to develop a text while maintaining cohesion.

We can also identify people or things by their spatial position, as in "this man" or "that man". THIS is also used in writing to refer to an idea that has just been mentioned, as in "this policy was very important", or simply "this was very important". When used on their own, THIS and THAT are called *demonstrative pronouns* and when used before a noun they are called *demonstrative adjectives*.

Exercise 2.2

1   Identify all the features Seb Coe uses in his speech to signal that (he expects that) the identity of a referent can be recovered in some way. Answer on p. 191.
2   Discuss the variety of ways in which Coe expects his audience to be able to identify the referents and consider.
3   What extra effect is created by Coe's use of reference to suggest shared knowledge in clauses 5, 20, 33, 39 and 40?

2.3.2 Motifs

Motifs are often developed through the expansion of *semantic domains*, where the words of the text share some feature of meaning or are the opposite of each other. Often the relationship between words will be something you can get from the dictionary and such relations are known as *synonymy* (the same meaning, or better, *nearly* the same meaning, as two words rarely if ever mean exactly the same thing); *hyponymy* (types of something); *meronymy* (parts of something); and *antonymy* (opposites). *Repetition* of the same word (not necessarily referring to exactly the same thing) is also included here.

For example, "Persian" and Manx" are both hyponyms of the *superordinate* "cat", and the relationship between "Persian" and "Manx" themselves is one of *cohyponymy*. "Hand" and "foot" are both meronyms of "body" (which is called the superordinate, as with hyponymy) and are *comeronyms* of each other. Sometimes it is hard to distinguish meronyms from hyponyms, but there is a simple test. Persians and Manx are both cats (hyponymy) but hands and feet are not both bodies, only parts of bodies (meronymy).

Relationships between words in a motif are, however, not always clear from their dictionary definitions but are construed within individual texts (Brazil 1995).

For example, in discussing a government failure, an author could start with the superordinate "catalogue of errors" and then list within this catalogue "bad schooling" and "failures in the health service" as *locally contingent* meronyms. A similar case, but one that it is useful to distinguish, is when specific people are referred to as *examples* of a category, as with Tony Blair and Margaret Thatcher as examples of the superordinate (again) category of "prime ministers of the UK". Somehow it just wouldn't seem right to refer to these people as hyponyms!

Similarly, locally contingent *contrasts* can be construed in a particular text. For example, a politician may contrast the achievements of one party with those of another (though most likely they will contrast what they see as achievements and failures). As the line between locally contingent contrasts and lexical antonyms (that is, from dictionary definitions) is sometimes hard to draw, we'll use *contrast* as the label for both in our textual analysis.

One final type of relationship in developing motifs is when there is a continuity or direct contrast in the attitudes that words express, as with "murder", "dictatorship", "human rights" and "the common good". These words all contain a moral evaluation and the use of such words in a text creates *semantic prosodies* at different levels (all relate to morality, two are positive two are negative), but this is the topic of a later chapter (Chapter 4).

We'll return to motifs after we've looked at reference in Seb Coe's speech in some detail.

2.4 Reference and motifs in Seb Coe's address to the IOC

2.4.1 Reference in Coe's address

The most common referents in Coe's speech are Coe himself (alone or with others), the International Olympic Committee (IOC), today's youth and the Olympic Games. This continuity is captured in Table 2.1. Note how this is set out, with the general term for the referent at the top of the column and then the actual word used to refer to them in a box (the *token*) under the general term in the row that corresponds to the clause they appear in (this makes it easier for whoever's looking at the table to check it against the text). When there is no referent given because *ellipsis* allows us to maintain reference without repeating a referent the "missing" word is placed in brackets. In clause 5 we see that the Subject "we" form the preceding clause is still understood; in clause 44 this is because "you", the IOC, is the implicit Subject of the imperative clause (see Chapter 4). Note that *possessive pronouns* such as "our" are also included. In some clauses the same referent will appear more than once, and all tokens are placed in the appropriate box. Note that in clauses 29 and 34 I have taken "we" to refer to both Coe and the IOC and have therefore included it in both boxes (see Table 2.1).

There are several points of interest that the table brings to light, both in terms of the way continuity is woven through the text, and also in the way the referential focus moves from one participant or group to another as the text develops.

TABLE 2.1 Reference in Coe's Olympic address

Clause	Coe (+ others)	IOC	Today's youth	Olympic sport
1	I			
2	I			
3	I			
4	we			
5	(we)			
6	our			
7				
8				
9	me			
10	I, my			
11	I			
12	I			
13	I			
14	I, my			
15				
16	I			
17	me, my			
18	I	you		
19	my			
20	me			Olympic sport
21	me, my, we		young people	
22			they	
23			they	
24			they	
25				
26			today's children	
27			their	
28			their	Olympic sport
29	we	we		
30	my			
31	my			
32				
33			millions more	
34	my, I, we	you, we		
35	I			
36	I			
37	we	we		
38		you	young people	
39			them	Olympic sport
40		you		
41				Olympic competition
42				the Olympiad
43	we			
44		(you)		
45		you	youth of the world	
46		You		

TABLE 2.1 Continued

Clause	Coe (+ others)	IOC	Today's youth	Olympic sport
47		IOC		
48		your		
49		you		
50		you		
51		your		
52				
53	us	us	a new generation	Olympic sport
54	we		the youth of today	
55	our			
56		you		

In terms of continuity, we can see that Coe himself provides an almost constant thread, and it is in relation to him that each of the other participants is first introduced: the IOC in clause 18; Olympic Sport in clause 20; and the youth of today in clause 21. Once introduced, these other referents can take on a life of their own and interact without Coe, whose presence is less intense as the address develops.

Also noticeable is the fact that there is only one clause in the whole address that does not include at least one of these four referents, clause 52. "The Olympic cause" in clause 52 is not coreferential with "Olympic sport", but it does form a semantic link as both form part of the Olympic movement, as discussed below.

In terms of development, there are interesting shifts between clauses 1 to 20 where most references to Coe are in the first person singular (I, ME or MY), clauses 21 to 37, where there is a mix of I/ME/MY and inclusive WE/OUR, and clause 38 to the end, where references to Coe shift to an exclusive WE/OUR referring to the London team and which contrasts with the IOC as YOU.

Also noticeable in Table 2.1 is how, after centring on Coe himself, the focus moves first to the youth of today, then briefly to sport, and then to the IOC as the address draws to a close.

Exercise 2.3

Discuss how the textual patterns described above, and any other features you notice, might contribute to the text as an effective piece of oratory.

As well as a means of highlighting patterns of interest in its own right, identifying reference in texts forms the basis for undertaking a transitivity analysis in order to explore the different ways in which the referents participate in the events described and how their actions impact upon one another. Transitivity analysis will be covered in Chapter 3.

2.4.2 Motifs in Coe's address

Table 2.2 demonstrates a different kind of textuality in construing a field. Rather than tracking the same referents as they reoccur across the text, the table shows how ideas (not specific referents) are taken up and expanded upon as the text develops.

I have chosen as my motifs Coe's journey from his schooldays to presenting the London bid, which seems to me to be the unifying narrative of the address; athletes as a class of people, which includes any specific referents; the Olympic Movement and all its manifestations; and problems and solutions, as opposing ends of the same idea.

Starting with the first reference to any of these ideas, Table 2.2 then tracks any concept from later in the text that is connected through any of the sense relations that were outlined above: synonymy, repetition and contrast; meronymy, hyponymy and superordination; cohyponymy, comeronymy and examples. After the first mention, the token identified is labelled according to its relation to the immediately previous token in the chain and in this way we can see how concepts are broken up and grouped together, how speakers develop one angle at the expense of another, and how different concepts are brought together.

As you will notice, the dividing line between referents and motifs is not always clear cut. In the case of an individual person, such as Seb Coe, it is relatively straightforward to identify reference to him as a specific person, but with a referent such as Olympic Sport it is a bit harder to draw the line between a single referent an abstract idea – would mention of "the discus" count as the same referent or an extension of the idea, for example? The line I have taken is that reference should be, as far as possible, to exactly the same thing; if this is divided up or lumped into a bigger category, then we can treat this as developing a motif.

As mentioned above, it is also important to bear in mind that many of the relationships established in a text are locally contingent: that is, the relationships between them are specific to the field being construed and even to the individual text. Returning to a point made at the beginning of the chapter, it is this freedom in construing a field in different ways that is of interest to us as discourse analysts trying to get to grips with the whys and hows of text in context.

Table 2.2 reveals a complex patterning of ideas in which Coe's life story, sport, the Olympic ideal, the problems facing today's youth and London's bid for the 2012 games are all construed as intimately and intricately interrelated. This effect is achieved by developing different aspects of the various motifs and bringing them into play with each other so that associations are made between the different strands of the argument. Many of the associations that are made are therefore locally contingent and it often requires a bit of thought to decide how the ideas are being made to fit together – but that often reveals the most interesting insights. For example I have analysed "the Olympic Games are for you" in clause 46 as being construed as synonymous with "London's vision of inspiration and legacy" in clause 43 because Coe, in clauses 44 and 45, has done the linguistic work necessary to link these two concepts. This shows not only how relations between ideas can be locally

TABLE 2.2 Motifs in Coe's Olympic address

Clause	Coe's journey	Athletes	The Olympic movement	Problems and solutions
1	I stand here today		Olympic movement	inspiration
2				
3				
4				
5			Mexico Olympic games (exa)	
6		Athletes		
7		John Sherwood (exa)		
8		Sheila (exa)		
9				
10				
11				
12				
13				
14		Sherwoods (rpt)		
15				
16				
17		Sheila (rpt)		
18	I stand before you (rpt)		This great movement (sup)	inspired (rpt)
19	My journey here to Singapore (sup)			
20	Life in Olympic sport (mer)	Sherwoods (rpt), Wolde, Gammoudi, Doubell and Hynes (exas)	That most potent celebration of humanity Olympic sport (mer)	
21	Doing whatever we can to inspire young people to choose sport (corner)			inspire (rpt)
22				

23				task (contr)
24				Conflicting messages and
25	task (syn)			competing distractions (mer)
26				Their landscape is cluttered
27				(syn)
28			Olympic sport (rpt)	Their path to Olympic sport is often obscured (mer)
29				A world we must understand and respond to (sup)
30		My heroes (sup)	Olympians (mer)	
31				
32				
33				Obstacles … models (mer)
34	My travels (corner)			This challenge (sup)
35				
36				
37	common good (contr)			Engage the hearts and minds of young people (syn)
38				Challenge of bringing them to Olympic sport (mer)
39			Olympic sport (sup)	
40				
41			Superb Olympic competition (syn)	This challenge (rpt)

TABLE 2.2 Continued

Clause	Coe's journey	Athletes	The Olympic movement	Problems and solutions
42			Olympiad (sup)	Broader vision (mer); global voice (mer)
43	We offer London's vision (comer)			London's vision of inspiration and legacy (exa)
44				
45				
46			Olympic games (mer)	Olympic games are for you (syn)
47			Mr President (comer); Members of the IOC (comer)	
48				Your decision today (sup)
49				Opportunity (syn)
50			The Movement (sup)	Bold decisions (hyp); decisions which have taken ... directions (exas)
51				Your decision today (exa)
52			The Olympic cause (mer)	Decision about ... cause (syn)
53			Olympic sport (mer); Olympic ideals (comer)	Decision about ... much (syn)
54	We humbly submit the bid of London 2012 (syn)	The athletes of tomorrow (contr); Olympians of the future (mer)	London 2012 (exa)	The bid of London 2012 (mer)
55	Our presentation (syn)		Mr President (comer)	
56				

contingent but also how speakers put their language to work in establishing these relations. Following this, I have suggested that "your decision today" is a superordinate of "the Olympic Games are for you". This might seem a little odd, but we can see that Coe defines the current decision as between five bids, one of which was London's "vision of inspiration and legacy", rephrased as "the Olympic Games are for you". So, the decision today comprises five possibilities: choosing that "the Olympic Games are for you" or one of the four other bids!

The important point to remember here is that the labelling of sense relations, by the very nature of discourse as locally contingent, is not an exact science but rather a way of thinking about the work that the speaker is making the concepts do and how they use other aspects of language to achieve this. In this regard tables such as 2.2 are just a preface to interpretation and explanation.

Exercise 2.4

1. Look though the sense relations as I have labelled them in Table 2.2. Do you see the relations I am trying to capture? What other linguistic features do you think might have contributed to my analysis? Do you agree with my analyses? What other relations would you suggest and why?
2. Look at the chain for "problems and solutions" and discuss how Coe draws connections between social problems, London's bid and the IOC decision.
3. What purpose do you think the chain for athletes serves in the discourse?
4. Discuss how the different motifs flow in and out of salience and whether you see this as effective.
5. In what way can Coe be said to be recalibrating the displaced storyline against which London's bid will be judged?
6. In what way can Coe be said to be recalibrating the immediate storyline in which he has the position of supplicant and the IOC that of the arbiter?
7. How do your answers to 5 and 6 work together to demonstrate how Coe is "managing the context"? What enables him to do so?

2.5 Summary

In this chapter we have looked at the difference between immediate and displaced contexts and the role of language as ancillary or constitutive in construing these. We considered how displaced contexts always played a role in some immediate activity and looked at the various ways in which different contexts work together. We saw how displaced contexts could be construed alongside the immediate activity in order to recalibrate interpersonal relations and so facilitate the activity itself and, conversely, we saw how ancillary uses of language in organising activities consisting mainly of displaced contexts could make salient certain features of interpersonal relations that might have repercussions on the main activity (to be followed up). We then looked at Sara and Uncle Henry's explanations of the SUA process to suggest that the borderline between displaced and immediate contexts was rather fuzzier than originally suggested (see Chapter 6 for an elaboration of this). In these texts we also saw how the different speakers recalibrated the storyline through different construals of the same concept. And finally we looked at Seb Coe's address to the IOC to see how a cohesive patterning of shifting contexts can be manipulated to great effect as texts go to work in the immediate context, construing and recalibrating storylines to open up new fields of discourse, fields which carry with them different histories and different ranges of rights and responsibilities for those involved. The take-home message of the chapter, and the basis of the whole book, is that speakers constantly recalibrate both the storylines that provide the backdrop to their discourse and the interpersonal relations between themselves and their hearers; crucially, though, these are not independent actions but are mutually reinforcing acts of discourse positioning. The goal of this book is to set out a method of textual and social analysis that will enable you to get a hold of these interrelations and to analyse their function in real time discourse.

Before leaving this chapter it would seem appropriate to reference the work of Bourdieu (1991) and Bernstein (1971, 2000) on field, and in particular on the potentially disabling effects of culturally specific fields for those who come from different cultural backgrounds. In this chapter we have looked at how speakers can construe and recalibrate fields to suit a particular purpose. Specifically, in the case of Uncle Henry, we saw how he construed the field of SUAs in terms that involved the community and drew on their experience as a valued form of knowledge. The flipside of such a process, however, is when the field is made strange to some of those involved in an activity – in Bourdieu's terms when the field of practise doesn't match that person's field of socialisation, so that they haven't developed the appropriate *habitus*, the subconscious feeling for what is going on and how to respond. In simpler terms they are not sure of "the rules of the game". In Bernstein's terms (2000:16–22), an acculturated speaker possesses both *recognition rules* that let them know what's going on and how to react and also the *realisation rules*, the culturally specific ways of performing the appropriate action. Speakers in unaccustomed fields are therefore at a double disadvantage to those who are operating in their comfort zone – a situation familiar to anyone who has tried performing a relatively simple task like booking a room or buying a tram ticket in a foreign country. Bernstein's focus was on the disadvantage of working class children on entering primary school and encountering the middle class rules of the game that were taken for granted there (see also Hasan and Cloran 1990); Bourdieu considers more generally how a dominant elite is able to impose its norms within state institutions so that they are able to maintain and reproduce their dominant status. While we will not be focusing on these themes directly, the concepts developed by Bourdieu and Bernstein are clearly relevant to the analytical framework developed in the book and you will be coming across their ideas later on.

Notes

1   Of course it could be argued that the washing-up talk also served a purpose within the political talk, perhaps defusing tensions.

2   Iwokrama is actually the name of the forest; the full name of the organisation is the Iwokrama International Rainforest Conservation and Development Programme.

3   All names from my Guyanese data are pseudonyms.

4   "Uncle" is a common term of respect for older family and community in Guyana.

5   However, the question of effect is not straightforward – we have to be careful to distinguish between what appears effective to us as discourse analysts and what is effective in actually achieving its goals. The latter, which should surely be the aim of applied linguistics, requires going beyond the text to try and ascertain how audiences respond to and take up the discourses they encounter.

6   I shall use the term speaker and hearer in reference to both spoken and written language, so that the terms are understood to include writers and readers as necessary.

3

CONSTRUING PARTICIPATION

The speaker as puppeteer

3.1 Introduction

In the previous chapter we looked in broad terms at how speakers construe fields of discourse within particular environments. We focused on complementary aspects of how fields of discourse are maintained and developed: through repeated *reference* to specific people and things and through the elaboration of thematic *motifs*. In this chapter we will look in more depth at the relationships that are construed between referents, particularly in terms of their participation in different activities, in terms of both the kinds of activities they are involved and the different roles they play within these activities. This will allow us to see who are being construed as the movers and shakers and who or what are being construed as the moved and shaken! Remember, though, that construal refers to the way that speakers use the resources of the language to make particular aspects of a field salient, so that the particular way they construe events tells you as much if not more about the speaker than the people and events they are talking about. So questions about why speakers construe an event in a particular way can become questions about the positions they are taking up and the status, or cultural capital, that might legitimate such a position before different audiences.

Our analysis of participation in events is centred, naturally enough, on the verb, as this is the lexicogrammatical resource most typically associated with actions, activities and states of affairs – all of which we can lump together under the technical term *processes*. Now, there are an awful lot of verbs in English, and if we took account of all the meaning differences they capture then it would be very hard to capture the patterns of construal that occur either within texts or between them. For that reason we have to decide on an appropriate degree of abstraction in differentiating **process types** into contrasting groups. There are different ways of doing this, some of which depend on locally contingent contrasts, such as processes of working in contrast to verbs of playing, which may be an important distinction to highlight within a particular research topic. At a general level, however, the grammar of the language provides basic distinctions between process types that capture fundamental distinctions in how different participants are involved in events and activities. Halliday has suggested (in Halliday and Matthiessen 2004, chapter 5) that all languages use the grammar (rather than the lexicon) to distinguish between *material*, *mental* and *relational* processes. The fact that these categories are most likely universal suggests that they capture distinctions which are basic to human understanding of participation and are therefore useful distinctions to capture in discourse analysis. As well as these three core categories, English includes *verbal*, *behavioural* and *existential* processes within the basic, or least **delicate**, **system** of process types. *Participants* can be involved in these process types in different ways, as, for example, the person who carries out a material action, such as hitting, or as the person getting hit. I'll discuss the different process types and the type of participation in some depth in section 3.1.

Once we've considered how the grammar distinguishes different process types, and therefore how we as analysts can distinguish the way in which speakers construe participation, we can look at the flow of such construals across a text and see how this varies in line with different topics and motifs. From there we can see how a complex picture can be woven together as a coherent whole in which different participants move in and out of prominence as the topic develops. At the end of the chapter we will consider how the linguistic resources for construing participation can be used by speakers to position themselves and others and how this positioning can work in tandem with features of the situational and social environment to make discourse effective or powerful.

3.2 Transitivity: process types

Transitivity is the technical term for the relationship between the roles different participants play within a process. You may have come across this term in traditional grammar where it is often used to distinguish between "verbs" that take an object and those that don't. For example, stroking is something you do to something else, so "stroking" is transitive in:

1.   Tom stroked the dog.

However, running is something you can do on your own, so "running" is intransitive in

2.   The dog was running.

You may also have heard of *ditransitive constructions* where three participants are involved and we need two objects, one direct and one indirect, as in:

3.   I gave my aunt the teapot.

Here "the teapot" is the direct object (it is the thing given) and "my aunt" is the indirect object (she is not given but has something given *to* her).

This is a very limited take on transitivity, however, as it only covers three possible grammatical patterns and it gives too little detail about the many different types of relationship that can be construed between participants by grammatical means. The more elaborate approach to transitivity that follows provides a much wider range of distinctions that can be used to analyse how speakers position themselves and others both in terms of the immediate event in which they are involved and in displaced fields which, as we have seen, also play a crucial role in acting out the immediate event.

As I said above, in English there are six broad process types, each construing different relations between the participants involved. Unfortunately this is quite a complex area of the grammar and it can be tricky to analyse clauses at times; however, as *tout se tient*, it's not really possible to present just a fragment of this system. From my experience of analysing texts, both those I have been working on and those students have selected, there are very rarely texts that rely on only simple and straightforward examples of transitivity. So, to avoid frustration later on, it's worth the effort of working through the various process types in some detail before undertaking the analysis of a text.

Transitivity analysis generally focuses on the processes that comprise the *main verbs* of each *clause*, but this is not necessarily the case and we shall discuss other possibilities below. An important point about transitivity analysis is that we do not talk about whether a *verb* is transitive or not, but whether the process that is being construed within the text involves more than one participant. For example, the same verb JUMP construes a process involving just one participant in example 4, but a process involving two participants in example 5:

4. Tom jumped when the television exploded.
5. The horse jumped the fence with ease.

From the perspective we are taking in this book it is the speaker's construal of events and the ***participant roles*** of different people and things within these events that is important. So it follows from this that it is impossible to say what process type is construed by a particular verb without seeing how that verb is being used in context.

Another aspect of transitivity that we will also look at briefly is the detail speakers add to their construal of actions and states of affairs, what are referred to generally as the **Circumstances** surrounding the process. These include information about the time or place something happened, the reason behind it or the effect it had. This should enable us to present a fuller picture of the fields being construed and provide further points of connection in moving from a description of text to a discussion of discourse and the positions taken up by speakers in different social situations. In general terms participant roles construe *who* or *what* is involved in a process while Circumstances answer the questions *why?*, *when?*, *where?*, *how?* (including compound questions such as *how much?* and *how often?*).

The text I will use to demonstrate the different process types and the participant roles they involve is Sebastian Coe's address to the International Olympic Committee, repeated here as Text 3.1. There are some points of interest in the clause breakdown which I will address in discussing the process types and particpant roles construed:

Text 3.1 Coe's Olympic address

1   I stand here today because of the inspiration of the Olympic Movement.
2   When I was 12, about the same age as Amber,
3   I was marched into a large school hall with my classmates.
4   We sat in front of an ancient, black and white TV
5   and watched grainy pictures from the Mexico Olympic Games.
6   Two athletes from our home town were competing.
7   John Sherwood won a bronze medal in the 400m hurdles.
8   His wife Sheila just narrowly missed gold in the long jump.
9   That day a window to a new world opened for me.
10 By the time I was back in my classroom,
11 I knew
12 what I wanted to do
13 and what I wanted to be.
14 The following week I stood in line for hours at my local track just to catch a glimpse of the medals the Sherwoods had brought home.
15 It didn't stop there.
16 Two days later I joined their club.
17 Two years later Sheila gave me my first pair of racing spikes.
18 35 years on, I stand before you with those memories still fresh. Still inspired by this great Movement.
19 My journey here to Singapore started in that school hall
20 and continues today in wonder and in gratitude. Gratitude that those flickering images of the Sherwoods, and Wolde, Gammoudi, Doubell and Hines drew me to a life in that most potent celebration of humanity: Olympic sport.
21 And that gratitude drives me and my team to do whatever we can to inspire young people to choose sport.
22 Whoever they are,
23 wherever they live
24 and whatever they believe.
25 Today that task is so much harder.
26 Today's children live in a world of conflicting messages and competing distractions.
27 Their landscape is cluttered.
28 Their path to Olympic sport is often obscured.
29 But it's a world we must understand and must respond to.
30 My heroes were Olympians.

31 My children's heroes change by the month.

32 And they are the lucky ones.

33 Millions more face the obstacle of limited resources and the resulting lack of guiding role models.

34 In my travels over the last two years, speaking with many of you, I've had many conversations about how we meet this challenge.

35 And I've been reassured

36 and I've been uplifted

37 we share a common goal for the future of sport.

38 No group of leaders does more than you to engage the hearts and minds of young people.

39 But every year the challenge of bringing them to Olympic sport becomes tougher.

40 The choice of Host City is the most powerful means you have to meet this challenge.

41 But it takes more than 17 days of superb Olympic competition.

42 It takes a broader vision. And the global voice to communicate that vision over the full four years of the Olympiad.

43 Today in Britain's fourth bid in recent years we offer London's vision of inspiration and legacy.

44 Choose London today

45 and you send a clear message to the youth of the world:

46 more than ever, the Olympic Games are for you.

47 Mr President, Members of the IOC: Some might say

48 that your decision today is between five similar bids.

49 That would be to undervalue the opportunity before you.

50 In the past, you have made bold decisions: decisions which have taken the Movement forward in new and exciting directions.

51 Your decision today is critical.

52 It is a decision about which bid offers the vision and sporting legacy to best promote the Olympic cause.

53 It is a decision about which city will help us show a new generation why sport matters. In a world of many distractions, why Olympic sport matters. And in the 21st century why the Olympic Ideals still matter so much.

54 On behalf of the youth of today, the athletes of tomorrow and the Olympians of the future, we humbly submit the bid of London 2012.

55 Mr President, that concludes our presentation.

56 Thank you.

3.2.1 Material processes

The most common, and perhaps the easiest to analyse, of the process types are *material processes*. These always involve, as the name suggests, an action in the material world in which someone or something does something, often but not necessarily to somebody or something else. An example of this occurs in Clause 6, where Coe says:

6.   Two athletes from our home town were competing

Clearly, competing is doing something physical, it is a material action; but to ana-lyse clauses on appearance alone would be a mistake as many processes are not so clear cut, often because, as language develops, it borrows features from one area of the grammar and puts them to work in new places or plays about with its resources to create special effects. It is necessary, therefore, to use grammatical **probes** to test for process types. As process types are categories that are distinguished by the grammar, it is logical that we as analysts can use grammatical probes to distinguish them. Judging by impression alone is called a *notional* approach, and while a cen-tral tenet of functional grammar is that grammatical categories relate to meaning differences, such an approach can miss seemingly slight yet significant differences between process types. Probes involve rephrasing the sentence using *agnate clauses*, clauses that are similar in meaning to the original clause but which differ from it in a particular way. The basic probes for material processes are as follows.

Basic Probes for material processes:

Can the process be rephrase in the form "What X did[1] was (to) ... "? Material processes can be rephrased this way.

Is the present continuous[2] form the form most naturally used to refer to the process if it is taking place *right now*? Material processes behave this way.

Note that DO in this sense is a *grammatical word*, signifying an action but having no specific content, so that the first probe is just as "grammatical" as the second. Applying these probes we find that "compete" in the clause is a material process:

7.   What the athletes did was (to) compete.
8.   The athletes are competing right now.

I said above that these were the "basic" probes for material processes; that is because these probes provide necessary but not sufficient bases for analysing a process as material. As we shall see below, two other process types can pass these probes: verbal and behavioural processes. This is because these two types also encode a degree of materiality. As Halliday says, our way of experiencing and representing the world does not always have neat boundaries. However, as verbal and mate-rial process types encode very specific types of actions they are subject to further probes. These probes, introduced below, grammatically distinguish verbal, behav-ioural and "mainstream" material actions and activities, and this is the basis for considering them different process types.

The first probe for material processes, above, also allows us to distinguish one of the participant roles (PRs) in material process, that of *Actor*: the person or thing that can be said to DO the competing, or whatever process is involved. Please beware, DO has many uses in English, so it's important to phrase the probe correctly. For example, we can say "I do love you", but it would be highly marked, or possibly a bit saucy, to say "What I did was love you". Note that an Actor in English doesn't necessarily have control over their actions and isn't necessarily responsible for them. This may be something that can be marked grammatically in other languages, in which case it would introduce a different participant role, or at least a subcategory. So, for example, when Coe says in Clause 9 that:

9. That day a window to a new world opened for me

it is "the window" that is the Actor, the thing that carries out the action (what the window **did** was open), although we understand that it was the Olympics that caused the metaphorical window to open. Coe could have said "That day opened a window to a new world for me", in which case "that day" would be the Actor; but he did not construe the event in that way, and it is Coe's construal that is of interest in this text. (For a complementary perspective see Halliday and Matthiessen 2004: 280–302 on ergativity.)

A different point of interest arises in Coe's opening clause:

10. I stand here today because of the inspiration of the Olympic Movement

In this clause "stand" looks like a material process; but notice the use of the present simple to refer to something happening *right now*. The use of this tense (or aspect, depending on your point of view) suggests that "stand" is not construing a material process here. The use of the simple present with material processes suggests habitual or repeated actions or activities, but Coe is clearly referring to a single event. Compare Coe's words with the following examples. * signals a poorly formed example and ? signals a dubious one:

11. I stand up whenever the teacher comes in.
12. I'm standing up right now.
13. *I stand up right now.

In these examples "stand up" is a material process, it's an action I habitually **do** whenever the teacher comes in or something I **am doing** right now (or **was doing** or **will be doing** at a specific time). In Coe's address, however, "stand" is a behavioural process, referring to his bodily posture. We'll look at behavioural processes in more detail below, but we can note in passing that behavioural processes can often be distinguished from material processes in that they do not refer to actions but states (or something between the two, like breathing) and so the present simple can be used to refer to **right now**. This is a good example of why it is necessary to go beyond a notional approach in analysing process types.

As well as construing a participant as doing something, material process also often construe the Actor as doing something **to someone or something**. In these cases, we have a *Goal* as well as an Actor. More specifically, we can say that in such processes an action is performed by an Actor which carries over to and impacts upon a Goal. This idea captures why such processes are traditionally called "transitive" (referring to a transition of action from one participant to another) and why Goal is the term used for the endpoint of the action.[3] Interestingly, Coe's address contains few examples of Goals, a point I will return to later. One example is found within Clause 20, though not a full clause in itself, where Coe says:

14. ... those flickering images ... drew me to a life in that most potent celebration of humanity: Olympic sport.

The probe for the Goal of a process is as follows:

Probe for Goal of a process:

Can the process be rephrased in the form "What X did to Y was ..."? If so, Y is Goal.

We can paraphrase Coe's clause using this probe as well as the second probe for material processes, above, as:

15. What those flickering images **did to me** was draw me to a life in that most potent celebration of humanity: Olympic sport.
16. Right now those flickering images **are drawing** me to a life in that most potent celebration of humanity: Olympic sport.

These probes show us that "those images" are the Actor in the process (they did the drawing) and that Seb Coe (realised here by the token "me") is the Goal (the person having the drawing "done to" them, the person who is impacted upon by the action). The following invented clauses show more obvious cases. The Actor is followed by (Ac), the Goal by (Go):

17. Tom (Ac) stroked the dog (Go).
18. The dog (Ac) ate my oatcakes (Go).

In example 17, Tom carries out the action of stroking, but the endpoint is the dog, and it is the dog that is impacted upon by the action. Impact can also be probed by using the passive form with GET rather than BE, as in "The dog **got** stroked". In example 18, the dog carries out the action of eating, but the endpoint was (it's a true story!) my oatcakes, which **get** eaten.

Note that in the passive, the Actor is either omitted or appears after the word BY, while the Goal is given Subject status (see Chapter 4 for a fuller description of the Subject):

19. The dog (Go) was stroked (by Tom (Ac)).
20. My oatcakes (Go) were eaten (by the dog (Ac)).

All material processes have an Actor either as a specified participant or implied in a passive clause. Example 21 is still a material clause, for example, despite the lack of overt Actor.

21. My oatcakes (Go) have been eaten.

No participant apart from an Actor is *necessary* for a clause to be material.

So far, relatively simple and common sense ... but there is, of course, a catch: some participants look like Goals, but are not, because they do not have anything **done to** them, they are not an endpoint and they are not impacted upon. For example, in clause 7 Coe says:

22. John Sherwood won a bronze medal in the 400m hurdles.

Here we can say that "What John Sherwood did was win the bronze medal", so showing that "John Sherwood" is construed as the Actor, and you might think that "a bronze medal" is the Goal of the process to win. However, if we apply the **DO TO** probe, we see that it does not fit:

23. *What John Sherwood did to a bronze medal was win it.

So, while "John Sherwood" is the Actor here, there is no Goal. This is because the nominal group "a bronze medal" is describing the extent of his victory, it is not having anything **done to** it. Note we can say "The bronze medal was won by John Sherwood" but not "The bronze medal **got** won by John Sherwood". We refer to participants of this type as the *Scope* of the process.[4] Perhaps the clearest example of this idea Scope as the extent of action rather than as Goal is in clause 24:

24. We (Ac) ran three miles (Sc).

There is another, more complex, and potentially less obvious and reliable, probe for Scopes in material clauses. All material clauses construe a participant as "changing" in some way, as having something **happen to** them. And note that HAPPEN is another grammatical word. In material processes with only a single participant the Actor has something happen to them. In processes with a Goal, it is the Goal that has something happen to them. When there is an Actor and a Scope, it is the Actor who has something happen to them. And when there is an Actor, a Goal and a Scope, it is the Goal that has something happen to them. In the clause above it is John Sherwood who has something happen to him, not the medal:

25. ?What happened to John Sherwood at the Olympics? He won a bronze medal.

Compare this with the following clauses:

26. What happened to John Sherwood in the 400m? He (Ac)won.
27. What happened to Tom Bartlett in the race yesterday? He (Ac) fell over.
28. ??What happened to the medal? John Sherwood won it (Sc).
29. What happened to the medal? Someone (Ac) stole it (Go).

One explanation for this is that a process with a Scope can be said to be just an extended form of the process rather than a process and a Goal. In these terms "winning a bronze medal" is the process, the same as "coming third" would be. Another way of understanding this is that the Scope is really in a circumstantial relation with the process. That is to say, it construes where, when or how much something happens (see below for further discussion of circumstantial elements). For example, in clause 16, Coe says:

30. Two days later I joined their club.

Note that we can say that "What Coe **did** was join their club" but not "What Coe **did to** their club was join it". This is because "their club" is a Scope in this process, it is not impacted upon. An alternative phrasing of the same idea would be:

31. Two days later I enrolled in their club.

In this construal of the event "their club" is a circumstantial element, marked by the preposition "in". However, while circumstantial elements are generally not essential for the process, Scopes are inherent elements. Scopes are therefore halfway between circumstantial elements and "full" participants in the process. But as they are construed by the grammar as Complements (that is, a necessary participant in the clause), we say that they are grammatically realised as participants, while we distinguish them from Goals to capture their "borderline" status.

Another function of a Scope is to complete the meaning of *bleached verbs* as parts of processes. In example 32 (clause 34 or the original text) Coe says:

32. … I've had many conversations about how we meet this challenge.

Here the verb "had" has been bleached of its original meaning "to possess" and has no real meaning without the addition of the Scope "many conversations". Again we see how Scopes can function to complete the meaning of processes rather than to construe a Goal. Common examples of this are:

33. I (Ac) had a bath (Sc).
34. John (Ac) gave Peter (Go) a kick (Sc).

These can be rephrased (despite the very dated style of 35!) as:

35. I (Ac) bathed.
36. John (Ac) kicked Peter (Go).

Let's compare clause 37 with clause 38:

37. John gave Peter a kick.
38. Two years later Sheila gave me my first pair of racing spikes.

Superficially, these two clauses look the same; yet there are *cryptogrammatical* differences between them. This wonderful word, introduced by Whorf, refers to grammatical differences that are not immediately obvious ("crypto" is the Greek for "hidden", often in reference to corpses ...) but are only revealed when we apply probes and consider variants (agnates) of the original clause. So let's do that, with a slight variation, altering the **do to** probe slightly as **do with**. This often produces a more natural sounding variant, and while a claim could be made on this basis that we have a different type of participant, in SFL the similarities rather than the differences are considered the criterial factor here.

39. *What John **did to** the kick was give it to Peter.
40. *What John **did with** the kick was give it to Peter.
41. What John **did to** Peter was give him a kick.
42. What Sheila **did with** the racing spikes was give them to Seb.
43. ??What Sheila **did to** Seb was give him his first pair of racing spikes.
44. *What Sheila **did with** Seb was give him his first pair of racing spikes.

What these probes show us is that "kick" is clearly a Scope in examples 39 to 41, where "Peter" is the Goal. In contrast, in example 42, "the racing spikes" pass the **do with** probe and can therefore be considered the Goal. We also see in examples 43 and 44 that "Seb" doesn't pass either test easily, and this is because Seb is construed as the *Recipient* (Rect) in the process, the one who receives something that is genuinely "given" in the full sense of the word (unlike a kick). In examples 39 to 41 GIVE is bleached of its original meaning, or perhaps we could say that it is being used metaphorically, and as a result "Peter" is the Goal of the extended process+Scope rather than a Recipient. This can be backed up by the following cryptogrammatical probes:

45. Sheila gave the racing spikes to Seb.
46. *John gave a kick to Peter.

Genuine Recipients, as opposed to Goals in metaphorical processes of giving, can appear in both forms "Give somebody something" or "Give something to somebody". This variation also explains why Example 47 is at least plausible, if a little forced: by construing the Recipient as a Complement, rather than using the preposition TO, the grammar is construing it as a little closer to a Goal, as someone or something that is impacted on by the process. This is backed up by the following examples of agnation:

47. ??What Sheila **did to** Seb was give him his first pair of racing spikes.
48. *What Sheila **did to** Seb was give his first pair of racing spikes to him.

There is thus a slight different in focus in the two construals "She gave the spikes to Seb" and "She gave Seb the spikes": in the first the spikes are seen as being impacted, in being transferred from one person to another; in the second there is *more of* an idea that Seb is impacted in becoming the new owner (and this is definitely the effect in Coe's address). However, SFL has tended to overlook these different nuances and in both cases the participant labelling is the same:

49. Two years later Sheila (Ac) gave me (Rect) my first pair of racing spikes (Go).
50. Two years later Sheila (Ac) gave her old racing spikes (Go) to Seb (Rect).

Notice how I've had to change the wording of the example 50 to make it more natural. This is occasionally necessary when features other than transitivity are at play in determining the way an idea is expressed.

We can now state the probe for the Recipient of a process.

Probe for Recipient of a process:

Can the participant be expressed using the form "to X" in processes of giving? If so, X is Recipient.

There is another optional participant in material processes that in some way resembles the Recipient, and that is the *Client* (Cli). Unfortunately, there are no examples in Coe's address, so I'll have to take liberties with an old song:

51. If I'd known you were coming I'd have baked you a cake.

Taking the second clause "I'd have baked you a cake" we can see that "I" is the Actor (what I **did** was bake a cake). A little more tricky is "cake": I didn't really do anything **to** it, as it didn't exist before I baked it. However, in Halliday's version of SFL only a secondary distinction is made between Goals that are *transformed* (have something **done to** them) and those that are *created*. These are both classified as Goals, though they can be more *delicately* classified (that is, subcategorised) as Go:transformative and Go:creative respectively.[5] The colon is used in SFL to signal more delicate distinctions such as these. But what of the "you" in "I'd have baked you a cake"? This looks a little like a Recipient, and both are referred to as *indirect objects* in traditional grammar, but closer examination (cryptogrammar again!) reveals that Clause 51 can't be rephrased using the preposition TO but the preposition FOR.

52. If I'd known you were coming I'd have baked a cake for you.
53. *If I'd known you were coming I'd have baked a cake to you.

This is the probe for Clients.

Probe for Client of a process:

> **Can the participant be expressed using the form "for X"? If so, X is Client.**

So, the analysis of the cake clause is:

54. I (Ac)'d have baked you (Cli) a cake (Go:cre).

Different dialects of English vary in terms of when it is okay to realise a Client as a Complement rather than with the preposition FOR. For example, my wife will say:

55. Put me (Cli) one of those on the table.

This sounds a little odd to me, but so do many of the things my wife says.

A final participant that we find in material processes is seen in clause 21 of Coe's address:

56. And that gratitude drives me and my team to do whatever we can to inspire young people to choose sport.

Taking the first half of this clause first, we see a complex example of transitivity in which something (gratitude) causes some people (Coe and his team) to do something (whatever they can). In examples such as this we label the person or thing that makes someone or something else do something material the *Initiator*, with the person or thing performing the actual action as the Actor. There are various types of causation encoded this way, so that helping and forcing someone to do something or even tricking them into doing it all involve an Initiator as well as an Actor (and possibly also a Goal).

Probe for Initiator of a process:

> **Can the process be expressed using the form "X made Y do Z"? If so, X is Initiator if Y is Actor in a material process.**

In fact, Coe's clause is more complicated than this as it includes a second type of causation, inspiring young people to choose sport. So, Clause 21 construes something causing some people to do something to cause others to do something – a complex transitivity chain, but one that is very important for the analysis that follows. The second type of causation is a little different, as choosing is a mental process (see below), and the people or things that induce someone to carry out a mental process are classified, naturally enough, as *Inducers* (In). We'll also see a third type of causation, verbal causation, below.

In example 56 the Inducer in "to inspire young people" is understood to be the same as the Actor of the previous process, "do what we can", and as it is not visible in the text we have to represent it in square brackets with two αs showing the relation. The full analysis is as follows. Note that "whatever we can" is a Scope, completing the meaning of "do"; Sen is Senser and Phen is Phenomenon, terms which will be explained in the following section:

57. And that gratitude (In) drives me and my team (Ac α) to do whatever we can
(Sc) to [αInd] inspire young people (Sen) to choose sport (Phen).

As this section has shown, there are various different ways in which participants can be involved in material processes – or more correctly, there are various ways in which participants can be construed as being involved. While each such construal is of interest, the focus of this book is more on how different participants are construed across whole texts (or at least significant stretches of text). For example, in Bartlett 2012a I analyse the 1977 Amerindian act of Guyana to explore the complementary rights and obligations of the Government of Guyana on the one hand and the indigenous Amerindian population on the other as these are construed in the Act. Material processes in the text are very important here in that they give us an insight into who the Government, as authors of the Act, see as Actors in various activities and who as Goals – the doers and the done to, respectively, the active and the passive. I then compared the material processes in a text written by the local population, the NRDDB Constitution, which sets out the complementary rights and obligations from the local perspective.[6] The results were very interesting in that they showed a clear symmetry between how the Government and the Amerindian population *positioned themselves and each other* as participants in the legal, economic and social activities that are seen as central to the good running and development of the Amerindian territories. In relation to material processes (though I looked at all process types), in the Amerindian Act the Government predominantly construe themselves as Actors and Initiators and the Amerindian population as Goals, Recipients of goods and money and Clients on whose behalf activities are carried out. The picture is very much one of the Government acting on and on behalf of a largely passive Amerindian population. In contrast, the NRDDB Constitution portrayed the local community as predominantly acting on their own behalf and often for the benefit of the Government. So much, of course, is only text analysis; but when we see the two texts as part of an ongoing legal discussion that is situated within the social history of the region, we are dealing with discourse.

Exercise 3.1

In the following extract, the opening of Martin Luther King's famous "I have a dream ..." speech, I have underlined all the material processes. Analyse the different participant roles for each process as they appear in the text and consider which referents fill these roles. See page 193 for the answers. Then consider the relationship between Black Americans and the US state and society as construed in material terms:

Text 3.2 Martin Luther King's *I Have a Dream* speech

1   I am happy to <u>join</u> with you today in what will <u>go down</u> in history as the greatest demonstration for freedom in the history of our nation.
2   Five score years ago, a great American, >< <u>signed</u> the Emancipation Proclamation.[7]
3   >in whose symbolic shadow we stand today,<
4   This momentous decree <u>came</u> as a great beacon light of hope to millions of Negro slaves who had been <u>seared</u> in the flames of withering injustice.
5   It <u>came</u> as a joyous daybreak to <u>end</u> the long night of their captivity.
6   But one hundred years later, the Negro still is not free.
7   One hundred years later, the life of the Negro is still sadly <u>crippled</u> by the manacles of segregation and the chains of discrimination.
8   One hundred years later, the Negro <u>lives</u> on a lonely island of poverty in the midst of a vast ocean of material prosperity.
9   One hundred years later, the Negro is still <u>languishing</u> in the corners of American society
10 and finds himself an exile in his own land.
11 So we have <u>come</u> here today to <u>dramatize</u> a shameful condition.
12 In a sense we have <u>come</u> to our nation's capital to <u>cash</u> a check.
13 When the architects of our republic <u>wrote</u> the magnificent words of the Constitution and the Declaration of Independence,
14 they were <u>signing</u> a promissory note to which every American was to fall heir.
15 This note was a promise that all men, yes, black men as well as white men, would be guaranteed the unalienable rights of life, liberty, and the pursuit of happiness.
16 It is obvious today that America has <u>defaulted</u> on this promissory note
17 insofar as her citizens of color are concerned.
18 Instead of <u>honoring</u> this sacred obligation, America has <u>given</u> the Negro people a bad check, a check which has <u>come back</u> <u>marked</u> "insufficient funds."
19 But we refuse to believe

20 that the bank of justice is bankrupt.
21 We refuse to believe
22 that there are insufficient funds in the great vaults of opportunity of this
    nation.
23 So we have <u>come</u> to <u>cash</u> this check – a check that will <u>give</u> us upon demand
    the riches of freedom and the security of justice.
24 We have also <u>come</u> to this hallowed spot to remind America of the fierce
    urgency of now.

(Source: www.usconstitution.net/dream.html © 1963 Dr Martin Luther King Jr ©
1991 Coretta Scott King)

3.2.2 Mental processes

In the last section I described material processes as construing actions in the material world. In contrast to these are *mental processes*, which construe processes that are not actions and that do not take place in the material world. Rather they are inner states, processes that involve thoughts, perceptions, emotions and desires. In fact, the grammars of thinking, perceiving, emoting and desiring are all realised a little differently from each other in English, giving us four subcategories, though they all share the same feature in needing a sensate participant – that is, someone who can feel or think, or something that is construed as being able to, as in:

58. I decided to buy a cake.
59. The old tree had seen many a battle fought around it.

The participant doing the sensing is called the Senser (Sen), and if what they sense is construed as a thing, rather than another process (see below), it is called the Phenomenon (Phen). So, in Coe's clause 21, discussed above and repeated here, "young people" are the Senser and "sport" is the Phenomenon. And, as discussed above, "we" is the Inducer, the participant construed as causing a mental process:

60. And that gratitude drives me and my team to do whatever we can to [Ind]
    inspire young people (Sen) to choose sport (Phen).

Here "choose" is an example of the subcategory of mental process known as *desiderative*, as choosing is a type of desiring or wanting. Examples for the subcategories *cognitive* (thinking), *perceptive* (perceiving with the senses) and *emotive* (liking or disliking) are as follows. Only the first of these is from Coe's address:

61. … whatever (Phen) they (Sen:cog) believe.
62. I (Sen:perc) can see the sea (Phen).
63. I (Sen:em) hate The X-Factor (Phen).

One interesting feature of emotive processes in particular is that either the Senser or the Phenomenon can be the Subject of active clauses:

64. I (Sen) like/hate/fear spiders (Phen).
65. Spiders (Phen) please/disgust/terrify me (Sen).

These variants are referred to as the *like-type* and the *please-type* respectively and such complementary pairs exist in a lot of languages, as if human experience has led us to understand emotive activities equally as reactions of the Senser (the like type) or as effects of the Phenomenon (the please type). Speakers construe one perspective or the other depending on the needs of their discourse at each point.

As mental processes refer to what happens in our minds, this means that they can construe not only what we think, feel, want or perceive with respect to individual things, but also what we think, feel want or perceive about complete events or activities. And as events and activities are typically realised as clauses in English, the different subcategories of mental processes combine with clause-like structures in a variety of ways.

Taking *emotive processes* first, rather than saying that chocolate as a food is something I like, I can say that it is the act of eating chocolate that I like:

66. I like eating chocolate.

The phrase "eating chocolate" in example 66 is not a full clause, but it does have certain features of a clause in that the material process "eating" is followed by "chocolate" as a Goal. And we can add further clausal elements if we want to say not that we like doing something ourselves but that we like it when somebody else does something:

67. I like you buying me jewellery.

Clauses or partial clauses that act as participants in a full clause are called **rankshifted clauses**. In cases like these, where the Phenomenon is an action or activity in itself, we refer to a **macrophenomenon**. For the purposes of marking up text it is easiest just to mark off the clausal elements in double square brackets and to label the whole bracketed element as the Phenomenon, as below (in this way you don't need to remember the term macrophenomenon!):

68. I (Sen) like [[you buying me jewellery]] (Phen).

Another complex type of Phenomenon is a **metaphenomenon**, which can alternatively be realised by a complete clause introduced by (THE FACT/IDEA) THAT. Again, we will just bracket these and mark them as Phen:

69. I (Sen) now regret [[that he bought me so much jewellery]] (Phen)
70. I (Sen) now regret [[the fact that he bought me so much jewellery]] (Phen)

This is quite a natural structure with like-type emotive processes. It is also possible with please-type processes but the structure is generally more awkward sounding:

71. [[The fact that he bought me the necklace]] (Phen) surprised me (Sen) greatly.

Clause 35 of Coe's address contains an example of the please type of mental processes, with the Senser as the Subject in the passive clause:

72. And I've been reassured
73. and I've been uplifted
74. we share a common goal for the future of sport.

We could add the phrase "by the fact that" to the coordinated clause 75, which suggests that we are dealing with metaphenomena:

75. And I've been reassured and I (Sen)'ve been uplifted by [[the fact that we share a common for the future of sport]] (Phen).

There is a little more than meets the eye to this sentence, however, and I'll return to this later.

Prepositions are omitted in English before that-clauses, and this can make metaphenomena hard to spot. So, as shown below, 76 represents a mental process and a metaphenomenon despite the ungrammaticality of 77:

76. I was angered that he should have acted that way.
77. *I was angered the fact that he should have acted that way.
78. I was angered by the fact that he should have acted that way.

Perceptive processes can take macrophenomena as Complements in a similar way to emotive processes:

79. I (Sen) saw [[you crossing the road]] (Phen).

However, a distinction is made with perceptive processes between whether someone or something is perceived in the process of doing something, as in example 79, or whether the complete action or event is perceived, as in example 80. The structure in example 81 is not possible with emotive processes:

80. I (Sen) saw [[you cross the road]] (Phen).
81. *I (Sen) like [[you cross the road]] (Phen)

There is an important semantic distinction here: the *bounded* clause in example 80 entails that you finished crossing the road and that I saw the whole process, while the *unbounded* clause in example 81 makes no such claim. This might seem like a small difference but it could be important when analysing legal discourse, for example, and distinguishing between what sort of events are seen either partially or in their entirety, or what sort of witness is construed as seeing whole or partial events.

As the Phenomena of perceptive processes are whole events (macrophenomena) rather than facts or ideas (metaphenomena) they cannot be introduced by THE FACT THAT:

82. *I saw [[the fact of you crossing the road]].
83. *I saw [[the fact of you cross the road]].

A further distinguishing feature of perceptive processes is that they generally take the modal auxiliary CAN (or COULD for the past) when they refer to an ongoing state:

84. I (Sen) can smell gas (Phen)!
85. I was always happy as long as I (Sen) could see the sea (Phen).
86. I (Sen) can feel a stone (Phen) in my shoe.

When we talk about the beginnings of a perception we generally don't use CAN:

87. I was excited when I (Sen) saw the sea (Phen).
88. Dick (Sen) suddenly felt [[a sharp object being pushed into his back]] (Phen).

Note that for perceptive process a whole event can be construed as a kind of thing, in which case it is just a simple Phenomenon:

89. The old tree (Sen:perc) had seen many a battle (Phen).

When *cognitive processes* relate to actions and events they *project* these as complete clauses, optionally introduced by THAT. Although they relate to ideas, mental projections are different from other metaphenomena in that they refer to ideas in the mind of the Senser, whereas other metaphenomena are construed as pre-existing ideas or presupposed facts (a very important category in philosophical and legal discourse). I'll use two slashes // to mark a projection:

90. I (Sen) think //(that) it will rain tomorrow.
91. *I think the fact that it will rain tomorrow.

However, if it is a question rather than a statement that is being projected then we use IF or WHETHER, not THAT, for yes–no questions and a wh-word for wh-questions. An example of this type appears in Clause 10 of Coe's address:

92. By the time I was back in the classroom I (Sen) knew //what I wanted to do and what I wanted to be.

Here the clause can be seen as a response to the unasked question "What do you want to be?"

This clause also includes the final type of cognitive processes: *desiderative processes*, or processes of wanting and hoping. When these refer to us wanting whole events or actions to take place they project a slightly reduced clause with a TO-infinitive:

93. England (Sen) expects //every man to do his duty.

Note that EXPECT can also be used in a cognitive sense, meaning roughly the same as THINK rather than WANT. This distinction is captured in the grammar, as in clause 94:

94. I (Sen) expect //that it will rain tomorrow.

When the event or action that is desired is to be carried out by the Senser themselves there is no Subject in the projected clause:

95. I (Sen) wanted// to be a runner.[8]

We saw above that LIKE generally realises an emotive process. However, in the following examples the semi-prefabricated phrases WOULD LIKE and WOULD HATE are functioning in a desiderative sense (you could paraphrase the clauses with WANT or NOT WANT) and this is reflected in the grammar:

96. Would you (Sen:desid) like //to go to Spain this year?
97. I (Sen:desid) would hate //to be all alone.

Compare these with the following emotive uses (as construed by the grammar):

98. Do you think you (Sen:em) would like [[living in Spain]] (Phen)?
99. She always said she would hate [[us saying goodbye]] (Phen).

As mental processes are states rather than activities, all four subtypes take the present simple tense even when referring to "right now":

100. At the present moment I (Sen) think //it was a mistake.

This contrasts with

101. At the present moment I'm thinking about my holidays.

which is a behavioural process, see below.

Similarly, mental processes are not things that you "do" and they therefore fail the do-probe while behavioural processes pass it:

102. *What I did was think it was going to rain.
103. What I'm doing is thinking about my holidays.

Probes for mental process:

Is one Participant in the process necessarily sensate? Can the process be phrased so as to either (i) project a separate event as a clause; or (ii) take a rankshifted clause as a participant? Mental processes behave this way.

Is the present simple form the form most naturally used to refer to something happening *right now*? Mental processes behave this way.

Does the process fail the DO-test? Mental processes fail it.

The following are the probes for distinguishing between mental process types, assuming that the general probes for mental processes have been passed.

Probes for distinguishing between mental processes:

Can the clause be phrased in such a way that the Phenomenon is a rankshifted clause with –ing for unbounded events or the infinitive for bounded events? If so, the process is perceptive.

104. I (Sen:perc) saw your brother (Phen).
105. I (Sen:perc) saw [[your brother buying sweets at the corner shop]] (Phen).
106. I (Sen:perc) saw [[your brother buy some sweets at the corner shop]] (Phen).

Can the clause be phrased in such a way that the Phenomenon is expressed by either (i) a rankshifted clause with the –ing form only; or (ii) a full clause potentially preceded by THE FACT? If so, the process is emotive.

107. I (Sen:em) like your brother (Phen).
108. I (Sen:em) like [[tickling your brother]] (Phen).
109. *I like [[tickle your brother]].
110. I (Sen:em) like [[your brother tickling me]] (Phen).
111. I (Sen:em) now regret my actions (Phen).

112. I (Sen:em) now regret [[(the fact) that your brother ever tickled me]] (Phen).

Note that emotive clauses can take a rankshifted clause with TO+infinitive (in contrast to the base infinitive of perceptive clauses):

113. I like to tickle your brother.
114. *I saw to tickle your brother.

There is a contrast in that the −ing form implies enjoyment or lack of enjoyment of the activity itself whereas the TO form implies (dis)satisfaction that it should happen:

115. I like to do my homework as soon as possible because I hate doing it!

> **Can the process project a full clause (where inclusion of THE FACT is not possible), potentially introduced by THAT, IF or a WH-word, in place of a Phenomenon? If so, the process is cognitive.**

116. She (Sen:cog) doesn't even know my name (Phen).
117. She (Sen:cog) knows // (that) I am called Tom.
118. *She knows the fact that I am called Tom.
119. I (Sen:cog) wonder // if it will rain.
120. I (Sen:cog) can't imagine // why you would do that.

> **Can the process project a clause which includes a TO-infinitive in place of a Phenomenon, but not an −ing clause? If so, the process is desiderative.**

121. Do you (Sen:desid) want an apple (Phen)?
122. Do you (Sen:desid) want//to eat an apple?
123. Or do you (Sen:desid) want//me to eat it?
124. I (Sen:desid) decided//to go.
125. *I want going.
126. *I decided going.

Mental processes can be used to construe different participants as thinking, being emotional, sensing things or wanting things. This can be an important distinction, especially if it is different classes of people who are regularly construed as having different mental reactions or who react mentally rather than acting in material processes. However, once again this is a textual distinction, and we have to consider any textual analysis within the wider environment to discuss the relevance of a speaker construing men or women, for example, as people of action or thoughtful, emotional or sensitive types and whether this construes them in a positive light at each point. To jump to a pair of terms from Chapter 4, there is no positive or negative attitude *inscribed* in the terms THINKING and FEELING, though there may be certain attitudes that are *evoked*. Similarly, we have to consider power relations in deciding the force of different participants wanting something to happen.

3.2.3 Verbal processes

Verbal processes are very similar to cognitive processes except they construe an idea or a thought as being put into words rather than staying in someone's head as, for example, when Coe states in clauses 47–48:

127. … Some might say that your decision today is between five similar bids.

Verbal processes always involve a *Sayer*, the person or thing who passes on the information, *as well as a representation in some form of the information relayed*. In example 127 the Sayer is the hypothetical "some" and their imagined words are projected in the clause "that your decision today is between five similar bids". As with cognitive mental processes the word THAT is optional in projections but THE FACT that cannot be used:

128. … Some might say your decision today is between five similar bids.
129. … *Some might say the fact that your decision today is between five similar bids.

Verbal processes can also include a *Receiver* (Recr), the person who picks up the message, but this is not essential, as example 128 shows, though. Coe could have included a Receiver:

130. … Some (Sayer) might say to you (Recr) //that your decision today is between five similar bids.

Note that it is the Receiver that must be sensate in verbal processes, not the Sayer:

131. The sign (Sayer) announced to passers-by (Recr) //that this was private land.

Receivers can be realised as Complements or after the preposition TO. However, many processes have restrictions on which forms they can take:

132. He (Sayer) swore to me (Recr) // that he was innocent.
133. *He swore me that he was innocent.
134. He (Sayer) told me (Recr) // that he was innocent.
135. *He told to me that he was innocent.

As with mental processes, if it is a question rather than a statement that is being projected then we use IF or WHETHER, not THAT, for yes–no questions and a wh-word for wh-questions.

136. He (Sayer) asked me (Recr)//whether I liked it or not.
137. May I (Sayer) enquire//when you are leaving?

Note that ENQUIRE rarely takes a Receiver and when it does it is the rather formal sounding OF:

138. Might I (Sayer) enquire of you (Recr) when you are leaving?

When a command is being projected the clause includes an infinitive with TO, rather like desiderative mental processes (as both convey the idea that someone wants someone to do something):

139. The boss (Sayer) ordered me (Recr)//to clear my desk immediately.

You will see that we often use different verbs such as INFORM, ENQUIRE or ORDER depending on whether we are projecting a statement, a question or a command. TELL is unusual in that it can be used for all three, with appropriate grammar for each:

140. He [Sayer] told me [Recr]//that he was called John,
141. [Sayer] Tell me (Recr)//if you want it or not.
142. I (Sayer) told him (Recr)//to get lost.
143. I was hoping you (Sayer) could tell me (Recr)//why you did that?
144. The dying cowboy (Sayer) told me (Recr)//what he was called.

Note that in example 141 the *projecting process* "tell" is an imperative with the Sayer understood as "you" and so we have to write this in square brackets.
    There is another potential example of a verbal process with a Receiver in Coe's address, and this appears in the coordinated clause we looked at above:

145. And I've been reassured
146. and I've been uplifted
147. we share a common goal for the future of sport.

Given that the previous clause refers to conversations, I think Coe is using "reassure" as a verbal process to mean:

148. People (Sayer) have reassured me (Recr) //that we share a common goal for the future of sport.

"Reassure" also, however, contains ideas of emotional reaction, an idea Coe takes up with "uplifted", which is an emotive process of the please type and cannot be a verbal process. However, as both take superficially similar that-constructions, this difference in process type is blurred in Coe's final utterance. So my reading of "that we share a common goal for the future of sport" is that it is functioning simultaneously as a projection of "reassured" and the Phenomenon of "uplifted". The full meaning would thus be:

149. And (Recr) I've been reassured//that we share a common goal for the future of sport and I(Sen)'ve been uplifted by [[the fact that we share a common goal for the future of sport]] (Phen).

Unfortunately (or fortunately?) for the analyst, such slippage often occurs in natural speech!

Sometimes the content of what is said can be condensed into a nominal group which is referred to as the *Verbiage* (Vb):

150. The dying cowboy (Sayer) told me (Recr) his name (Vb).

Verbiage also includes "units of information" as in:

151. [Sayer] Tell me (Recr) a story (Vb).
152. He (Sayer) barely said a word (Vb) all night.

The basic probes for verbal processes are as follows.

Basic probes for verbal processes:

Can the process project a separate event as a clause?[9]

Can the process have a Receiver that must be sensate?

If yes to both, then the process is verbal.

A rather different form of verbal process is where a *Target* is evaluated in speech:

153. ... activities (Tg) which have been highly praised by the Government (Sayer).

Targeted verbal processes are often followed by a circumstantial element explaining the reasons for the evaluation:

154. The Goverrment (Sayer) praised the activities (Tg) as daring and innovative.
155. Everybody (Sayer) blamed her (Tg) for the accident.
156. I (Sayer) can't thank you (Tg) enough for what you have done.

The probe for Targets is as follows.

Probe for Targets:

> **Does the process simultaneously construe an act or speaking and some evaluative content? Does the process involve two participants, one of which (X) is responsible for making the evaluation and the other of which (Y) is the entity evaluated? If so X is Sayer and Y is Target.**

Notice also that, in contrast to mental processes which refer to non-material states, verbal processes, as the material manifestation of ideas, both pass the DO test and usually take the progressive tense when referring to right now:

157. What's he doing? He (Sayer)'s telling them (Receiver) the time (Vb).

All verbal processes construe the passing on of information of some sort: either to the world in general, in which case no Recipient is expressed, or to a specific Recipient. This has two significant consequences. First, although we refer to these as verbal processes, they do not always construe the passing on of information by verbal means. And second, not all acts of speaking are construed as verbal processes. The names of the process types are convenient labels, but occasionally they can be misleading, which is another reason why we rely on grammatical probes rather than intuition in labelling them. Perhaps *informative processes* would have been a better term.

There is an example of a non-verbal verbal process (!) in clause 53 of Coe's address:

158. … which city will help us (Sayer) show a new generation (Recr)//why sport matters.

This could also be phrased with Verbiage in place of the projection:

159. … which city[10] will help us (Sayer) show a new generation (Recr) the importance of sport (Vb).

Although "showing" is used here for the passing on of information by material means, it is still a verbal process. As for acts of talking that are not verbal processes, these are covered in the following section on behavioural processes.

Verbal processes are useful in analysing position and power for three reasons: first, and most obviously, they construe certain people as speaking rather than doing, thinking or feeling (and as above the relative merits of each in a given environment is a locally contingent matter of discourse); second, they can suggest whose words as worthy of repetition; and third and related, they can be used as a means of crediting or discrediting a particular idea (see the discussion of attribution in Chapter 4).

3.2.5 Behavioural processes

In clause 34 of his address Coe says that:

160. In my travels over the last two years, speaking with many of you, I've had many conversations about how we meet this challenge.

While there are two examples of talking here, "speaking" and "having conversations", in neither case is the transfer of information itself represented. Clearly there must have been such a transfer, but as text analysts we are interested not so much in actions in the real world but in how events are construed in particular contexts, how writers focus on and interpret specific aspects and details of the events they represent. In the present example Coe represents his talk as a form of activity rather than as an exchange of information. It is possible to close in on the subject matter of the talk, as in "how we meet this challenge", above, and to include interlocutors in the construal but, as there is no reproduction of the actual content of the talk, these processes cannot be categorised as verbal processes by the definition and criteria provided in the previous section. Rather they are a type of behavioural process,[11] which Halliday and Matthiessen (2004:248) describe as "processes of (typically human) physiological and psychological behaviour", often the material manifestations of mental processes. In this sense "talking" and "chatting" are behavioural processes, focusing on the activity of speaking, in contrast to verbal processes, which construe the act of saying something as a transfer of information. Returning to the example above we can suggest that what Coe is emphasising here is the fact that he has been heavily involved in the activity of talking, with the suggestion of a two-way exchange of information, but without the specific details of what was said.

Taking this a little bit further we can talk about clauses as a whole representing different degrees of information transfer.

161. Gerard (Beh) was talking.
162. He (Beh) was talking to his colleague (Recr).
163. He (Beh) was talking about football (Circ:matter).
164. He (Sayer) was slagging the game (Tg) off.
165. He (Sayer) told me (Recr) the score (Vb).
166. He (Sayer) told me (Recr) // that the score was five-nil.

In example 161 Gerard is construed as being involved in a behavioural process, one up from a material one in evolutionary terms, but without any specific transfer of information being mentioned. In 162, we have a Receiver, but there is still no transfer of information construed. In 163 we are getting closer in that there is a topic introduced, but this is still vague and does not constitute a transfer of information. In 164 a transfer of information is construed, but in fairly vague terms: we know that Gerard said something bad about the game, but we don't know what exactly. In 165 we are given more detailed information, but we don't get a construal of Gerard's exact words until clause 166. So across the clauses we see a gradual increase in the degree of information exchange construed, but it is only from 164 on that we are dealing with a verbal process type as this means that the process encodes the transfer of information as part of its meaning. These distinctions show that the construal of meaning across the clause is a combination of various elements: the nature of the process itself and also the nature of the participants and Circumstances (see below) which are also parts of the transitivity system.

Other behavioural processes are closer to mental process of cognition. In these cases they refer not to our hopes and beliefs but to the temporary focus of our attention:

167. I (Beh) was just thinking about my holidays.

Similarly, there are behavioural processes relating to the deliberate focusing of our perceptions:

168. What are you (Beh) looking at?

Behavioural processes involving speaking, thinking and perceiving almost always encode only a single participant, the human *Behaver* (Beh). When there is a focus on the behaviour this is generally introduced by a preposition, as in 167 and 168 above and, potentially, in clause 34 of Coe's address ("had conversations about"). Halliday (Halliday and Matthiessen 2004:251) cites WATCH as an exception as this encodes two participants, the Behaver and a Phenomenon. Clause 5 of Coe's address is an example of this:

169. and [we (Beh)] watched grainy pictures from the Mexico Olympic Games (Phen).

Despite Halliday's claim that WATCH is an exception here, the action senses of SMELL, FEEL and TASTE would also seem to fit into this category:

170. I got my nose stung when I (Beh) was smelling the flower (Phen).

A further type of behavioural process refers simply to physiological processes such as breathing, coughing or farting. Slightly further along the evolutionary scale are processes which reflect conscious states, as with laugh, smile and frown. Interestingly, such processes can be used as quotatives after direct speech:

171. "I feel a little queasy", she frowned.

And as discussed above, processes referring to bodily posture are analysed as behavioural:

172. I (Beh) stand here today.

Given the range of meanings of behavioural processes and their similarity at times to mental and verbal processes, it is useful from the point of view of text analysis to distinguish between behavioural:mental (or more delicately still, as behavioural: cog, etc.), behavioural:verbal and other behavioural processes. Taking this angle, we can analyse example 167 above as:

173. I (Beh:cog) was just thinking about my holidays.

As behavioural processes are forms of activity they take the continuous form when referring to "right now":

174. Shut up, will you? I'm (Beh:cog) thinking.

As you can see behavioural processes are a bit of a mixed bag with only a single common feature that can be probed, the need for a Sensate participant (and even here this probe on its own cannot distinguish behavioural processes from cognitive processes, for example).

Probe for behavioural processes:

Does the process encode a participant that must be sensate?

However, as behavioural processes are seen as sensate activities, they usually take the continuous form with the "right now" test. There are exceptions, though these sound dated or formal:

175. I (Beh) stand here today.
176. She (Beh) breathes!
177. Why do you (Beh) laugh?

The DO-test can also provide unconvincing results:

178. ??What he did next was breathe.

Halliday and Matthiessen (2004:248) admit that behaviourals are "the least distinct of the six process types", and some analysts do not agree on the need for such a category at all (for example, Banks *forthcoming*). However, from a discourse analytical point of view, I think there is a worthwhile distinction to be made between, for example, the conveying of information, talking as an activity, and laughing and belching as non-verbal human behaviour.

Exercise 3.2

Look at the following text, Tony Blair's response to the London bombings of 7 July 2005, in which I've underlined material, mental, verbal and behavioural processes. Identify the different participants involved in these processes as well as any projected clauses. Then discuss how Tony Blair develops his response in terms of thought and action and why this rhetorical strategy may have been effective.

To contextualise Blair's response you should read up on the events and do some background reading on Tony Blair and his relationship with the electorate and more generally on what the US called the "War on Terror". This information will be helpful when we analyse the text as discourse in more detail later on. It would also be interesting to see how commentators in the press evaluated Blair's speech at the time and to see if their evaluations match the linguistic insights gained from the transitivity analysis and other analyses in later chapters.

Text 3.3 Blair's 7/7 response

1 I am just going to <u>make</u> a short statement to you [[on the terrible events that have <u>happened</u> in London earlier today]],
2 and I <u>hope</u>
3 you <u>understand</u>
4 that at the present time we are still trying to <u>establish</u> exactly [[what has <u>happened</u>]],
5 and there is a limit to [[what information I can <u>give</u> you]],
6 and I will simply try and <u>tell</u> you the information as best I can at the moment.
7 It is reasonably clear that there have been a series of terrorist attacks in London.
8 There are obviously casualties, both people [[that have <u>died</u>]] and people seriously <u>injured</u>,
9 and our thoughts and prayers of course are with the victims and their families.
10 It is my intention to <u>leave</u> the G8 within the next couple of hours and <u>go down</u> to London and <u>get</u> a report, face-to-face, with the police, and the emergency services and the Ministers [[that have been <u>dealing with</u> this]], and then to <u>return</u> later this evening.
11 It is the will of all the leaders at the G8 however that the meeting should <u>continue</u> in my absence, that we should continue to <u>discuss</u> the issues that we were going to <u>discuss</u>, and <u>reach</u> the conclusions which we were going to <u>reach</u>.
12 Each of the countries round that table have some experience of the effects of terrorism
13 and all the leaders> < share our complete resolution to <u>defeat</u> this terrorism.
14 >as they will <u>indicate</u> a little bit later<
15 It is particularly barbaric that this has <u>happened</u> on a day [[when people are

meeting to try to help the problems of poverty in Africa, and the long term problems of climate change and the environment]]

16 Just as it is reasonably clear that this is a terrorist attack, or a series of terrorist attacks,

17 it is also reasonably clear that it is designed and aimed to coincide with the opening of the G8.

18 There will be time to talk later about this.

19 It is important however that those engaged in terrorism realise

20 that our determination to defend our values and our way of life is greater than their determination to cause death and destruction to innocent people in a desire to impose extremism on the world.

21 Whatever they do,

22 it is our determination that they will never succeed in destroying what we hold dear in this country and in other civilised nations throughout the world.

You may have noticed some other words connected with knowledge, hopes and desires at the beginning of clauses 7 to 11 and again in clauses 20 to 22. I have not analysed them here as they are not functioning as processes in a clause. They are, however, play a very important role in the interplay of thought and deed that Blair is developing here and we'll return to look at these in detail in Chapter 5.

3.2.6 Relational processes

Up to this point we have looked at ways in which speakers can construe the inner and outer experiences of others. Another class of process is exemplified in clause 25 of Coe's address:

179. Today that task is so much harder.

This is an example of a *relational process*. These are processes which relate referents and concepts in terms of the logical relationships that hold between them. Here Coe is not talking about "that task" as being involved in any activity, he is describing it in terms of one of its attributes or defining features, that of being harder than previously. As relational processes construe states rather than activities they use the simple present even for "right now", as a paraphrase of 179 shows:

180. Right now that task is so much harder.

A few clauses later Coe expands upon his idea, describing the lives of today's children in ways that explain why the task is now harder:

181. Their landscape is cluttered.[12]
182. Their path to Olympic sport is often obscured.

In each of these examples we have a participant being described and a term describing them, and we can label these as Carriers (Ca) and the Attributes (At) that they carry:

183. Today that task (Ca) is so much harder (At).

In passing it's worth noting that the term "participant" seems a little counter-intuitive for the Attributes in the relational processes above. This is because it is being used in a specific grammatical sense. In the following examples it sounds more natural.

    Attributes often refer to qualities, as above, but they can also refer to categories, as with this example from just two clauses later in Coe's address:

184. My heroes (Ca) were Olympians (At).

This is the structure that is most commonly used to say what someone does for a living, as in 185, but it can be used for other purposes too:

185. My grandfather (Ca) was a doctor (At).
186. You're (Ca) a bloody idiot (At)!

As well as Attributes which are qualities (realised by adjectives) or categories (realised by nominal groups), as above, we can have attributes expressing relations such as time, place, manner and cause, concepts usually realised by Circumstances. There is an example of this use in Coe's address where he describes himself in terms of his location:

187. By the time I (Ca) was back in my classroom (At:Circ)

Examples of matter (that is, topic) and cause would be:

189. This book (Ca) is about text analysis (A:Circ).
190. The delay (Ca) was because of leaves on the track (At:Circ).

As you will have seen, attributive processes generally involve the verb to be; however, sometimes ideas of time and location etc. are included in the process itself:

191. The voyage from Oban to Castlebay (Ca) takes about five hours (At).

A very similar example to this appears as clause 41 of Coe's address:

192. But it (Ca) takes more than 17 days of superb Olympic competition (At).

In English age is also an attribute, as in clause 2 of Coe's address:

193. When I (Ca) was 12 (At)

Relational processes might additionally include an idea of change, in which case the continuous forms are possible:

194. He's (Ca) growing old (At).

As transitivity refers to the relation between the participants examples such as 194 are still relational even though growing old could be considered a material process in notional terms. Similarly, relational processes can contain an element of perception. In these cases they still encode a relationship between a Carrier and an Attribute:

195. This all (Ca) seems/looks/sounds quite complicated (At).

In these cases it is useful to add the idea of perception as a subclassifier

196. This all (Ca) looks (relational:perc) quite complicated (At).

Attributive processes can occur in progressive tenses when there is an element of control suggested. In such cases they usually also pass the DO-test:

197. He's (Ca) just being silly (At)!
198. When they are frightened what some animals (Ca) do is play dead (At).

Attributive processes can occasionally take a Client:

199. He'll (Ca) make someone (Cli) a good husband (At) one day.

In many other languages age is expressed by a verb that has the general meaning "to have", as are emotions and fears. In English "to have" is used to express a different type of attributive relation, that of possession:

200. My friends (Ca:pos) have all got Porsches (At:pos)

There is an example of possessive attribution in Clause 37 of Coe's address:[13]

201. ... we (Ca) share a common goal for the future of sport (At:pos) ...

Attributive clauses can involve an extra participant – the one responsible for the attribution, called the *Attributor* (Attr), as in:

202. Why did you (Attr) call me (Ca) stupid (At)?
203. You (Attr) could always paint them (Ca) green (At).

Attributes occasionally appear in a similar construction after material processes:

204. They (Ac) built the wall (Go) too high (At).

Attributive clauses such as those we have just seen are one type of *relational clause*, another type is ***identifying clauses***. Whereas attributive clauses describe someone or something in terms of features, identifying clauses are used to state that two things are in some way the same thing. So, to give a fairly straightforward example, let's look at Clause 32 of Coe's address, where he says:

205. And they are the lucky ones.

Here the lucky ones are Coe's kids. Notice Coe doesn't simply say that they are lucky, but rather that they comprise one group," the lucky ones", with the "millions more" he talks of comprising the alternative group of unlucky ones. And as, according to Coe, "the lucky ones" and "my children" are the same thing, it doesn't matter which way we phrase the relationship:

206. My children are the lucky ones.
207. The lucky ones are my children.

Another example of an identifying process is in Clause 40 where Coe, after discussing the nature of the challenge ahead of the Committee, goes on to identify how best to meet the challenge:

208. The choice of Host City is the most powerful means you have to meet this challenge.

Once again, this clause can be "reversed":

209. The most powerful means you have to meet this challenge is the choice of Host City.

This idea of "reversibility" doesn't hold for attributive processes. Example 210, as a reversal of example 185 above, would be a highly marked usage:

210. *A doctor (At) was my grandfather (Ca).

In contrast identifying clauses with BE reverse very easily, as we have seen. However, not all identifying clauses are realised by BE, and whenever a different verb is used then reversibility entails using a passive form. Imagine I am describing a battle using anything available on my kitchen table. I could say:

211. The salt cellar is the HQ.
212. The HQ is the salt cellar.
213. The salt cellar represents the HQ.
214. The HQ is represented by the salt cellar.

We can therefore distinguish between the participants in an identifying clause, despite the fact that they are being construed as the same thing! The participant that represents something else is called the *Token* (Tk) – as in a token of my affection – and the participant that is represented by something is called the *Value* (Val). We can even do this for clauses using BE by paraphrasing them using REPRESENT. Though this is sometimes awkward-sounding it's always understandable. Remember: Token represents Value. This gives us the following analyses:

215. My children (Tk) are the lucky ones (Val).
216. The lucky ones (Val) are my children (Tk).
217. My children (Tk) represent the lucky ones (Val).
218. The lucky ones (Val) are represented by my children (Tk).
219. The salt cellar (Tk) is the HQ (Val).
220. The HQ (Val) is the salt cellar (Tk).
221. The salt cellar (Tk) represents the HQ (Val).
222. The HQ (Val) is represented by the salt cellar (Tk).

As with attributive processes it is possible to have a circumstantial element included in an identifying process. The following example includes a temporal meaning of duration:

223. The meeting (Tk) takes up the whole afternoon (Val).
224. The whole afternoon (Val) is taken up by the meeting (Tk).

In these clauses the whole afternoon and the meeting are seen as coextensive, and this identity relationship is captured by the grammar here. Coextension can relate to space as well as time, as in:

225. Trees (Tk) line the road (Val).
226. The road (Val) is lined by trees (Tk).

Here the trees are seen not just as features of the road but as marking off its boundaries – tokens of its limits. Compare this with the more descriptive attributive variant:

227. The road (Ca) is lined with trees (At).

Identifying processes can be very hard to analyse as they are often realised by metaphorical extensions of other process types, particularly verbal processes. For example, and just to add a little to the confusion caused by describing SHOW[14] as a non-verbal verbal process above, in the following example "show" is an identifying process:

228. The arrows (Tk) showed where we should walk (Val).

Example 228 reverses very naturally, as opposed to the verbal use of SHOW:

229. Where we should walk (Val) was shown by the arrows (Tk).
230. The teacher showed us why he was wrong.
231. ?? Why he was wrong was shown (to us) by the teacher.

Note also that, as a subcategory of relational clauses describing states, identifying clauses take the simple tenses, while verbal processes tend to take continuous forms for "right now":

232. *Trees (Tk) are lining the road (Val).
233. The teacher (Sayer) was showing us (Recr)//why he was wrong.

Identifying processes can have a macrophenomenon as the Token or Value:

234. [[(The fact) that he's stupid]] (Val) is shown by his behaviour (Tk).
235. His behaviour shows (Tk) [[(the fact) that he's stupid]] (Val).

Identifying clauses can also involve the participant responsible for the identification, called the *Assigner* (Assr), as in:

236. Why on earth did they (Assr) elect you (Tk) as the president (Val)?

As this example shows, the Value can be explicitly signalled by the preposition AS (which is optional here).

Let's note in passing that we can also have possessive identifying clauses, as shown by their reversibility, though I must admit I am yet to get my head around the semantics of this category:

237. George Washington once owned these false teeth.
238. These false teeth were once owned by George Washington.

Probes for relational processes:

If the unmarked form of the process for the "right now" test is the simple present and if the process cannot project, then it is relational. If the process cannot reverse it is attributive and Subject is Carrier; if the process is reversible it is identifying and Token is Subject in active form.

Attributive relational processes can take continuous tenses when there is an element of change or an idea of control.

3.2.7 Existential processes

The last process types we will look at *existential processes*, which take the Subject THERE (or can have it inserted with no change of meaning) and a verb, with the whole structure followed by the single participant, which is called the *Existent* (Ex).

Be careful to distinguish the existential Subject THERE from the demonstrative pronoun THERE. The existential form can be pronounced with a short vowel, the pronoun cannot. Existential processes are often used along with a Circumstance of location to introduce new participants into a text. Compare the existential process in 239 and the relational process in 240:

239. There was a strange-looking man (Ex) on the corner.
240. The strange looking man (Ca) was there (At:circ).

They are also, as the name suggests, used to construe the existence of something either in general or in a specific place:

241. Is there any sugar (Ex)?
242. Is there a God (Ex)?
243. There are no chocolates (Ex) in the chocolate box.

Be careful though: the verb EXIST construes a one-participant relational process!

The Circumstance can be placed before the existential structure. When it is, then the process precedes the Existent. In contrast, when the demonstrative article THERE is placed first then the process follows the Carrier:

244. In the room there was a cat (Ex).
245. There (At:cicr) the cat (Ca) is!

The verb realising existential processes is generally the verb BE. Verbs other than BE can be used when the Circumstance comes first. Other relational processes, intransitive material processes of moving or appearing and, occasionally, agent-less passives can be used and in such cases the process construed is considered existential:[15]

246. In the room (there) stood a single bookshelf (Ex).
247. Over the mountain (there) flew an eagle (Ex).
248. Into the room (there) ran a small boy (Ex).
249. Out of the dark (there) appeared a grim figure (Ex).
250. Onto my lap (there) was placed a small child (Ex).

When the Circumstance is placed before the existential structure it is possible to omit THERE – but it is always possible to insert it, as signalled by the brackets, and this is the probe for existential processes.

Existential processes are always third person even if the Existent is YOU or I. It is always singular with pronouns even when these are plural:

251. There's me (Ex) and there's you (Ex).
252. There's them (Ex) and there's us (Ex).

The contracted singular form of BE is also often used in existential structures even when the Existent is plural:

253. There's no chocolates (Ex) in my chocolate box.

Probe for existential processes:

If the Subject THERE is present or can be inserted without changing the sense the process is existential.

Existential processes take the simple present in the "right now" test.

Exercise 3.3

I've underlined all the relational and existential processes in Tony Blair's speech. Identify the different process types and the participants involved (answers on p. 195) and discuss how this adds to your understanding of the text so far.

1 I am just going to make a short statement to you on the terrible events that have happened in London earlier today,
2 and I hope
3 you understand
4 that at the present time we are still trying to establish exactly what has happened,
5 and there is a limit to what information I can give you,
6 and I will simply try and tell you the information as best I can at the moment.
7 It is reasonably clear that there have been a series of terrorist attacks in London.
8 There are obviously casualties, both people that have died and people seriously injured,
9 and our thoughts and prayers of course are with the victims and their families.
10 It is my intention to leave the G8 within the next couple of hours and go down to London and get a report, face-to-face, with the police, and the emergency services and the Ministers that have been dealing with this, and then to return later this evening.
11 It is the will of all the leaders at the G8 however that the meeting should continue in my absence, that we should continue to discuss the issues that we were going to discuss, and reach the conclusions which we were going to reach.
12 Each of the countries round that table have some experience of the effects of terrorism
13 and all the leaders> < share our complete resolution to defeat this terrorism.
14 >as they will indicate a little bit later<

15 It is particularly barbaric that this has happened on a day when people are meeting to try to help the problems of poverty in Africa, and the long term problems of climate change and the environment

16 Just as it is reasonably clear that this is a terrorist attack, or a series of terrorist attacks,

17 it is also reasonably clear that it is[16] designed and aimed to coincide with the opening of the G8.

18 There will be time to talk later about this.

19 It is important however that those engaged in terrorism realise

20 that our determination to defend our values and our way of life is greater than their determination to cause death and destruction to innocent people in a desire to impose extremism on the world.

21 Whatever they do,

22 it is our determination that they will never succeed in destroying what we hold dear in this country and in other civilised nations throughout the world.

3.2.8 Summary of probes

Table 3.1 presents a summary of the probes (or potential grammatical patterns) of the different process types – have fun trying them out!

TABLE 3.1 Summary of probes

	DO-test	Projection or macrophenomenon?	THERE as Subject	Right now-test	Receiver	Recipient	Client
Material	√	X	X	cont.	X	√	√
Mental	X	Cognitive and desiderative– projection; Perceptive and emotive – macrophenomenon	X	simple	X	X	X
Verbal	√	Projection	X	usually cont.	√	X	X
Behavioural	?	Only after preposition except for WATCH and FEEL	X	usually cont.	X	X	X
Relational: attributive	For control or change only	X	X	simple except for change or control	X	X	Rare
Relational: identifying	X	Macrophenomenon only	X	simple	X	X	X
Existential	X	X	√	simple	X	X	X

3.3 Transitivity: circumstances

As stated earlier transitivity involves not only process types and participants, which form the *nucleus* or necessary elements of the events described, but also the circumstantial elements that provide additional optional details. For example, in the following example, the word slowly could be omitted, whereas the other elements of the clause are all necessary to describe the event fully:

254. The coachman slowly rang the doorbell.

In example 254, then, the process is "rang" and the participants involved in the ringing are "the coachman" and "the doorbell". All three elements are therefore necessary to represent the event. "Slowly", in contrast, is an optional extra telling us "how" he rang the bell.[17] As such it is referred to as a Circumstance of manner. These are often realised by adverbs ending in –ly in English. There is not room to discuss Circumstances in depth here but Table 3.2 gives a summary of the nine basic types as at least a passing familiarity will be needed. An analysis of Circumstances is particularly important when analysing how texts develop, and we'll return to them in Chapter 5. They also form part of a full transitivity analysis, as we'll now see in relation to Seb Coe's address, which is analysed in Table 3.3. For fuller treatments of Circumstances see Martin, Matthiessen and Painter 1997:127–130 and Halliday and Matthiessen 2004:259–279).

3.4 Transitivity analysis of full text

In this section I'll present and discuss an analysis of Coe's address in its entirety. An important point to note here is how I've based the transitivity analysis around the most important referents identified in Chapter 2. An alternative method is to analyse the main verb of each clause, and there are advantages to each approach. Analysing the main verbs of each clause can tell us a lot about the *style* of individual texts and about genres of language, but this approach misses out on a lot of the action, which often appears in embedded clauses. Analysing by referent allows us to see how that person or thing is being construed by the speaker and this is of interest when discussing how position and power are realised in discourse. When analysing by referent we look at every process in which that referent is involved, no matter its function within the clause. This means that we will sometimes have clauses where there are no relevant processes and, conversely, clauses where we analyse several. We will also include cases where the referent appears as a personal pronoun, as in "their lives", and those cases where the referent appears in Circumstances rather than in the nucleus of the clause. These additions provide an extra angle for analysis. I've provided notes for the less straightforward examples (and at least once where I have taken a justifiable liberty!). Have a good look at the text and Table 3.3 together and then move on to the discussion that follows.

TABLE 3.2 Types of circumstance

Type	Subtype	Question answered	Example
Extent	Distance	How far?	He jumped <u>three metres</u>.
	Duration	How long?	The film lasted <u>(for) three hours</u>.
	Frequency	How often?	She comes <u>every second Thursday</u>
Location	Place	Where?	I stroked the dog <u>on the ear/in the park</u>.
	Time	When?	He got promoted <u>last year</u>.
Manner	Means	By what means?/How?	He blew it up <u>with dynamite</u>.
	Quality	How?	He rang the bell <u>slowly</u>.
	Comparison	Like what?	She ran <u>like the wind</u>.
	Degree	How much?	Tom loves Mary <u>more than anything</u>.
Cause	Reason	Why?	She ran <u>because she was scared</u>.
	Purpose	For what purpose?/To what end?	She ran <u>to raise money</u>.
	Behalf	On whose behalf?/Who for?	She died <u>for the cause</u>.
Contingency	Condition	Under what conditions?	<u>In the event of fire</u> leave the building.
	Default	Under what negative conditions?	<u>Without an agreement</u> the plan will fail.
	Concession	With what concessions?/Despite what?	<u>Despite my advice</u> the plan failed.
Accompaniment	Comitative	(Along) with who/what?	I saw him walking <u>with Jane</u>.
	Additive	Who/what else?	I like my gin <u>with tonic</u>.
Role	Guise	What as?	He came <u>as a pumpkin</u>.
	Product	What into?	She turned him <u>into a mouse</u>.
Matter	Matter	What about?	We were talking <u>about the game</u>.
Angle	Source	According to whom?	<u>According to the papers</u> the game was fixed.
	Viewpoint	In whose view?	<u>To me</u> it's all a load of rubbish.

3.5 Discussion of analysis

A transitivity analysis adds another dimension to the texturing of continuity and change we saw with regard to reference and motifs in Chapter 2. For longer texts it might be most appropriate or practical to consider the overall *method of development* (see also Chapter 5) of a text by identifying sizeable sections of the text in which

TABLE 3.3 Transitivity analysis of Coe's Olympic address

Clause	Process	Coe (and others)	Athletes	Olympic Games/sport	Community	IOC
1	stand	Beh		Circ:cause		
1	inspiration[1]	(Sen[2])		Phen		
2	be 12	Ca				
3	march	Go				
4	sit	Ac				
5	watch	Beh:perc		Phen		
6	compete		Ac			
7	win		Ac	Circ:loc		
8	miss		Ac	Circ:loc		
9	open	Cli				
10	be back in classroom	Ca				
11	know	Sen:cog				
12	want	Sen:desid				
12	do	Ac				
13	be	Ca				
13	want	Sen:desid				
14	stand	Ac				
14	catch a glimpse of	Cog:perc				
14	bring		Ac			
16	join	Ac				
17	give	Rect	Ac			
18	stand	Beh				
18	inspire	Sen		Phen		
19	started	my journey Ac				
20	continues	my journey Ac				
20	draw	Go	Ac	Circ:loc		
21	do	Ac				

TABLE 3.3 Continued

Clause	Process	Coe (and others)	Athletes	Olympic Games/sport	Community	IOC
21	inspire	Ind		Phen	Sen	
22	be				Ca	
23	live				Ca[3]	
24	believe				Sen:cog	
26	live				Ca	
27	be				their landscapes Ca	
28	be			Circ:loc	their path Ca	
29	understand	Sen:cog			their world Phen	
29	respond	Ac			their world Circ:cause	
30	be Olympians		At			
31	change				My children's heroes Ac	
32	be the lucky ones				Tk	
33	face				Sen:perc[4]	
34	my travels	Ac[5]				
34	speak	Beh:verbal				Recr
34	have conversations	Beh:verbal				
34	meet	Ac[6]				Ac
35	reassure	Recr				(Sayer)
36	uplift	Sen				Ind
37	share	Ca[7]		Common goal for the future of sport At:pos		Ca
38	do					Ac
38	engage				The hearts and minds of young people Go	Ac
39	bring			Go		
40	have				Rect	Ca:pos
40	meet	Ac				Ac

No.	Process				
41	take		At	Global voice At	
42	take			Global voice Sayer	
42	communicate		Circ:temp		
43	offer	Ac			Rect
44	choose				Sen:desid
45	send a message			Recr / Circ:Cli	Beh:vbl
46	be		Ca		
48	be				Your decision Ca/ Sen:desid[8]
50	make bold decisions				Beh:desid
50	take forward				Go
51	be				Your decision Ca/ Sen:desid
52	promote		Tg/Go[9]		Your decision At/ Sen:desid
53	be				Sayer
53	show	Sayer[10]		Recr	
53	matters		Ca[11]		
53	matters		Ca		
54	submit	Ac			
55	conclude	Our presentation Go/Sayer		3xCirc:behalf	

Notes

1 Although not a grammatical process and already signalled as the Circ:cause above, I have included inspiration as it construes a relationship between Coe and the Olympics.

2 Coe as Senser is implicit.

3 This meaning of LIVE is "be resident"; it is necessarily followed by a Circumstance of location or preceded by a wh-word of location; and the unmarked tense is the present simple, so I analyse it as relational.

TABLE 3.3 Continued

4 "Face" could take "the fact that they have limited resources" or "having limited resources" as Complement so I see it as a mental process.

5 This is a metaphorical phrase and means "while travelling", so I have decided to label Coe the Actor here as this best suits the angle of analysis. A different analysis might have been appropriate if we were discussing the method of construal rather than the content.

6 This is similar to "face" in clause 33 but can't take a that clause as a Complement. It has an added idea of "tackle" and takes the progressive tense naturally so I have analysed it as material.

7 Though this might be an identifying possessive clause, introduced later, as there are some agnate clauses which are reversible.

8 Here and in several of the following clauses I've analysed such examples for both the role of the IOC and/or Coe and for the whole nominal group "your decision" or "our presentation".

9 I see this as a borderline case between extolling the virtues of the Olympic cause (which would be a Target) and increasing the profile of the cause (which would be a Goal). In practice it probably suggests a bit of both.

10 See the discussion of "show" in the chapter.

11 A relational process with unmarked simple tense, meaning "be important".

specific configurations of participant relations predominate and seeing how these shift as the text develops. In a shorter text, with a more focused research question, it is may be necessary to look at smaller movements. Our angle of analysis here is to see the different positions Coe construes for himself within the immediate context and the ways in which he construes and recalibrates the storyline (including his own part in it) in order to legitimate the London bid before the IOC. We can therefore focus in some detail on how and where these construals occur rather than on broader patterns.

Let's look first at the various positions Coe construes for himself. In the opening line we see Coe placing himself in the immediate context and, given the conventions of the event, we know that his position is as a supplicant, representing London's bid, though the reason he gives is "the inspiration of the Olympic Movement". So, from the very start, we have Coe positioned in two different ways with regard to the Olympics: as a supplicant before the IOC and as someone inspired by the Movement.

Coe then builds on this second position through the displaced context of his childhood experience of the Games: first as an observer, then as knowing his future, and finally as acting on his experience. This pattern of Coe being given inspiration by the Games and then acting on the inspiration is mirrored in material terms through his construal of Sheila Sherwood, one of the athletes at the Games, giving him his first set of running spikes and Coe joining the Sherwoods' club. Interestingly, while athletes are almost exclusively construed as Actors in Coe's address, this rarely involves a Goal as an impacted participant; rather it is the athletes themselves who are transformed by their actions (see above). Notable exceptions are the Sherwoods bringing their medals home and Sheila giving her running spikes to the young Seb – both of which are acts symbolising the passing on of their success to the next generation (and remember that leaving a "legacy" is an important criterion in bidding to host the Games at the present time). In this section, then, we see Coe truly as someone "inspired", first simply as the Senser of inspiration as a mental reaction and then as an Actor with the Games inspiring him to do take up the material activity of running. In clause 18 Coe returns to the immediate context with the simple phrase "35 years on", but everyone listening will know that in those 35 years Coe became a double gold medallist and one of the all-time greats of the Games. Coe's *embodied capital* as an Olympic athlete is so great here that he can invoke it without mentioning it! Coe rounds off this *phase* of his address in clauses 19 and 20. So, after introducing the notion of inspiration in his opening words, Coe has established his position as an example par excellence of someone inspired to greatness by the Games and so a worthy supplicant. In terms of the Positioning Star, we can say that in recalibrating the storyline Coe has increased the symbolic capital of his words before this particular audience as part of the immediate event of the London bid. In this way we can see how the points of the Star can be seen as affordances as well as constraints.

In Clause 21 Coe once again uses the term "inspire", but now it is his turn to inspire the youth of today – in return for the inspiration he received and the life he was inspired to lead. This strategy allows Coe to shift the storyline from his own youth and successes to the youth of today and their more troubled lives. Here Coe also construes a position for himself as a parent, someone who is capable of responding to the problems of today's youth.

From clause 34 Coe construes yet another position for himself, as someone who has shared talk and experiences with the IOC themselves both as provider (Beh: verbal) and recipient (Rect, and Sen in complex clauses). As a result he and the IOC can be construed as equal in sharing "a common goal for the future of the sport", and by implication the youth of today. In praising the work of the IOC in clause 39, then, Coe is promoting his own (and London's) vision by implication. Coe now has an impressive array of positions: supplicant; child inspired to greatness; parent; and colleague of and covisionary with the IOC.

Coe then introduces a new storyline (though one hinted at earlier) when he talks of the challenge of the Olympic movement as lasting beyond the Games themselves. This is captured in clauses 41 to 43 where Coe, returning to the immediate context and his role as supplicant, mentions the idea of a "legacy" explicitly for the first time as part of London's vision in the bid he represents. He then builds on this motif, recalibrating the London bid as a bid for the youth of today (45–46), and positioning the IOC as responsible for making this vision come true, a construal he builds on until clause 53. And remember, he has already construed the IOC and himself as sharing the same vision. And it might not be too far-fetched to see a parallel in his use of the word "offer" with Sheila Sherwood's giving Seb his first spikes as a means of inspiration. Coe finishes with a return to the immediate context and the job at hand, construing the London bid as being "on behalf of the youth of today, the athletes of tomorrow and the Olympians of the future" – that is, those inspired today to greatness tomorrow, just as Coe was. Throughout his address, therefore, Coe has recalibrated the storyline of what a bid should represent away from "17 days of superb Olympic competition" to a vision for the youth of today to act and change themselves just as he and the athletes before him did. Given this storyline, Coe's self-construed positions as inspired youth, Olympic great, parent and covisionary with the IOC all serve to legitimate his position in the immediate context as a supplicant before the IOC representing the London bid, construed as one of "inspiration and legacy", and as advocate on behalf of today's disadvantaged youth.

Though Coe construes several positions for himself as he recalibrates the storyline through the displaced contexts he describes, his immediate position, that of supplicant before the IOC, never changes, it is just consolidated by the multiple positions he brings together into a single unit. In later chapters we will look at more complex cases in which a speaker takes up multiple *roles* in the immediate context. These different roles can form part of a single *role set*, as when a doctor switches between the roles of diagnostician and counsellor, or relate to different social positions, or *statuses*, which the speaker holds simultaneously.

In the next chapter we move on from the discussion of experiential meaning and the construal of fields and participant roles to look at interpersonal meaning and the tenor of context. We will also consider how interpersonal and experiential meaning, though theoretically independent in linguistic terms, are inextricably linked in social practice.

Notes

1 Or "will do" or "is doing", etc.
2 Halliday and Matthiessen (2004:335–354) calls this the present in the present, but I shall use the more familiar term.
3 Not all approaches to grammar use this term. However, the terms used by different schools in some way capture more general differences in the approach to transitivity adopted. Terms from different schools should not, therefore, be mixed.
4 Note that Halliday earlier used the term Range for these participants. This term is now used when we are analysing for *ergativity* (Halliday and Matthiessen 2004:280–303).
5 In the Cardiff Grammar, another "dialect" of SFL, however, a separate category of Creators and Created exists to distinguish what Halliday labels Actor and Goal in effective material processes.
6 To produce a fuller analysis I used linguistic features other than transitivity, such as prepositions. For example, "on behalf of" was interpreted as construing the same Client role as we saw construed by an indirect object in this section. This use of prepositions is discussed in the section on Circumstances.
7 When a full clause appears in the middle of another clause the symbol > < signals where it appears in the original text while the clause itself appears below as >xxx<.
8 An alternative interpretation of clauses such as 95 as single clauses with modality is presented in Chapter 4.
9 UTTER might be an exception here in that it only seems to be used with Verbiage of the unit of information type.
10 "Which city" is a verbal Initiator, but unfortunately there is no special term for this – perhaps *Prompt* would work?
11 If we take the bleached verb and Scope of 160 as a single lexical item.
12 This looks superficially like a passive. However, time-sequencing means that the passive would be "their landscape has been cluttered".
13 Though this might be an identifying possessive clause, introduced later, as there are some agnate clauses which are reversible.
14 SHOW can also construe a material process as in "He showed us the book".
15 In cases such as these it might be an idea to provide a dual label for the process type. This would square with other views of existential clauses as interpersonal variations.
16 The use of the present tense suggests this is an attributive relational use rather than a passive.
17 The necessary elements are referred to as the nucleus of the clause and the optional extras as Adjuncts.

4

INTERPERSONAL MEANING

Text as interaction and alignment

4.1 Introduction

In the previous chapter we saw how writers and speakers can represent the type and degree of activity of different participants across a text, drawing on the lexicogrammatical resources of transitivity at the clause level or below. It was argued that this was an act of construal, one possible representation of events amongst many, and that the way in which events are construed by particular authors needs to be interpreted in terms of the contexts/environments in which the texts are produced. However, while these representations are those chosen for specific purposes by specific speakers, they can be more or less evaluated in terms of how closely they correspond with real or imaginary events. That is to say experiential meaning is largely concerned with objective truths (or falsehoods), though this is, of course, a misleadingly simple statement. As such, experiential meaning was the sole object of early linguistic research, falling within the philosophical study of truth conditions. In general, modern linguistic theories see the experiential as only one of several types of meaning, as we saw in Chapter 1, and in this chapter we will look at what Halliday calls *interpersonal meaning*, where language is a resource for building identities and forging relationships, concepts which are largely subjective. This means that they cannot really be judged in terms of truth values.

There are various interrelated ways in which interpersonal meaning is construed through language in discourse and in this chapter we will consider:

- the speech roles (for example, teller, enquirer, commander) adopted by different speakers
- the degree of certainty and the evidential base speakers provide for their assertions

- the degree of possibility or necessity speakers assign to events
- the different standards of evaluation speakers use when appraising people, things and actions

As you will have noticed, these categories *do* touch on truth and falsehood, but they are concerned with the speakers' own subjective assessments, the truth of which cannot be objectively verified. That is to say, if I declare "The moon is made of cheese", you can prove or disprove this claim; but you cannot prove whether I believe it or not. And if I ask you if it is raining or tell you to buy me a pint, how can you test the truth of a question or a command? For this reason the speech philosophers began to talk of the *felicity conditions* of *speech acts*: that is, the conditions necessary for these acts to be effective rather than true. And this, you will remember, is the central theme of the book, as set out in the Positioning Star, only with a focus on whole texts rather than individual utterances. Halliday (1978:117) refers to interpersonal meaning as the *intruder function* of language, as it is here that speakers' personal judgements are most explicitly allowed to intrude into the text. However, you should remember that any representation of an event is already a speaker's personal construal, as discussed in the previous chapters, so that interpersonal meaning is by no means the only way in which a speaker can be said to intrude.

Once we have looked at the grammatical resources for realising interpersonal meaning in isolation from other types of meaning (which is nothing more than a handy theoretical abstraction), we will begin to consider how these features interact with the variables of field we discussed in the last two chapters and how different combinations relate to different positions speakers can take up in relation to the symbolic capital they control for different audiences.

In Chapter 2 I made a distinction between immediate events and displaced events and we saw how displaced events can be put to use in the immediate environment. In contrast, interpersonal meaning is always related to speakers' positioning within the current discourse event (though possibly with an eye on the long term …). As such it is one of the means for signalling the role that constitutive text is playing within that immediate event. Consequently, and as we shall see, interpersonal meaning is just as important as experiential meaning in determining the type of activity that is being construed by language.

4.2 Mood and speech function

Let's now look again at the text from the Management Workshop (reproduced here as Text 4.1) and consider some of the basic form-function relationships that contribute to interpersonal meaning:

Text 4.1

1 S: The second thing is is whether or not we want to continue with drinking water,
2 (xxxxxxx). Now (xxxxx) topic of discussion, where do we go from here? (xxx).

3   What = what is, what kind of thing you've put together so ↑far and what is the
4   future ... next steps of activity? (xx) remember, this is just the beginning, it's a
5   (?step) assessment. Of (x) developing a management plan ... erm, what does T- ...
6   what does T- want to do ... and to what extent would you like to ... continue to
7   have Iwokrama involved in ... in ... in facilitating it? And in ... in building
8   capacity to to (xx)? ((data omitted))
9 S: Okay, so you're prepared to finish off the water? [Okay.]
10 W: [I feel] the whole point (xxxx).
11   ((unclear background discussion))
12 S: I wish ... I was hoping that maybe you could (xx) do it (to the other xx room).
13   Just kind of get one person to do what er ... what ... er er I was hoping (?to be)
14   facilitator and one (person xx) to do the planning (xxxxx). Yeah?
15 W: Okay.
16 S: Right, Walter, you in shape for this?
17 W: A'right.
18 S: (Or we could) try ...
19 W: (xxxxx).
20 S: (xx) did you want (xxx)? So we need ... two other people ... Vanessa ... Nicholas ...
21 W: VANESSA! COME NOW! °(xxxx)°.
22   ((shuffling)) (12s)
23   Come here and do some writing.
24   (9s)
25 S: Here, Vanessa, (you could do with this pen).
26   ((mumbling)) (50s)
27   So ...

The language of this stretch of text, as we saw in Chapter 2, is ancillary to other activities in organising participants and the setting in order to establish the context as a meeting. This stage of the activity therefore involves different speakers providing and checking organisational details, getting other people to do things for them and offering to do them themselves. These different activities correspond to what Halliday and Matthiessen (2004:107–108) call the four basic **speech functions**, or the **discourse roles** speakers take up. These can be organised in a grid to highlight the semantic similarities and differences between them (see Table 4.1).

The four terms *statement*, *offer*, *question* and *request* are no more than catch-all glosses and cover a wide range of related speech acts. For example, commands,

TABLE 4.1 Speech roles

	Information (saying)	Goods and services (doing)
Give	Statement	Offer
Demand	Question	Request

injunctions and exhortations are all types of demanding goods and services (as are prohibitions, as demands not to do something). Various attempts have been made to define and categorise speech acts in much greater detail (for example, Hasan 1996, in press) but for the purposes of this book we will stick with this basic four-way distinction. This means that in Hasan's work, for example, the term *question* has a more specific meaning than I am giving it here – so beware! And in your own work you might wish to use more delicate descriptions – it's all a question of the right level of detail in your *mappa mundi*: do you want, metaphorically speaking, to walk from your house to the supermarket or fly from Oslo to Berlin?

Now, statements, offers, questions and requests are all semantic categories which we recognise by the combination of intonational and lexicogrammatical features that realise them. At a very basic level of description, we can distinguish between a question and a statement in English because the **Subject** and the **Finite** appear in different orders in each. The following examples are modified forms of Sara's "You in shape for this?" in line 16 (we'll return to the actual form in a bit):

1. Are (F) you (S) in shape for this?
2. You (S) are (F) in shape for this.

Grammatically these **structures** are known as **interrogative mood** and **declarative mood** and they are the **congruent** (of which more below) realisations of questions and statements respectively.

Finite and Subject are best described together. The Subject is the person or thing we are making a statement about and the Finite is the part of the verb that signals time (or possibility, see below) and agrees with the Subject in English and many other languages. Between them they anchor an utterance in (hypothetical) space and time and are jointly referred to as the **Mood element**. So, in examples 1 and 2, "are" signals present time (*cf.* "were") and agrees with the Subject "you" (*cf.* "He is"), which signals the space of the act as centred around "you". In general English does not mark much for agreement except in the third person singular (I go, you go, he/she/it goes, we go, they go), but it is still a relevant factor. A further complication in English is that the Finite is often *fused* (that is, combined) with the *main verb* (the word that describes the process), as in the regular "He walked" and the irregular "He went". Here the words "walked" and "went" include both the semantics of the main verbs, "walk" and "go", and the Finite element, the reference to time. In both cases the Finite signals past time. In interrogatives and some other forms the two elements are separated, as in "Did he walk?" and "Did he go?" Here "did" is the Finite form of the *auxiliary verb* DO, and is used here to mark past tense. But notice that in both cases the ordering of Subject and Finite is still the F^S of interrogative clauses (where ^ indicates necessary sequencing).

The Mood element therefore does a lot of work: it signals time of reference, who or what we are making a statement about, and the speech function of the clause, as well as other types of meaning that we'll discuss below. These are all elements of interpersonal meaning (how speakers *orient themselves and others* with regard to the experiential meanings being exchanged), so analysis of the Mood element of different clauses is central to describing the interpersonal meaning of texts and how they function with respect to speaker positioning in discourse.

There is, however, a slight complication (isn't there always?), in that there are two main categories of questions that are realised by different structures. First there are **polar interrogatives** that are generally looking for a yes/no answer to verify if an idea is true or not. The example we've been looking at, "Are you in shape for this?", is an example of a polar interrogative. But there are also detail-seeking questions, or **wh-questions**, that don't ask about the truth of falsehood of an idea but are requests for more specific information. There are a couple of examples of this in Text 4.1:

3. What is the future?
4. ... to what extent would you like to continue to have Iwokrama involved in facilitating it?

Wh- questions include a wh-word (where, why, what, when, which, who – and how!), usually at the beginning of the clause but sometimes preceded by a preposition (as in example 4). When the wh-word is the Subject of the clause the word order is S^F, not the expected F^S of polar interrogatives, as in:

5. What (S) is (F) the future?

Note, however, that this is still referred to as an interrogative.

When the wh-word is anything other than the Subject, then the same order as polar interrogatives applies:

6. ... to what extent would (F) you (S) like to continue to have Iwokrama involved in facilitating it?

Note that in 6 the Finite element does not refer to time but to degree of possibility, an aspect of modality, which we shall look at shortly. In brief, Finites can locate an utterance in either time or in alternatively possible worlds.

So far we have seen three Mood types: declarative, polar interrogative and wh-interrogative. There is one further main type,[1] the **imperative** (from the same Latin root, meaning "to order" as Emperor). There is a double example of this in line 23 of Text 4.1 when Walter says to Vanessa:

7. Come here and do some writing.

Here the imperative is realised by the main verb with *no visible Mood element*. In some cases it is possible to include either the Subject, as in:

8. You (S) come here!

or the Finite, as in:

9. Do (F) come here ...

It's better to think of these variants as extra resources rather than exceptions to the rule – they do create different meanings after all. In example 8 the inclusion of "you" involves an extra level of emphasis, probably creating a contrastive meaning suggesting "... because *I'm* not going to!" In example 9 the inclusion of "do" suggests that an extra level of insistence is being added for some reason.

When we have a negative imperative the negative auxiliary DON'T is added as the Finite, just as DO was added with some interrogatives:

10. Don't (F) come here.

Generally imperatives are directed solely at our *interlocutors* (the people we're speaking to) so we can refer to them as second person imperatives. However, as this category comprises the vast majority of cases, we generally just say imperatives. But it is also possible to direct an imperative towards a group that contains the speaker. We'll see an example later in the chapter on Martin Luther King's famous "I have a Dream" speech:

11. Let us not wallow in the valley of despair.

There are several names, such as jussive, exhortative and suggestive, for the discourse function typically realised by the structure "LET'S" followed by the infinitive; we will refer to the structure itself as *first person plural imperative*. Be careful to distinguish these from the second person imperative of the verb LET:

12. Please let us stay up late tonight, mum!

There are also, very rarely, similar *third person imperative* forms:

13. Just let him try!!!
14. Let them eat cake.

In more formal language MAY can be used:

15. May he rest in peace.

For the purposes of this book we can mark up occurrences of these forms in text as 1plimp, 3simp and 3plimp (first person plural imperative, third person singular imperative and third person plural imperative) without worrying about whether LET or MAY is used. Second person imperatives will just be labelled as imp.

The different Mood types can be positive or negative (a distinction known as *polarity*). In this way example 11 is neg 1plimp. As positive polarity is far more common than negative polarity, example 2 will just be labelled as decl and example 13 as imp.

As you will probably have realised by now, this is all a rather idealised picture, and the time has come to explain what is mean by *congruence*. When we say, for example, that questions are congruently realised by interrogative structures, we are saying that this is the *unmarked* form (that is, the form with nothing extra going on). Unmarked forms are generally the commonest and simplest structures realising the function and are usually the earliest forms to have come into the language and to be learnt by children. For our purposes the most important aspect is that marked forms often take more work to produce and carry extra meaning. So, when Sara says:

16. I was hoping you could do it to [in?] the other room.

she would appear to be making a suggestion as a way of indirectly requesting other participants to carry out some action rather than just letting them know her immediately prior state of mind. Indirectness usually means that there is extra meaning at play (for example, allowance for other possibilities, hedging, politeness and facework of all kinds) and this is mirrored in the extra linguistic work being carried out in comparison with the use of the congruent imperative form (Brown and Levinson 1987):

17. Do it in the other room.

It is sometimes difficult to state precisely what speech acts are being performed in real-time discourse (which is perhaps why the speech philosophers invented examples and contexts); however, it is generally clear when a stretch of text can be characterised as functioning primarily to give information, to demand action or as a mix of these. Similarly, it is usually quite clear whether these speech acts are being performed directly or indirectly (that is with the congruent or non-congruent grammatical structures). What is a more complex question is in what contexts it is unmarked behaviour to use the marked form (Watts 2003)

There are two further indirect demands for goods and services in text:

18. Could we try ... ?

and

19. So we need two other people.

As you'll see these indirect realisations include some idea of possibility or necessity, realised by the verbs "could" (which is a form of CAN) and "need". There is a whole group of verbs, called modal auxiliaries, which encode ideas such as possibility and necessity, and they typically interact with choices in Mood to realise different speech acts. For that reason "mood and modality" are often treated together in descriptions of language use and we'll look at modality in more depth in the following section.

The observant (and not so observant) user will have noticed that I have not discussed the fourth speech function in Table 4.1, "offers". This is because English has no congruent structure for realising offers (unlike, Spanish and French, say, which use the present simple tense). The most common way of making an offer is through combining the interrogative mood with the modal auxiliary SHALL (particularly in British English) or WILL, as in:

20. Shall I open the window?

However, different modal verbs are also regularly used to make offers, as is the declarative:

21. Can I help you?
22. I'll do that for you.

In the following section we will look at modality in some depth. Before that we'll quickly look at two further examples from Text 4.1. The first comes from line 9:

23. Okay, so you're prepared to finish off the water? Okay.

The complete sentence is declarative in form; however, Sara uses a rising intonation (signalled in the transcript by the question mark), which is the congruent intonation pattern for demanding information, not giving information. The effect is that Sara is both making a statement and asking if it's true at the same time, a speech act that is sometimes labelled a *check*. The combination of declarative structure grammatically with rising intonation is often referred to as a *queclarative* form in order to capture this hybridity. For the purposes of the book, however, it will be sufficient to label the structure as declarative and the speech function as demand information. This will signal the non-congruent pairing of form and function. Looking at example 23 in full we see that Sara adds a second "okay", without rising tone, which suggests that the lack of a response can be taken as confirmation. This backs up the analysis of her first sentence as a demand for information rather than as a statement. Looking at the surrounding text often provides clues such as this for analysts.

Unfortunately, there is not enough space to discuss intonation patterns in detail. For a full description of intonation in English (which, as you've probably guessed, is far more complex than is hinted at here), see Halliday and Greaves (2008), Tench (1996) or O'Grady (2010).

Sara also produces the following "sentence" (a manipulated version of which was discussed above) in line 16:

24. Right, Walter, you in shape for this?

Here the Finite verb has been omitted and so it is not strictly possible to say whether it is a declarative or interrogative clause and we have to rely on our intuition in testing the plausibility of the two possible full forms in context. (This "missing out" of words is known as *ellipsis*.) To me "Are you in shape for this?" fits better that "You're in shape for this?" in context, probably because there is no previous discussion about Walter's readiness which would prompt Sara to use the checking form. Sometimes identification of a full form is easier, as with the informal:

25. You go to the shops yesterday?

As ellipsis involves the missing out of words rather than changing their form (you'll just have to believe me on this …), so ruling out the possibility of "went", then the interrogative "Did you go to the shops yesterday?" is generally a far more likely candidate for the full form than the highly marked declarative "You did go to the shops yesterday?" with its contradictory use of "did", which suggests certainty in sentences such as this, and the rising intonation, which suggests uncertainty. Such forms will be marked as declarative or interrogative according to their full, or *unellipted*, form, though it may be useful to add a note that the utterance is informal.

Exercise 4.1

In Text 4.1 we see how Sara is controlling the immediate context through the discourse roles she takes up. It was suggested in Chapter 2 that the position Sara construed for herself in this immediate context might have repercussions later in the Management Planning Meeting and in Bartlett 2012a, where this whole stretch of discourse is analysed in depth, I show how this appears to be the case, as control over the meeting, despite having formally been ceded to Walter as a central purpose of the exercise, gradually reverts to Sara. I suggest that this is because her role as organiser of the activity, highlighted in the setting up of the exercise, combined with her capital as a professional development worker, meant that when problems arose it became almost inevitable that her immediate role would change from that of facilitator to that of organiser, taking over from Walter. In Text 4.2 we can see that that is what has happened as Sara is firmly back in control. Read through the text and answer the questions below.

Text 4.2

1 S: Okay, so … so the activity … is … to do what?
2   >To get a reservoir … set up … in the village?< Right?
3   That's the activity?
4 N?: Yeah.
5 S: Right.

6		And then ... how does that fit with ... .with all these other things in terms of
7		of agricultu:re, health, and all of those ... is the next thing you're talking about?
8		Makes it more accessible, makes it easier ... maybe healthier, those kind of stuff,
9		right?
10		So ... so, let's just back up.
11		So, you wanna do ... three.
12		(15s)
13		And remember this from yesterday ... the various points we've built, right?
14		(5s)
15		Right?
16		And re ... re ... and so ... that's one, it is "How does it fit with other things in the
17		village?",
18		and you're saying it makes it more accessible an' easier.
19		So ...
20		(6s)
21		Any other ... things [to go with]
22	N:	[Safer], it was safer.
23	S:	Sa:fer. ((writing it down?))
24	W:	(xxx) safer (xxx).
25	S:	(xxx).
26		(9s)
27	S:	Because drinking water is such a straightforward thing, these two collapse into
28		one basically.
29		I mean 'cause it's not like you're talking about lo:gging or ... or cutting
30		down trees to do agriculture, right?
31		So 1 and 2 would ...
32	N:	Less time taken to ... t= =for your water.
33	S:	Yeah. 1 and 2. Less time taken to acquire (our) water.
34		So, less labour, right?
35	?:	((grunt of assent))
36		(14s)
37	S:	Mm-hmm. Anything else?
38		(6s)
39	W:	Encourage agr ... kitchen gardens.
40	S:	Encourage agriculture, right?
41		(20s)
42		Anything else?
43	W:	Is it okay that hoping they erm ... a flush toilet system (xxxxx)?
44	S:	In the future?
45	W:	Mm-hmm.
46	S:	But that's not meant to be activity right now?
47		(Eh,) the activity right now is to find somebody to fund ... the reservoir. .and the
48		pipes ... to certain points, right?
49		So, potential future ... so that's potential.

50 N: I think maybe we should put that part.
51   ((W and N mutter a while)) (12s)
52 S: We have … you talked about this yesterday, activity (xx), How it's going to each
53   ↑ home and … and …
54 N: We could have taken it from under … easier access, (xxx).
55   (12s)
56 S: (What about other) sanitation, Walter?
57   Flush toilet system, (?sanitary towel) system. (This is to put under) positive=
58 N: =We don't see water in the home as something that should be automatic.
59   ((mumbling from floor)) (16s)
60 S: They would get what?
61   ((further mumbling, with N's voice suddenly becoming prominent.)) (6s)
62 N: … not a necessity,
63   you could collect (more than) water from outside).
64   I mean, which can happen,
65 S: [Could everyone]
66 W: [When we] talked about the flush toilet, it was the … around the nearby
67   well … (xxxxx). Nearby homes to the wells, because of er … (away then
68   from) the shit-juice bringing into the wells and the water stream.
69 S: Right.
70   So it links (xxxx).
71   Sanitation, right?
72 W: Right.
73 S: We also talked yesterday about ecotourist things … having better water supply.
74   So that if we collapse … in here we could do one and two together, kind of
75   collapse it in … okay?
76   So …
77   ((mumbling leading to laughing, especially from N)) (23s)

Questions

1. Identify both the mood and speech function of all the utterances in Text 4.2 that are not declaratives functioning as statements. Mark where short utterances like "right" or nominal groups check or confirm an idea. See p. 197 for answers.
2. Identify those utterances where Sara is genuinely seeking information that is unknown to her and those where she already knows the answer.
3. Provide more delicate labels, such as suggestion, for some of the utterances and say what features of the statement and/or the cotext led you to choose the name.
4. Can you find any examples where Sara *reformulates* the answers given to her?
5. How would you describe the overall *tenor* of the text as relationships construed between the participants and the way Sara engages the community – does it remind you of any other contexts?

6. Relate your answers in 1 to 5 to the Positioning Star, taking the semantic features of Sara's talk as aspects of the acts she is performing.

4.3 Modality, attribution and evidentiality

I said above that interpersonal meaning is not concerned with truth conditions, which were once the central focus of work on sentence semantics within philosophical linguistics. However, this is not quite true, though the approach we'll explore here has a rather different focus to that of the philosophers. In this section we won't be considering the experiential truth or otherwise of speakers' utterances in relation to "objective real-world facts" but instead we will look at the speakers' own judgements of the truth or otherwise of various ideas, as these appear in their real-time discourse. This is a very important means of using text analysis as a bridge to discourse analysis as it can reveal how speakers position themselves with respect not only to specific aspects of the storyline as it is construed but also with respect to other speakers in terms of their respective rights and abilities to act as arbiters of truth. There are obviously connections to be made here with respect to the relative cultural capital of the different speakers, not only in terms of the positions of knowledge or authority they hold before a given audience or audiences but also in terms of new positions they are trying to *appropriate* for themselves. The negotiation of truth and the right to act as arbiter are key battlegrounds in the struggle for power, and not just linguistic power (Bourdieu 1991). There are both short- and long-term considerations here, as being successful in a particular struggle over "the truth" can feed into a speaker's cultural capital in future discussions, though not necessarily with positive effects, as we'll see.

I've been using the term "truth" here, but let me expand upon this and relate it both to mood and speech role, discussed above, and to modality, which will be the focus of this section. Let's consider the following utterance:

26. Vanessa is writing.

This is a statement realised by declarative mood. We can say that it is a *proposition* put forward as true without any contestation or engagement with alterative possibilities. Compare this with a polar question realised by interrogative mood:

27. Is Vanessa writing?

We can say that this utterance functions to check on the truth or otherwise of the proposition put forward. Questions therefore introduce other possible truths and serve to engage others in the construal of truth. There are other ways of engaging with alternative truths, such as introducing hypothetical statements with an "if" clause. There is not room to deal with engagement as a semantic category here, but it is one of the central systems of *discourse semantics* as elaborated by Martin, White and Rose and others, with excellent overviews provided in Martin and White (2005) and Martin and Rose (2003).

Imperative clauses, or commands, are related to truth values in a slightly different way. Consider the following example:

28. Do some writing, Vanessa.

Here we can say that the speaker is requesting that Vanessa makes a proposed state of affairs (or *proposal*) come true. In the case of offers the speaker is stating their willingness to make the proposed event true themselves:

29. I'll do the writing.

This distinction between the truth of propositions and proposals true also applies to *modality*. Compare the following two examples:

30. You must be home by ten.
31. He must be home, the light's on upstairs.

In example 30 the speaker is imposing an obligation on the hearer to make a proposal come true; in example 31 the speaker is offering their own evaluation of the proposition as very probably being true. These two examples therefore represent two different *types* of modality, which go under a variety of names in the literature. For utterances concerned with the desirability or necessity of hypothetical proposals, the terms *deontic modality*, *event modality* and *modulation* are used. We'll use the term *deontic modality* in this book. For utterances concerned with whether propositions are factually true or not, the terms *epistemic modality*, *propositional modality* and *modalisation* are used. We'll use the term *epistemic modality* in this book. Notice also that some modal auxiliaries, such as MUST, can be used with both deontic and epistemic meaning, whereas in other cases a different auxiliary might be used to distinguish these ideas. Let's add another couple of examples to the mix:

32. You should be home by ten.
33. He might be at home, I suppose.

Here we see again the difference between deontic and epistemic modality as *types*, but in both cases there is less strength to the speaker's utterances than in examples 30 and 31. That is to say the speaker shows less commitment to the need for the proposal in 32 to come true or to the truth of the proposition in 33. As we shall see, we can generally grade this commitment, or *value*, as high, median or low, which means we now have six subcategories of modality (three values x two types).

However, it should be noted that it is not always easy to distinguish between instances of epistemic and deontic modality, as in:

34. Taxis from Cardiff Central should cost no more than £5.

Is the speaker here evaluating the probability of their proposition being true or expressing their opinion on the desirability or necessity of a proposal coming true? Such **blending** of modal meaning is quite common and tells us something about society and out tendency to consider something that usually happens (that is, that is very probably true) as being desirable. Consider, for example, the evaluative load of "He's not normal!" and the use of "You don't do that" as a means of controlling behaviour.

Another very important aspect of modality is that it reflects the speaker's orientation to propositions or proposals *within the ongoing discourse* and as such it is always realises a speech act in the immediate context. For example, when a speaker says "You must be home by ten", the event itself might be in the future, but the imposition of the obligation takes place at the time the speaker makes the utterance. Similarly, current modal evaluation of past events is possible, with the "pastness" of the event signalled by use of the *perfect infinitive*:

35. He must have fallen down a hole.

In this example the speaker is making a current evaluation of the possibility of a past event having taken place. This is an important point with regard to texts that construe displaced context, such as journal articles, where the language is overwhelmingly constitutive. The use of modality in these texts signals the writer's positioning in terms of the act of giving the information, which is the immediate context of the article even though it doesn't happen in real time.

Note that modality can appear in interrogative clauses as well:

36. Could he have come back in through the window?

Here the speaker is simultaneously construing a certain degree of possibility to the proposition through their use of "could" while engaging the hearer as partner in this construal. And note that when we have a modal auxiliary this acts as the Finite and so comes before the Subject in interrogative clauses. Finites can therefore mark either for tense (as discussed above) or for modality, depending on whether the speaker wants to place an event in time or to evaluate the probability, desirability or possibility of it being true. Modality is therefore one further aspect of interpersonal meaning that is realised in the Mood element of the clause.

So far we have looked only at modal auxiliaries and at the two main types of modality, but things get more complicated. Consider the statement I made a little whole ago:

37. We can generally grade this commitment as high, median or low.

What is the word "generally" doing here? It is signalling that the proposition is not always true. So, we have different but related types of epistemic modality, which can be labelled *usuality*, as in example 37, and *probability*, as in example 35.

Similarly, for deontic modality we can distinguish between inclination, as in example 38 (the modal auxiliary WILL is historically related to the adjective WILLING), and obligation, as in example 39.

38. I'll do that for you.
39. Thou shalt not steal.

So now we have 12 categories of modality: 4 types x 3 values. And there's more …

As example 37 shows, modality can also be expressed through *adverbs*. This means that modality is an area of semantics rather than grammar *per se*, as it can be realised by various grammatical means (Halliday and Matthiessen 2004:613–625). However, as grammar carries its own type of meaning (Halliday 2002:291–322), there is a certain correspondence in the type of modality being expressed and the grammatical form being used. More on this later!

Let's now turn to a textual example to see modality in action as part of discourse.

Text 4.3

1 **G:** Added to that, then, there's the whole question of (who owns) agriculture,
2   we talked about (xx) and (xx) … Another one was the land, the whole question
3   of the relationship between Toka and the Government and what land was
4   available for use … and that's tied in with (xxx), tied in with long-term
5   security … ?
6 **N:** That's … that should be tied in to ownership of other resources like water,
7   (xxx) …
8 **G:** Ownership and use of management (product). Management (rights xx).
9   (p)
10   The target (h)as communication we've got in … which I think comes into
11   the first thing, that's called mechanisms how … > how your views can be
12   reflected both < with the government, with UNDP,[2] with Iwokrama, with
13   everybody.
14   (p)   ((some mumbling))
15   Another big one … we've seen … that seems to affect a lot of things is creek,
16   your ideas of creek management … (detay) reforestation.
17 **N:** I think it's a whole restoration process.
18 **G:** Restoration (xxxx)?
19 **N:** Not only that. But the (xxxx). Because of cultural restoration. Maybe
20   you couldn't finance that, you know? Because what we find there's
21   disadvantage when we've been government, erm, driven programmes, they've
22   been … financially supported properly … and our erm programmes are not,
23   traditional ways are not supported so. They have an advantage right away
24   there (xx) find that … they actually killing … government is (xx) not knowing

25   (they) erm killing culture.
26 **S:** °Not knowing?°
27 **?:** °(xx)°
28   (p)
29 **G:** I'm not sure if this doesn't (xxxx) my interpretation.
30 **N:** (What your interpretation is?)
31   ((Interference, pauses and muttering.))
32   I think one of the things we have to do (actually) is we have to be ...
33   (adventure,
34   you know) with a (pi xx). When we develop plans that erm ... the government
35   na[3] see it as being, you know, complementary ... complementary with the
36   present development strategies of the government, so ... we're not supported,
37   but
38   it should be supported, (na?)
39 **G:** But this comes back again to this whole question of whether or not anybody's
40   listening to what you're saying. Which doesn't appear to be the
41   case. At <u>all</u> levels. Sometimes because before in our communities they don't
42   know how to listen. Sometimes they're just not terribly interested in listening.

This text comes from the same Management Planning Workshop as Text 4.1, but comes from the day before and is a smaller group discussion. The speakers here are Nicholas, Gordon and Sara, each with high status in their own communities and institutions. Nicholas is a prominent elder in the local community and Gordon and Sara are a scientist and social scientist with Iwokrama respectively. The different speakers' knowledge and evaluation of each other's status are part of the non-material environment of the discourse as they are likely to provide both constraints and affordances in the way the speakers set about *managing the context* – that is recalibrating the storyline and their respective positions and symbolic capitals. The topic of discussion is local development and the participation of local communities, the government and other organisations in promoting this. Local development is thus the displaced field and is constituted by language. However, as this meeting is also part of the local development process and the speakers are all prominent actors in this area, we have a case where the immediate and displaced fields *coincide*. This means that ancillary and constitutive language interact to construe, enact and recalibrate both the history of the groups' involvement in local development (the storyline) and the status relations within this field in complex ways. We'll discuss this further after looking at a few examples of modality in the text.

In line 6 Nicholas says:

40. That's ... that should be tied in to ownership of other resources like water ...

Here we have a use of "should" to signal what Nicholas thinks is to some degree necessary. It is therefore an example of obligation as one of the types of deontic modality. "Should" expresses median value here, as compared with MUST or

COULD, which he could have used in the same context for high or low force respectively. However, I would say that, while "median obligation" captures the systemic contrast in the modality system, it doesn't capture the full idea of "should" here, which seems to relate to what would be "appropriate". This shows us the distinction between what modals mean in relation to each other in the language system and the specific uses they have in language use. Sometimes a further gloss, such as "appropriate", helps to capture the usage in a way the high/medium/low distinction doesn't. *We'll see this again with respect to modals of probability*. However, in categorising the types of modality used over a whole text and their effect on the discourse as a whole, rather than their specific local meanings, the terms high, medium and low provide us with a useful level of generalisation in grouping modals together for comparison.

The next use of modality introduces another angle to our discussion and a further set of features for distinguishing the modality speakers have at their disposal Remember I said above that modality is a semantic area that can be realised by different parts of the grammar. This is shown in lines 10–11, where Gordon says.

41. The target (h)as communication we've got in ... which I think comes into the first thing, that's called mechanisms ...

Gordon's "I think" here functions as a **hedge**, it downplays the force of his assertion, construing it as *possibly true* rather than *definitely true* (as "I know" would have done). So, while "I think" is clearly an example of transitivity grammatically, it is functioning here within the semantic domain of modality to express median possibility and is classified as a **pseudomodal**. There is, however, a significant distinction in meaning between the use of pseudomodal forms such as "I think" and the modal auxiliaries themselves. If Gordon had said "it could come into the first things, called mechanisms" this would have been a subjective claim, an expression of his personal opinion (see below), but the subjective nature of the claim would have been **implicit** (that is, not stated overtly); by using "I think" instead, he makes the subjective nature of his claim **explicit** through the use of "I". We see here how the grammatical differences in form create important semantic distinctions in a motivated way, as was suggested above. This introduces a new variable into the equation so that we now have 24 kinds of modality (keep up!): 3 values x four types x 2 levels of **investment**.[4]

Notice how a few lines later Nicholas mirrors Gordon's usage with:

42. I think it's a whole restoration process.

This is very interesting, as Nicholas is in effect contradicting what Gordon has said, but his use of *modal alignment* serves to keep things on a relatively even keel interpersonally – though the explicit use of "I" might add a little spice in making it personal! We can see in these examples how the speakers play a game of cat and mouse in offering alternative construals of events while downplaying their suggestions in deference to each other's status. There is a lot of mutual positioning going on here.

Lines 32 to 33 from Nicholas also supply an interesting interplay of modal forms. I've normalised the example a little make it easier to understand the points that follow without altering the sense of the modality here:

43. I think one of the things we have to do, actually, is we have to be adventurous, you know …

Here Nicholas's use of "have to" signals high obligation, but it contrasts with MUST in this sense in that it carries less of an idea of Nicholas stating his own **subjective** opinion and more an idea that he is stating the necessity as an **objective** fact. Consider the following minimally contrastive pair of utterances and say which is more likely to be said by a classmate rather than a teacher:

44. You must hand your work in by the 15th.
45. You have to hand your homework in by the 15th.

The first of these would be very marked if said by a classmate. This is because, as we discussed briefly above, modal auxiliaries realise speech acts in the immediate context, so that 44 is the laying down of the obligation while 45, by contrast, is merely reporting an obligation imposed by some unnamed other. Let's explore this a bit further by looking at the two forms with relation to the past:

46. You must have passed your driving test to apply for this job.
47. He had to leave his job immediately …

In the first, while passing the driving test is in the past, the obligation is set out in the statement itself. There is no past tense form of MUST. In example 47, in contrast, we see that HAS TO can be used in the past to state a previous necessity. So HAVE TO, although it is concerned with the semantic area of obligation, is not a true modal and is often referred to as a **semi-modal**. This is also reflected in the fact that it is not the finite of the clause (in all but a decreasing number of dialects, anyway, and this for a different linguistic reason), as example 48 demonstrates:

48. Do we have to go to the shops?

Interestingly, NEED has both full modal and semi-modal forms:

49. Need I say more?
50. Do you need to do that?

Perhaps this make it three-quarters modal?

The difference between MUST and HAVE TO then is one of **subjective** as opposed to **objective orientation**. The two are similar, however, in that the source of the obligation is not explicitly stated. We have already seen how "I think" contrasts with MUST as an example of explicitly subjective modality, and an example of explicitly objective modality would be:

51. It was necessary for us to leave the following day.

The objective nature of the modality in such cases is clearly signalled with "it", which contrasts with the use of the first person "I" or "we" in explicitly subjective forms. This brings up a grand total of 48 types of modality: 3 values × 4 types × 2 levels of investment × 2 orientations. And that, you'll be pleased to know, is where we stop. Usually it will be the contrast across only a couple of these parameters that is of interest in comparing texts.

As well as the explicitly subjective orientation of pseudomodal forms, we can explicitly present the views of someone other than the speaker:

52. John thinks it's a good idea.

This is an example of **attribution**. In cases such as these the speaker is attributing the proposition to a third party, with varying degrees of certainty expressed. Attribution is therefore closely linked to modality:

53. John's adamant that it's a good idea.
54. John suggests it might be a good idea.

For fuller discussions of the many variables involved in attribution see Bednarek (2006). For the purposes of this book we will just consider whether propositions or proposals are attributed or not and how attributing them to particular kinds of people affects the positioning of the speakers themselves.

Note that with interrogative forms of implicit subjective modality it is the hearer's subjectivity that is involved, not the speakers:

55. Must we go?

Here the speaker is asking about the hearer's imposition of obligation.

In Text 4.3 there is another example of explicitly subjective modality, this time concerning probability, when Gordon says:

56. I'm not sure if this doesn't (xxxx) my interpretation.

Here we would label "not sure" as low possibility because of the negative, which reverses the high modality of "sure" on its own.

There is also an example of an implicitly objective evaluation of median usuality in the text:

57. Sometimes they're just not terribly interested in listening.

"Sometimes" here is what's called a *Modal Adjunct*. These behave rather like adverbs or *adverb phrases*, but with important differences. First, unlike a true adverb phrase such as "during meetings", "sometimes" cannot be used to answer the question "When are they not interested in listening?", at least not without a level of ironic word play. Second, they can appear between the Subject and the Finite in cases where this is not possible with true adverbs or adverb phrases. This is particularly the case when the Finite is stressed:

58. He sometimes <u>does</u> eat like a bit of a pig, I agree.
59. He at every meal <u>does</u> eat like a bit of a pig.

This is a good test when you are in doubt about the function of an adverb-like word or phrase in your analysis and shows once again the important connections between semantics and grammar. In this case "sometimes" can go between Subject and Finite, and hence within the Mood element, because it carries interpersonal meaning, not experiential meaning.

Returning to Text 4.3, there are one or two further examples of modality:

60. ... how your views can be reflected both with the government, with UNDP, with Iwokrama, with everybody.

Here Gordon uses "can" to consider the possibility of local views being reflected by other groups. In other cases the meaning of CAN is ability, as in "I can swim", which has borderline modal meaning in that ability is a type of possibility, but it does not reflect speaker assessment in the way modality usually does. We will return to this central meaning of CAN when we look at Appraisal.

CAN is occasionally used to express median usuality, as in "linguistics can be fascinating". The past tense form COULD is used to express lower possibility, as when Nicholas says:

61. Maybe you couldn't finance that, you know?

This form of this sentence is a little unusual, but Nicholas appears to be assessing the proposition as having low probability (because of the negative). Alternatively, it could be argued that this is an example of CAN in the sense of ability (COULD is the hypothetical form of CAN, the only example of a special hypothetical form in English). It is not always possible to make a clear judgement because, as suggested with SHOULD above, one type of modality often blends into another – something that is occasionally put to good use by skilled speakers, consciously or otherwise.

With positive polarity COULD expresses low probability, as in:

62. It could rain tonight.

A similar meaning could also be construed with:

63. It might rain tonight.

Both modal auxiliaries express low probability, but this is a case where there is a subtle distinction, which is brought out in the following examples:

64. It could rain tonight, but it won't.
65. ??It might rain tonight, but it won't.

Example 64 makes sense because "could" here signals *hypothetical possibility*. So the speaker is saying it could conceivably rain but in my opinion it won't. Example 65 is very odd as "might" is a subjective assessment of roughly 50/50 probability, so to follow it with a subjective assessment of zero possibility is a contradiction! When considering the force of speakers' statements over a text it is sufficient to class these both as median modality, but when we look at short sections of the text in detail then the more delicate distinctions are useful.

Table 4.2 sets out the different categories of modality we have been looking at. For a fuller discussion see Halliday and Matthiessen 2004:613–625. Note that not all cells are full and that some examples are more natural-sounding than others. You might also notice that there are often more than three values, as for example with "She's desperate/determined/keen/willing to do it".

As well as modality, Text 4.3 also contains an example of the related resource **evidentiality** when Gordon says:

66. Which doesn't appear to be the case.

Here Gordon is making his statement on the basis of the available evidence. Evidentiality is like modality in that it relates to speakers' assessments of the truth of a proposition. However, whereas modality relates to the level of certainty, etc., evidentiality refers to the nature of the evidence supporting a proposition. This can be very vague, as in example 66, where Gordon is suggesting that his claim is based on available evidence but is not being very explicit about exactly what sort. The verb SEEM is also used for non-specific evidence:

67. She seems very nice.

However, we can be more specific and make it clear how we came across the evidence, as in example 68 where the evidence was heard:

68. She sounded like she was very upset.

In example 66 Gordon's claim is implicitly subjective. Compare this with:

69. I can see that this isn't the case. (explicit subjective evidentiality)
70. Apparently this isn't the case. (implicit objective evidentiality)
71. It appears that this isn't the case. (explicit objective evidentiality)

TABLE 4.2 Summary of modality

		Explicit subjective	Implicit subjective	Implicit objective	Explicit objective
Deontic: obligation	High	I order you to leave!; I insist you leave.	You must leave.	You have to leave; you're required to leave.	It's essential you leave.
	Median	I suggest you leave; I want you to leave.	You should leave.	You're supposed to leave.	It's advisable you leave.
	Low	I don't mind if you leave.	You can leave now.	You're allowed to leave.	It's okay for you to leave.
Deontic: willingness	High			Mick's desperate to do it.	It's our determination that they will not defeat us
	Median		Mick'll do it.	Mick's keen to do it.	It's our wish that they win.
	Low			Mick doesn't mind doing it.	It's okay with Mick to do it.
Epistemic: probability	High	I know he'll be home by now.	He must be home by now.	He's definitely home by now.	It's certain he'll be home by now.
	Median	I think he'll be home by now.	He'll be home by now.	He's probably home by now.	It's probable he'll be home by now.
	Low	I guess he could be home by now.	He might be home by now.	He's possibly home by now.	It's possible he'll be home by now.
Epistemic: usuality	High	I expect it to rain in July.	On sunny days my folks will just sit outside and snooze.	It always rains in July.	It's inevitable that it rains in July.
	Median		It can rain in July.	It usually rains in July.	It's normal for it to rain in July.
	Low			It sometimes rains in July.	It's rare for it to rain in July.

There is another form which can be used to attribute the perception of the evidence to some unnamed other:

72. He was seen to place the Buddha on the mantelpiece.

and

73. He was heard to have called her a liar.

Note that the mental processes in 72 and 73 do not take the particle "to" in the active form while they always do in the passive. This suggests that these passive forms are special evidential constructions (Fawcett 2007:935–938).

74. *We saw him to place the Buddha on the mantelpiece.
75. *He was seen place the Buddha on the mantelpiece.

This shows one again how the grammar rearranges itself to make different kinds of meaning.

And, finally, someone specific can be cited as perceiving the evidence. Example 76 is an example of such attributed evidentiality, a staple of newspaper reporting and court cases:

76. His neighbour heard him fire three shots.

Here the burden of truth is passed onto a third party. As with other uses of attribution it is often a reliable source who is cited in order to back up the speaker's proposition, as in:

77. Three police officers witnessed the defendant speeding.

There is an example of attributed evidentiality in Text 4.3, when Nicholas says in lines 33–34:

78. The government na see it as being complementary.

Here, however, Nicholas's attributed evidentiality seems designed to discredit the government rather than to lend authority to the proposition.

It should be noted that there is often very little use of modality, attribution or evidentiality in texts, which is a shame from the analyst's point of view. However, there are other resources available for speakers to evaluate individual actions, people and things (rather than the truth value of whole clauses as propositions or proposals), and these are much more commonly used (hurrah!). We will look at these when we discuss Appraisal, below.

As discussed earlier, *tenor* refers to the interpersonal aspect of context: the personal positions and the relations between them that are brought out in the text. Note here that, as tenor is an aspect of context, not the environment,[5] it does not refer to any other relations that might be expected to hold between the speakers – though the speakers' understandings of these social relations will influence the possible tenors construed and being aware of these features will be helpful to analysts in reaching a rich interpretation of the text as discourse, particularly when there are tensions between the expected relations and the tenors actually construed in the discourse.

Indirect speech acts can be used to mitigate the force of *face-threatening acts* (Brown and Levinson 1987) or they can be used by speakers who are aware that their social position will make it likely that their proposal will be accepted and their proposals acted upon. This means that an informal and egalitarian tenor is not necessarily an indication of a balance of power in discourse. Similarly, while we can make a distinction between subjective and objective modality in a speakers' utterance, even with objective modality we have to ask what it means for a speaker to state an obligation as a self-evident fact, what social position entitles them to do this or what position they are appropriating to themselves in doing this.

Exercise 4.2

1. Discuss Text 4.3 in terms of the overall tenor of the discourse, the interpersonal feel. Mention mood, modality and speech roles as well as any other features you see as relevant.
2. Given what you know of the speakers, what would you say is happening in this text as discourse?

4.4 Appraisal

Modality, attribution and evidentiality, as we have discussed them so far, relate to the assessment of the truth of entire clauses. However, the focus of these resources can be limited to a participant or a process, as in:

79. a visibly inferior team
80. the probable cause of the accident
81. the alleged culprit
82. a man described as inspirational by his students

As with other forms of assessment these can be attributed to a specific person, as in 82, or (for various discursive reasons) leave the source unnamed, as in 79 to 81.

These assessments all have their counterparts at clause level (evidentiality in 79; modality in 80; and attribution in 81 and 82). Capturing how these meanings are repeated, intensified and distributed across texts is the focus of *Appraisal*, a text analytical framework originally developed by Peter White and Jim Martin (for example, 2005). It is now very significant method in SFL theory, particularly in research into *genre theory*. We will only cover some of the most basic distinctions here, but a wider reading of Appraisal is highly recommended in order to supplement the analytical approach outlined in this book.

Although Appraisal is the name generally given to the framework as a whole, Appraisal is in fact only one category of evaluative language that is covered by the theory, with others being Engagement and Graduation. Engagement includes attribution, covered above. In this section we will focus on the categories of Appraisal and the three subcategories of which it is comprised; Affect, Judgement and Appreciation.

Affect is concerned with emotional responses, and is related to emotive processes at clause level; Judgement is concerned with assessments of behaviour, and is related to modality at clause level; and Appreciation is concerned with the worth of various phenomena in terms of their aesthetics, coherence, value or effectiveness (see Martin and White 2005:57):

83. Sometimes they're just not terribly interested in listening. (Affect)
84. They don't really <u>want to</u> listen.

85. They have an advantage right away there (xx) find that ... they actually killing ... government is (xx) not knowing (they) erm killing culture.   (Judgement)
86. the government is behaving in ways that it <u>shouldn't</u>

87. When we develop plans that erm ... the government na see it as being, you know, complementary ... complementary with the present development strategies of the government ...   (Appreciation)
88. the strategies don't <u>look</u> good to the government/the government doesn't think these strategies will be <u>effective</u>

Each of these categories can be subclassified at a more delicate level. In this book we will consider one extra degree of delicacy for Affect and two degrees of delicacy for Judgement and Appreciation as I find these the most useful and the most workable distinctions (see Figure 4.1).

The labels within Affect and Judgement are fairly self-evident but those within Appreciation need some glossing. Reaction refers to the property of someone or something to cause an affective reaction, either because it "grabs" you in some way (Martin and White 2005:57), or fails to grab you (+/- impact) or because you like or dislike it (+/- quality). This contrasts with Affect, which refers to the emotion felt by the human senser, rather than the property of the phenomenon: so, "interesting" or "delightful" would be (+Appreciation:reaction:impact) and (+Appreciation:reaction:quality) while "interested" or "delighted" would be (+Affect:satisfaction) and (+Affect:happiness) respectively. Composition is made up of the fairly self-evident categories "balance" (how well something hangs together) and "complexity". Valuation is a much more catch-all and subjective category, referring to our considered opinions of whether something is valuable in some way. As Martin and White (2005:57) put it: "Of these variables valuation is especially sensitive to field since the value of things depends so much on our institutional focus."

Each category can be positive or negative, and the polarity is marked in the analysis, as with:

89. a weak government (-judgement:social esteem:capacity)
90. an honest man (+judgement:social sanction:veracity)
91. dangerous times (-affect:security)

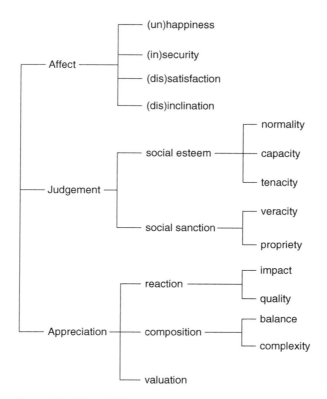

FIGURE 4.1   Categories of appraisal

As with modality, evaluation can be expressed by use of an Adjunct:

92.   Thankfully, no one was hurt. (+affect:happiness)
93.   Disgracefully, he voted against the proposal. (-judgement:social sanction: propriety)

Adjuncts such as these express the speaker's evaluation of the whole proposition and are called *Comment Adjuncts*. The word "hopefully" is often used as a Comment Adjunct, much to the annoyance of pedants who do not understand grammar very well. They complain about sentences such as:

94.   Hopefully Man City will lose tonight.

on the spurious grounds that Man City will not be likely to lose "in a hopeful fashion". They don't follow up on this flawed logic, however, to suggest that

95.   Admittedly, Man Utd have as good as won the title.

on the grounds that Man Utd are unlikely to win an "in admitted fashion"! Another argument against their pedantry is provided by the flexibility of positioning in the clause of Comment Adjuncts:

96. Man City will hopefully lose tonight.
97. Man City hopefully <u>will</u> lose tonight.

Such flexibility is not possible with adverbs of manner and clearly signals the function of the term. For a fuller list of Comment Adjuncts and their subclassification see Halliday and Matthiessen 2004:608–612).

As with modality, evaluations can sometimes be expressed in an "it's clause" in a way that makes them sound more objective, or with common agreement presupposed, as with example 98 (for more on this see Chapter 5):

98. It's great news that you can come.

Exercise 4.3

Look at the following text, Tony Blair's response to the London bombings of 7 July 2005 once again, and answer the questions below.

Text 4.4 Blair's response to 7/7 bombings

1 I am just going to make a short statement to you on the terrible events that have happened in London earlier today,
2 and I hope
3 you understand
4 that at the present time we are still trying to establish exactly what has happened,
5 and there is a limit to what information I can give you,
6 and I will simply try and tell you the information as best I can at the moment.
7 It is reasonably clear that there have been a series of terrorist attacks in London.
8 There are obviously casualties, both people that have died and people seriously injured,
9 and our thoughts and prayers of course are with the victims and their families.
10 It is my intention to leave the G8 within the next couple of hours and go down to London and get a report, face-to-face, with the police, and the emergency services and the Ministers that have been dealing with this, and then to return later this evening.
11 It is the will of all the leaders at the G8 however that the meeting should continue in my absence, that we should continue to discuss the issues that we were going to discuss, and reach the conclusions which we were going to reach.
12 Each of the countries round that table have some experience of the effects of terrorism

13 and all the leaders> < share our complete resolution to defeat this terrorism.
14 >as they will indicate a little bit later<
15 It is particularly barbaric that this has happened on a day when people are meeting to try to help the problems of poverty in Africa, and the long term problems of climate change and the environment.
16 Just as it is reasonably clear that this is a terrorist attack, or a series of terrorist attacks,
17 it is also reasonably clear that it is designed and aimed to coincide with the opening of the G8.
18 There will be time to talk later about this.
19 It is important however that those engaged in terrorism realise
20 that our determination to defend our values and our way of life is greater than their determination to cause death and destruction to innocent people in a desire to impose extremism on the world.
21 Whatever they do,
22 it is our determination that they will never succeed in destroying what we hold dear in this country and in other civilised nations throughout the world.

Questions

1. Identify and label the examples of modality and appraisal according to the various subcategories discussed. Answers on p. 199.
2. Discuss the use of implicit/objective and subjective/objective modality – what do you think is its effect in terms of Blair's positioning given the social environment at the time of the bombings and the various audiences Blair is addressing (you might like to make comparisons with Bush's "Bring it on" speech, see pp. 146–147).

Returning to Text 4.3, there is one more important distinction to be made when labelling for Appraisal. Consider the following words from Nicholas:

99. Because what we find there's disadvantage when we've been government, erm, driven programmes, they've been … financially supported properly … and our ermprogrammes are not, traditional ways are not supported so.

Do you think Nicholas's use of the word "traditional" is evaluative here? In what way? Would a dictionary include such evaluation in the definition of "traditional"? My own view is that Nicholas intends the term to carry positive evaluation, where "authentic" and "fake" are useful glosses for the positive and negative poles. However, this positive evaluation is only *evoked* by the use of the word in context rather than being *inscribed* as an essential part of its dictionary meaning. This gives us 48 different labels for evaluation: 12 subcategories of evaluation type x two polarities x inscribed/evoked.

Evoked categories are a fuzzy area, though, and the analyst has to be careful to account for what effect evoked evaluation can reasonably be assumed to achieve rather than relying on their own intuitions. Two excellent articles by O'Halloran and Coffin (2004 and Coffin and O'Halloran 2006) exemplify the dangers well. In one (Coffin and O'Halloran 2006), they take exception to an analysis by Fairclough in which he labels the verb "flock" as carrying negative connotations. Coffin and O'Halloran use corpus evidence to show that "flock" does not carry negative overtones in the majority of cases and so cannot be expected to evoke negative evaluations without further evidence. From a rather different perspective, they show that the term "Eastern Europeans", while apparently neutral, will carry negative associations for readers of the *Sun* by demonstrating that within a corpus taken from that newspaper "Eastern Europeans" nearly always *collocates* with extremely negative terms. But this takes us to another point: if a word such as "flock" appears in relation to Eastern Europeans in a subcorpus in which Eastern Europeans are overwhelmingly negatively evaluated, or within a text that is **saturated** (Martin and White 2005:19) with negative evaluations, then we can suppose that "flock" itself will carry negative evaluations within that text. As subcategories of evoked evaluation we can therefore have *corpus-based*, *subcorpus-based* and *text-based evocation*.

Saturation is an extreme case of what is called **semantic prosody**. While some authors have used the term prosody to refer to the evocative load of single words,[6] for Halliday and others it refers more to the evaluative feel of a whole text or stretch of text:

> The interpersonal component of meaning is the speaker's ongoing intrusion into the speech situation. It is his [sic] perspective on the exchange, his assigning and acting out of speech roles. Interpersonal meanings cannot easily be expressed as configurations of discrete elements ... The essence of the meaning potential of this part of the semantic system is that most of the options are associated with the act of meaning as a whole ... this interpersonal meaning ... is strung throughout the clause as a continuous motif of colouring ... the effect is cumulative ... we shall refer to this type of realisation as 'prosodic', since the meaning is distributed like a prosody throughout a continuous stretch of discourse.
>
> *(Halliday 1979:66–67)*

This means that in a text which contains many potential examples of evoked evaluation, the saturation of the text with such meanings makes the negative readings *mutually reinforcing*.

Exercise 4.4

Have a look at the following text and then answer the questions that follow.

Text 4.5 Wikipedia entry for Chavs

1   Chavs have been noted to often don designer sportswear.
2   Brands such as Adidas, Burberry, Puma, Umbro, Ecko, Carbrini and Kappa are very popular,
3   with many chavs often wearing a full tracksuit or tracksuit bottoms, with a hoodie or polyester jacket, baseball cap and oversized trainers.
4   Clothing attire is usually navy, white, black, red or grey for the chav male,
5   and pink and white are very common with the "chavette", particularly jogging bottoms, velour tracksuits or shell suits.
6   Stereotypical attire might be accompanied by some form of bling, such as oversized gold hoop earrings and necklaces, bracelets and rings, and an abundance of tattoos.
7   Several stereotypical traits are associated with chavs;
8   smoking, drinking and taking drugs in gangs on street corners and outside shops, petty thievery and violence, vandalism and graffiti, an exaggerated "tough" gangster-like voice and lingo and foul, aggressive language (with common expressions such as "Am I bovvered" or "Warru on about"), council house/flat accommodation, unemployment and state benefits scrounging
9   (and despite this still appearing to have money for show),
10 teenage girls being sexually promiscuous and smoking whilst pregnant,
11 driving a highly modified and chromed up Vauxhall Nova (in particular), Vauxhall Cavalier, Ford Sierra, Ford Escort or Austin Metro,
12 usually souped up with alloys, stickers, oversized spoiler, side panels, exhaust pipe and engine
13 painted white or in some flamboyant colour,
14 enhanced speakers blasting hip-hop, R&B, garage, drum and bass or rave/jungle music
15 and chewing whilst being spoken to.
16 Stereotypical chavs tend to sport skinheads, or very short hair with short back and sides and fringe, usually gelled down.
17 In northern British cities such as Manchester, it is fashionable for some chavs to sport longer hair and sides in the Mod fashion.
18 Chavettes' stereotypically wear their hair tightly scraped back into a ponytail or bun,
19 known as the "Council house face lift"
20 Burberry is a clothing company
21 whose products became associated with the "chav" stereotype.
22 Burberry's appeal to "chav" fashion sense is a sociological example of prole drift, where an up-market product begins to be consumed *en masse* by a lower socio-economic group.[
23 Burberry has argued that the brand's popular association with "chav" fashion sense is linked to counterfeit versions of the clothing.
24 "They're yesterday's news", stated Stacey Cartwright, the CEO of Burberry.

25 "It was mostly counterfeit, and Britain accounts for less than 10% of our sales anyway."

26 The company has taken a number of steps to distance itself from the stereotype

27 It ceased production of its own branded baseball cap in 2004

28 and has scaled back the use of its trademarked checkered/tartan design to such an extent

29 that it now only appears on the inner linings and other very low-key positions of their clothing

30 It has also taken legal action against high-profile infringements of the brand.

31 The large supermarket chain Asda has attempted to trademark the word "chav" for a new line of confectionery

32 A spokeswoman said: "With slogans from characters in shows such as *Little Britain* and *The Catherine Tate Show* providing us with more and more contemporary slang,

33 our Whatever sweets – now nicknamed chav hearts – have become very popular with kids and grown-ups alike

34 We thought we needed to give them some respect and have decided to trademark our sweets

35 A BBC TV documentary suggested that "chav" culture is an evolution of previous working-class youth subcultures associated with particular commercial clothing styles, such as mods, skinheads and casuals.

36 The widespread use of the "chav" stereotype

37 has come in for some criticism

38 Some argue that it amounts to simple snobbery and elitism

39 Critics of the term have argued that its users are "neo-snobs",

40 and that its increasing popularity raises questions about how British society deals with social mobility and class

41 In a February 2005 article in *The Times*, Julie Burchill argued that use of the word is a form of "social racism", and that such "sneering" reveals more about the shortcomings of the "chav-haters" than those of their supposed victims

42 The writer John Harris argued along similar lines in a 2007 article in the *Guardian*

43 The Welsh rap group, Goldie Lookin Chain, have been described as both embodying

44 and satirising the "chav" aesthetic

45 though the group themselves deny any such agenda,

46 simply making a mockery of the subject

47 In the BBC TV series *Doctor Who*, Episode *New Earth*, 15 April 2006, the character Lady Cassandra is transplanted into Rose Tyler's body (Billie Piper)

48 When Cassandra sees herself in a mirror,

49 she exclaims "Oh my God … I'm a chav!"

50 Characters described as "chavs" have occurred in a number of British television programmes.

51 The character, clothing, attitude and musical interests of Lauren Cooper and her friends in the BBC comedy series *The Catherine Tate Show* have been associated with the chav stereotype.

52 The comedy series *Little Britain* features a character with some similarities, Vicky Pollard.

(Source: http://en.wikipedia.org/wiki/Chav)

Questions

1. Indicate as many examples of inscribed Appraisal in the text as you can and assign each to the appropriate subcategory.

2. Indicate as many examples of evoked Appraisal in the text and assign each to the appropriate subcategory.

3. Check some of these words in a corpus and see if they generally carry negative, positive or neutral evaluations.

4. Discuss the text in terms of saturation and text-based evocation.

5. Read Wikipedia's policy on neutrality, below, and discuss how linguistic resources such as modality and attribution are used in an attempt to make the entry comply with this policy. How successful do you think this strategy is?

> Editing from a **neutral point of view** (**NPOV**) means representing fairly, proportionately, and as far as possible without bias, all significant views that have been published by reliable sources. All Wikipedia articles and other encyclopedic content must be written from a neutral point of view. NPOV is a fundamental principle of Wikipedia and of other Wikimedia projects. This policy is nonnegotiable and all editors and articles must follow it.
>
> "Neutral point of view" is one of Wikipedia's three core content policies. The other two are "Verifiability" and "No original research". These three core policies jointly determine the type and quality of material that is acceptable in Wikipedia articles. Because these policies work in harmony, they should not be interpreted in isolation from one another, and editors should try to familiarize themselves with all three. The principles upon which this policy is based cannot be superseded by other policies or guidelines, or by editors' consensus.
>
> *(Source: http://en.wikipedia.org/wiki/Wikipedia:*
> *Neutral_point_of_view 12th No 2012-11-12)*

6. Consider the repeated use of the words "stereotypical" and "stereotypically" in terms of both modality and evaluation and discuss their usage here.

7. Look at the current entry for Chavs to see what changes have been made to make it comply better with NPOV.

For a fuller discussion of evoked and inscribed Appraisal in Wikipedia see Bartlett 2012b. For an excellent discussion of anti-Chavism see Jones 2012.

This text shows us how seemingly neutral terms can carry evaluative overtones in specific texts. A similar process occurs on a much wider and more significant scale when words can jump categories within whole language systems. Consider left-handedness. This could be considered as -social esteem:normality as the majority of the population is right-handed. Now consider the following words for left and right in different languages and think of the overtones these words or related words carry and the evaluative categories they belong to:

> Right: dexter (Latin), droite (French), derecho (Spanish), rechts (German)
> Left: sinister (Latin), gauche (French)

What does this tell you about historical attitudes to usuality (and compare this to the use of "You don't do that" as an injunction)? It is also interesting here to note that in some dialects of Scots Gaelic the left hand is referred to as "the wrong hand".

Appraisal analysis has been much used in recent years. Analyses of the opinions expressed in small talk, for example, has been used to suggest how customers and service providers align themselves in terms of their evaluative stances as part of the process of facilitating business transactions (*cf.* Chapter 2). More typical examples would be to compare the bases of evaluation between political parties, religious groups or newspapers, either within the same country or in different countries. A research question of interest, for example, would be the relative weight given to how well things function (Appreciation) and how things are judged in moral terms (Judgement) between political parties or between countries with a more or less secular political tradition of politics. Taking a more complex angle, an Appraisal analysis could show how shifts from one category to another are naturalised over texts and discuss how such muddying of the evaluative waters is relevant to the environment in which such texts are produced.

Exercise 4.5

To finish this chapter on interpersonal meaning and tenor we'll look in detail at Martin Luther King's "I have a dream speech" from 1963. Read up on the speech and on the US civil rights movement at the time. Then read the text and answer the questions that follow.

Text 4.6 Martin Luther King *I Have a Dream* speech

1 I am happy to join with you today in what will go down in history as the greatest demonstration for freedom in the history of our nation.
2 Five score years ago, a great American, >< signed the Emancipation Proclamation.
3 >in whose symbolic shadow we stand today, <
4 This momentous decree came as a great beacon light of hope to millions of Negro slaves who had been seared in the flames of withering injustice.

6　But one hundred years later, the Negro still is not free.

7　One hundred years later, the life of the Negro is still sadly crippled by the manacles of segregation and the chains of discrimination.

8　One hundred years later, the Negro lives on a lonely island of poverty in the midst of a vast ocean of material prosperity.

9　One hundred years later, the Negro is still languishing in the corners of American society

10　and finds himself an exile in his own land.

11　So we have come here today to dramatize a shameful condition.

12　In a sense we have come to our nation's capital to cash a check.

13　When the architects of our republic wrote the magnificent words of the Constitution and the Declaration of Independence,

14　they were signing a promissory note to which every American was to fall heir.

15　This note was a promise that all men, yes, black men as well as white men, would be guaranteed the unalienable rights of life, liberty, and the pursuit of happiness.

16　It is obvious today that America has defaulted on this promissory note

17　insofar as her citizens of color are concerned.

18　Instead of honoring this sacred obligation, America has given the Negro people a bad check, a check which has come back marked "insufficient funds."

19　But we refuse to believe

20　that the bank of justice isbankrupt.

21　We refuse to believe

22　that there are insufficient funds in the great vaults of opportunity of this nation.

23　So we have come to cash this check – a check that will give us upon demand the riches of freedom and the security of justice.

24　We have also come to this hallowed spot to remind America of the fierce urgency of now.

25　This is no time to engage in the luxury of cooling off or to take the tranquilizing drug of gradualism.

26　Now is the time to make real the promises of democracy.

27　Now is the time to rise from the dark and desolate valley of segregation to the sunlit path of racial justice.

28　Now is the time to lift our nation from the quick sands of racial injustice to the solid rock of brotherhood.

29　Now is the time to make justice a reality for all of God's children.

30　It would be fatal for the nation to overlook the urgency of the moment.

31　This sweltering summer of the Negro's legitimate discontent will not pass

32　until there is an invigorating autumn of freedom and equality.

33　Nineteen sixty-three is not an end, but a beginning.

34　Those who hope that the Negro needed to blow off steam and will now be content will have a rude awakening

35 if the nation returns to business as usual.

36 There will be neither rest nor tranquility in America

37 until the Negro is granted his citizenship rights.

38 The whirlwinds of revolt will continue to shake the foundations of our nation

39 until the bright day of justice emerges.

40 But there is something that I must say to my people who stand on the warm threshold which leads into the palace of justice.

41 In the process of gaining our rightful place we must not be guilty of wrongful deeds.

42 Let us not seek to satisfy our thirst for freedom by drinking from the cup of bitterness and hatred.

43 We must forever conduct our struggle on the high plane of dignity and discipline.

44 We must not allow our creative protest to degenerate into physical violence.

45 Again and again we must rise to the majestic heights of meeting physical force with soul force.

46 The marvelous new militancy which has engulfed the Negro community must not lead us to a distrust of all white people,

47 for many of our white brothers, >< have come to realize

48 >as evidenced by their presence here today,<

49 that their destiny is tied up with our destiny.

50 They have come to realize

51 that their freedom is inextricably bound to our freedom.

52 We cannot walk alone.

53 As we walk,

54 we must make the pledge

55 that we shall always march ahead.

56 We cannot turn back.

57 There are those who are asking the devotees of civil rights,

58 "When will you be satisfied?"

59 We can never be satisfied

60 as long as the Negro is the victim of the unspeakable horrors of police brutality.

61 We can never be satisfied,

62 as long as our bodies, heavy with the fatigue of travel, cannot gain lodging in the motels of the highways and the hotels of the cities.

63 We cannot be satisfied

64 as long as the Negro's basic mobility is from a smaller ghetto to a larger one.

65 We can never be satisfied

66 as long as our children are stripped of their selfhood

67 and robbed of their dignity by signs stating "For Whites Only".

68 We cannot be satisfied

69 as long as a Negro in Mississippi cannot vote

70   and a Negro in New York believes
71   he has nothing for which to vote.
72   No, no, we are not satisfied,
73   and we will not be satisfied
74   until justice rolls down like waters
75   and righteousness like a mighty stream.
76   I am not unmindful
77   that some of you have come here out of great trials and tribulations.
78   Some of you have come fresh from narrow jail cells.
79   Some of you have come from areas where your quest for freedom left you battered by the storms of persecution and staggered by the winds of police brutality.
80   You have been the veterans of creative suffering.
81   Continue to work with the faith that unearned suffering is redemptive.
82   Go back to Mississippi,
83   go back to Alabama,
84   go back to South Carolina,
85   go back to Georgia,
86   go back to Louisiana,
87   go back to the slums and ghettos of our northern cities, knowing that some-how this situation can and will be changed.
88   Let us not wallow in the valley of despair.
89   I say to you today, my friends,
90   so even though we face the difficulties of today and tomorrow,
91   I still have a dream.
92   It is a dream deeply rooted in the American dream.
93   I have a dream
94   that one day this nation will rise up
95   and live out the true meaning of its creed:
96   "We hold these truths to be self-evident:
97   that all men are created equal."
98   I have a dream
99   that one day on the red hills of Georgia the sons of former slaves and the sons of former slave owners will be able to sit down together at the table of brotherhood.
100 I have a dream
101 that one day even the state of Mississippi, a state sweltering with the heat of injustice, sweltering with the heat of oppression, will be transformed into an oasis of freedom and justice.
102 I have a dream
103 that my four little children will one day live in a nation where they will not be judged by the color of their skin but by the content of their character.
104 I have a dream today.
105 I have a dream

106 that one day, down in Alabama, with its vicious racists, with its governor having his lips dripping with the words of interposition and nullification; one day right there in Alabama, little black boys and black girls will be able to join hands with little white boys and white girls as sisters and brothers.

107 I have a dream today.

108 I have a dream

109 that one day every valley shall be exalted,

110 every hill and mountain shall be made low,

111 the rough places will be made plain,

112 and the crooked places will be made straight,

113 and the glory of the Lord shall be revealed,

114 and all flesh shall see it together.

115 This is our hope.

116 This is the faith that I go back to the South with.

117 With this faith we will be able to hew out of the mountain of despair a stone of hope.

118 With this faith we will be able to transform the jangling discords of our nation into a beautiful symphony of brotherhood.

119 With this faith we will be able to work together,

120 to pray together,

121 to struggle together,

122 to go to jail together,

123 to stand up for freedom together, knowing that we will be free one day.

124 This will be the day when all of God's children will be able to sing with a new meaning,

125 "My country, 'tis of thee, sweet land of liberty, of thee I sing.

126 Land where my fathers died, land of the pilgrim's pride, from every mountainside, let freedom ring."

127 And if America is to be a great nation

128 this must become true.

129 So let freedom ring from the prodigious hilltops of New Hampshire.

130 Let freedom ring from the mighty mountains of New York.

131 Let freedom ring from the heightening Alleghenies of Pennsylvania!

132 Let freedom ring from the snowcapped Rockies of Colorado!

133 Let freedom ring from the curvaceous slopes of California!

134 But not only that; let freedom ring from Stone Mountain of Georgia!

135 Let freedom ring from Lookout Mountain of Tennessee!

136 Let freedom ring from every hill and molehill of Mississippi.

137 From every mountainside, let freedom ring.

138 And when this happens,

139 when we allow freedom to ring,

140 when we let it ring from every village and every hamlet, from every state and every city,

141 we will be able to speed up that day when all of God's children, black men

and white men, Jews and Gentiles, Protestants and Catholics, will be able to join hands and sing in the words of the old Negro spiritual,
142 "Free at last! free at last! thank God Almighty, we are free at last!"

(Source: www.usconstitution.net/dream.html © 1963 Dr Martin Luther King Jr © 1991 Coretta Scott King)

Questions

1. Can you identify stretches of text which are characterised by particular features of mood and/or modality? How would you characterise these stretches in terms of their rhetorical effect?
2. Can you identify stretches of text which are characterised by particular configurations of evaluative language?
3. How do mood, modality and evaluation interact with shifts in field, including transitivity relations?
4. What different positions do you think Martin Luther King is construing for himself and for his audience?
5. How does King recalibrate the storyline at different points?
6. Do you recognise styles of rhetoric from different traditions in the speech?
7. Do you think the positions adopted by King all belong to a single role set appropriate to a single social status or is there a mixing here of different roles belonging to different role sets?
8. Relate the positions taken up by King to the historical context and King's status(es) and discuss why you think this speech is generally regarded as of great historical significance.
9. Relate your answers in 1–8 to the Positioning Star, remembering that all aspects of the language used are part of the act, but that they affect and are affected by the other points of the Star.

4.5 Conclusion

In this chapter we have looked at the resources speakers have available to signal and negotiate their role in ongoing interaction and to present subjective assessments and evaluations of the topics being discussed. These features, then, work together to construe what is known as the **tenor** of the discourse, the personal investment of the speakers as speakers and the social relations they establish and recalibrate with each other through their ongoing talk. In terms of the Positioning Star, interpersonal features of language, like experiential features, are part of the discourse act and they serve to construe one aspect of the speaker's position. As we have seen in the examples above, the negotiation of interpersonal position brings in issues of power and cultural capital which are, in turn, connected to the storyline(s) in different ways. We can see, then, that while we can separate the interpersonal from the experiential for ease of analysis, ultimately the two types of meaning, as well as textual meaning as we shall see later, cannot be considered in isolation. This is a theme I'll return to in more detail in Chapters 6 and 7.

Notes

1   There is also, rarely, the exclamative mood, as in "What an ass I am!"
2   The United Nations Development Programme, one of several UN organisations operating in Guyana, with a history of work in the North Rupununi.
3   "Na" is a general negative marker in Guyanese English.
4   This is my own term. Halliday and Matthiessen include this as one feature or orientation.
5   A lot of SFL literature, however, is indeterminate on this point
6   As in the work of John Sinclair and Bill Louw.
7   The symbols >< mean that a whole clause originally appeared in the middle of another clause but that it has been separated and placed below for ease of reference, so: >in whose symbolic shadow we stand today, <.

5

TEXTUAL MEANING

The speaker as weaver

5.1 Introduction

In previous chapters we have looked at the representational meaning and exchange value of individual clauses and how these are spread out across texts; in this chapter we will begin looking at how speakers and writers control this spread of meanings and signpost linkages to produce coherent and cohesive texts. This is what Halliday calls *textual meaning*, which he describes as the "enabling metafunction" as it is the means by which texts are organised so as to allow the interpersonal and experiential meanings to do their work more effectively. The term textual meaning (or the textual metafunction) can be a little confusing, however; as I've said above, the patternings of interpersonal and experiential meaning turn speech and writing into texts, so they clearly contribute to the "textuality" of texts. What we mean by the textual metafunction, however, are those resources that languages have developed to *explicitly signal* the way in which different aspects of a text are related either to each other or to the time and place in which they are produced. In this chapter we will focus on one of the principal resource for signalling how clauses, as chunks of text, fit together: the thematic organisation of the clause and the development of these thematic elements as the text progresses. If experiential and interpersonal elements are the threads of a text, we can say that the textual metafunction refers to the way in which these elements are woven together to make a patterned cloth.

5.2 Theme and Rheme

Let's look again at the most famous sections from Churchill's *On the Beaches* speech, the section which gives the speech its popular name:

... we shall not flag or fail.
We shall go on to the end.
We shall fight in France,
we shall fight on the seas and oceans,
we shall fight with growing confidence and growing strength in the air,
we shall defend our island,
whatever the cost may be.
We shall fight on the beaches,
we shall fight on the landing grounds,
we shall fight in the fields and in the streets,
we shall fight in the hills;
we shall never surrender

One of the most obvious features of this section is that every clause begins with the word WE as Churchill catalogues the efforts that he pledges will be undertaken in order to defend the country from Nazi invasion – a variety of actions, but all grouped together in terms of what "we" will do. From the point of view of the textual organisation of the speech, what Churchill has done is to anchor the text at this point on the idea of "we, the British people" and to develop this idea in a variety of ways, one after the other. In functional terms we refer to the anchor of the clause, or series of clauses, as the *Theme*, and we refer to the rest of the clause, what is said about the Theme, as the *Rheme*. In English, the Theme comes at the beginning of the clause, but this is not necessarily true of other languages.

More specifically, we can talk of the *experiential Theme*[1] as the first element in the clause which carries experiential meaning – that is, which refers to a participant, process or circumstantial element. The following clauses from Martin Luther King's speech show, respectively, a participant as Theme and a circumstance as Theme. We'll look at processes as Themes a little below:

1.   **Some of you** have come from narrow jail cells
2.   **One hundred years later**, the Negro lives on a lonely island of poverty ...

The experiential Theme can be seen as fulfilling a sort of subheading function, as introducing an angle or topic before developing on it. As the principle function of thematic information is to signal how speakers are maintaining, developing and shifting the topic from one stretch of text to the next, the experiential Theme is an essential element of the clause. However, it is also possible to increase the *thematicity* of some purely interpersonal and textual elements of the clause, highlighting these ideas before moving on to the main content of the clause. This is achieved by placing these elements before the experiential Theme itself as some kind of preface to the experiential content of the clause. So we can define the *thematic element*[2] of a clause as all those elements up to and including the experiential Theme. We will look at interpersonal and textual Themes in Section 5.4 below.

Returning to the Churchill extract above, we said that Churchill was maintaining thematic focus on 'we' as the British people, and when the experiential Theme is maintained from one clause to the next we refer to a **constant Theme**. An important point to remember here is that it is the *referent* that is the Theme, irrespective of the words used to refer to it. The repetition of the exact same word, such as "we" can be used for rhetorical effect; alternatively, if Churchill had varied the word "we" with phrases such as "the British public" or "our nation" we would have had an interesting combination of constant Theme with semantic development (see Chapter 2).

In English the Theme is usually the Subject of declarative or yes–no interrogative clauses, the verb itself in imperatives, and the wh-word in wh-questions (see Chapter 4). When this is the case we refer to the clause as having an **unmarked Theme**. The following clauses from Martin Luther King's speech have the Theme marked in bold:

3. **Some of you** have come fresh from narrow jail cells.
4. **Some of you** have come from areas where your quest for freedom left you battered by the storms of persecution and staggered by the winds of police brutality.
5. **You** have been the veterans of creative suffering.
6. **Continue** to work with the faith that unearned suffering is redemptive.
7. **Go back** to Mississippi,
8. **go back** to Alabama,
9. **go back** to South Carolina,
11. **go back** to Georgia,
13. **go back** to Louisiana,
14. **go back** to the slums and ghettos of our northern cities, knowing that somehow this situation can and will be changed.
15. **Let us not wallow** in the valley of despair.

Note that in clauses 3 and 4 the Theme is a phrase, as this refers to a single participant. Note also that lines 3–5 have, to some extent, a constant Theme, 'you' as King's audience, though there is a difference in that the first two clauses narrow down the reference. In this way there is both a degree of continuity and a degree of change – and that is what textuality is all about, cohesion and development.

In clauses 6 to 14, the Themes are the imperative verbs. As direct imperatives always imply a second-person Subject (YOU), we can again see both continuity and development here as this implicit Subject remains constant while the actions themselves, the focus of imperative clauses, can vary (though only slightly here). In clause 15, we have a first person plural imperative introduced by "let's". As both the implied Subject (US) and the process change here, we have a change in Theme, a change that allows King to reformulate the YOU of his audience to include himself also and so create a sense of solidarity between his audience and himself as representatives of the Black population of the USA.

As for example 16, below, remember that DO is an interpersonal element (see Chapter 4), marking the structure as interrogative, and this is not therefore part of the experiential Theme.

16. Do **you** want to talk about it outside?

This is also true of interrogatives involving the verb TO BE. Although BE has experiential meaning in relational clauses (see Chapter 3), it is a feature of English that interrogatives with BE are formed by placing the BE word first rather than by introducing the "dummy" DO as we do with other verbs. This is also true for HAVE in some dialects of English. This is a case where features of clause structure are in tension with textual structure, an inevitability in a constantly evolving system such as language. So, in the following cases the Theme is the Subject, not the process:

17. Are **you** an idiot?
18. Have **you** any eggs?

There is also a tension between clause grammar and textual development in wh-interrogatives (see Chapter 4). English has developed a system whereby question words appear at the beginning of clauses in order to signal from the outset that the speaker is asking a question rather than providing information. Therefore the wh-word is the Theme of the clause, as it also encodes experiential information in the form of an unknown participant or circumstantial element. So, in example 19 the unmarked Theme is "when". This makes sense in that it signals a change of textual focus to the circumstantial element, but it can also mask the fact that there may be a thematic continuity of reference that is realised in the Subject. That is to say that thematicity at clause level (focus on the question) and text level (focus on continuity) are in tension. In these cases it is therefore useful to mark up both the wh-word (bold) and the Subject (underlined) when carrying out a thematic analysis:

19. **When** did <u>you</u> get here?

Note here that in some wh-interrogatives with WHO and WHAT the Subject and the wh-word are the same, so that we only need to mark up one element:

20. **Who** saw you?
21. **What** happened next?

However, WHO and WHAT often refer to the Complement of the clause (see Chapter 4) and in these cases it is also useful to mark up the Subject, as above. In fact, whenever we have a Theme that is not the Subject, it is useful to mark the Subject also:[3]

22. **What** did <u>you</u> do next?
23. **Who** did <u>you</u> see?

5.3 Marked Theme

In the above section we have considered the unmarked Theme, so now it is time to consider what we mean by a **marked Theme**. In the following clause from King's speech we see that the first experiential element of the declarative clause is not the Subject, as in the unmarked case, but the temporal Circumstance "five score years ago":

24. **Five score years ago**, a great American, in whose symbolic shadow we stand today, signed the Emancipation Proclamation.

King could have said:

25. **A great American**, in whose symbolic shadow we stand today, signed the Emancipation Proclamation five score years ago.

In the modified example the circumstantial element is at the end and the Subject at the beginning, and this is the case in roughly 90 per cent of English clauses, which is why we call it the unmarked case. However, King "chose" to begin his clause with this phrase and, as this is marked behaviour, we need to seek additional explanations for the "choice". The first reason can be provided at the local level, as we see that King is contrasting the time reference of his own appearance at the Lincoln Memorial ("today") with the timeframe of Lincoln's own historic speech:

26. **I** am happy to join with you today in what will go down in history as the greatest demonstration for freedom in the history of our nation.
27. **Five score years ago**, a great American, in whose symbolic shadow we stand today, signed the Emancipation Proclamation.

Here we can see how using a marked Theme *explicitly signals* a shift in focus (very often a spatial shift or, as in this case, a temporal shift), and such explicit signalling of textual development is a type of textual meaning. A similar shift, this time back to the present, in order to contrast the high words of the decree and the miserable conditions of many Black people in the USA of King's day, occurs with clause 30 in the following section:

28. **This momentous decree** came as a great beacon light of hope to millions of Negro slaves who had been seared in the flames of withering injustice.
29. **It** came as a joyous daybreak to end the long night of their captivity.
30. But **one hundred years later**, the Negro still is not free.

The use of marked Themes is therefore a tool in explicitly shifting the focus of a text. However, as I've said above, textuality involves both continuity and development, and as we can see in the above lines, this continuity is captured, despite the shift in focus, through the reference to "Negroes" in lines 28 and 30. For this reason, as with similar cases above, it is useful to highlight both the Subject and the Theme when there is a marked Theme:

31. **This momentous decree** came as a great beacon light of hope to millions of Negro slaves who had been seared in the flames of withering injustice.
32. **It** came as a joyous daybreak to end the long night of their captivity.
33. But **one hundred years later**, <u>the Negro</u> still is not free.

We can thus see that there is a constant Theme between clauses 31 and 32, but in the following clause we have an explicit shift in focus, signalled by the marked Theme (I will discuss the thematic function of "but" below), and a new Subject, "the Negro", which links back to clauses 31 and 32. You may ask why, therefore, we do not mark "Negro slaves" in clause 31 as Theme, and I shall return to that later.

First, let's look at a bit more of this text, marked up for thematic development:

34. **This momentous decree** came as a great beacon light of hope to millions of Negro slaves who had been seared in the flames of withering injustice.
35. **It** came as a joyous daybreak to end the long night of their captivity.
36. But **one hundred years later**, <u>the Negro</u> still is not free.
37. **One hundred years later**, <u>the life of the Negro</u> is still sadly crippled by the manacles of segregation and the chains of discrimination.
38. **One hundred years later**, <u>the Negro</u> lives on a lonely island of poverty in the midst of a vast ocean of material prosperity.
39. **One hundred years later**, <u>the Negro</u> is still languishing in the corners of American society
40. and finds himself an exile in his own land.
41. So **we** have come here today to dramatize a shameful condition.

There are two grammatical features to comment on quickly here. First, the word "so" in clause 41 (as with "but" in clause 36) does not add experiential meaning to the clause and therefore is not part of the experiential Theme (see below). Second, clause 40 has a finite verb but no overt Subject. This is because clauses 39 and 40 comprise a single sentence with each clause having the same Subject. When this happens it is possible to ellipt, or miss out, the second Subject. The effect of this is strongly cohesive, suggesting that the two processes are closely related in some way, and ellipsis is therefore considered a cohesive device and as such part of textual meaning. We can therefore say that ellipsis is a very strong marker of constant Theme over two clauses and to show this we have to enter a Subject in brackets so that it can be marked as Theme. As Theme refers to referents rather than concepts the exact word we use to represent the ellipted Theme is not important as long as the reference is clear. Thus, for the sake of analysis, we can rewrite clauses 39 and 40 as:

42. **One hundred years later**, <u>the Negro</u> is still languishing in the corners of American society
43. and **[he]** finds himself an exile in his own land.

What is very unusual (and therefore worthy of comment) in the stretch of text from 36 to 39 is the repetition of both the circumstantial element "one hundred years later" as marked Theme and the Subject "the Negro". Having already explicitly shifted temporal focus, it is not strictly necessary for King to repeat the marked Theme, and similarly he could have replaced "the Negro" with HE, THEY or WE in all but the first case. What seems to be happening here is that King is repeating "one hundred years later" to emphasise and reemphasise the long gap between the words of Lincoln and their becoming reality while the repetition of "the Negro" similarly emphasises the gap between the lot of Blacks and Whites in the USA at that time. Also, this stretch of text presents a series of Generalisations (which we'll explore in Chapter 6), so the repeated use of the same structure serves to emphasise the idea that that this unhappy state of affairs is a general truth rather than an isolated event. Such repetition is part of the overall rhetorical effect of King's speech and is a feature that is generally only found in such dramatic and emotionally charged discourse as this.

Let's now look again at the following clauses, relabelled 44 and 45:

44. When the architects of our republic wrote the magnificent words of the Constitution and the Declaration of Independence,
45. they were signing a promissory note to which every American was to fall heir.

Here we see a *clause complex* (more than one clause in a single sentence) in which the *subordinate cause* has been placed before the *main clause* (the one that carries the thrust of the sentence). As subordinate clauses function to provide circumstantial information, and as the usual position for subordinate clauses is after the main clause, we can say that a subordinate clause that precedes the main clause is in its entirety a marked Theme. However, as both the main clause and the subordinate clause have their own clause structure, we can also analyse each for Theme. To capture this we can italicise subordinate clauses that precede the main clause and mark in bold the Theme of each clause:

44. *When **the architects of our republic** wrote the magnificent words of the Constitution and the Declaration of Independence,*
45. **they** were signing a promissory note to which every American was to fall heir.

Subordinate clauses have semantic functions very similar to that of Circumstances. Table 5.1 lists the main categories of subordinate clauses and the conjunctions that introduce them.

TABLE 5.1 Subordinate clauses

Category		Conjunction	Example
Temporal	same time	while, when	I called him while he was painting.
	preceding	before	The man was unconscious before he was shot.
	following	after	The man was shot after he was unconscious.
Spatial	same	where	I like to linger where the lovely lilies bloom.
Manner	comparison	as, like	She sings just like he does!
Cause	cause: reason	because	I love you because you understand me.
	cause: purpose	so (that)	We need to save up so we can all go on holiday.
	cause: result	so that	She was so tall that she could pick the apples from the tree.
Condition	positive	if	If it rains we'll stay indoors.
	negative	unless	We'll play football outside unless it rains.
	concessive	even if, although	We'll play football outside even if it rains.

In the above sections I've tried to show how marked Themes can signal a change in focus from one clause to the next, but I said above that they also had a function at a less local level, that is across a whole text or a section of a text. To see this, let's look at the first six marked Themes of the King speech:

> Five score years ago …
> one hundred years later …
> one hundred years later …
> one hundred years later …
> one hundred years later …
> When the architects of our republic wrote the magnificent words of the Constitution and the Declaration of Independence …

As you can see all of these Themes are temporal Circumstances, and this shows us that this whole section of the text is designed from a temporal perspective. A series of marked Themes therefore indicates the *angle of development* of a text or part of a text. King could have chosen instead to take up a spatial angle, highlighting how the lot of Black Americans was the same across the country. Had he done so, we might expect to have seen a series of Circumstances of location such as:

> In Alabama …,
> In Mississippi …,
> In Kansas …,
> And even in Washington DC …

However, King chose to take a historical angle, and this is reflected in the use of marked temporal Circumstances. Both strategies are very common in biographical notes and encyclopaedia entries – take a look and see how these tend to use marked temporal or locational Themes to mark transitions in the text. Staying with King's speech for a while longer, let's look at the clauses in 46 to 49:

46. **Now** is the time to make real the promises of democracy.
47. **Now** is the time to rise from the dark and desolate valley of segregation to the sunlit path of racial justice.
48. **Now** is the time to lift our nation from the quick sands of racial injustice to the solid rock of brotherhood.
49. **Now** is the time to make justice a reality for all of God's children.

Here we see that the idea of time is highlighted again, not by marked temporal Themes, but by the unmarked Theme "now" as the Subject of the four clauses. We can see, then, how King has used the temporal framing to lead on to a discussion of the current time, with "now" as the Subject and constant unmarked Theme in four consecutive clauses, a Theme which he builds on to contrast what must be done now with the lack of progress over the one hundred years since Lincoln's speech.

In sum, a marked Theme serves the dual purpose of shifting the focus of the clause at the local level and also to set out the angle of development of the text or part of the text. At the local level we may have a marked Theme followed by a Subject or series of Subjects in following clauses that refer back to the Subject or Theme of the clauses immediately prior to the shift in focus, signalling both a continuity and a change in development:

50. **We** cannot walk alone
51. *As **we** walk,*
52. **we** must make the pledge ...

Alternatively, the marked Theme might be followed by Subjects/Themes that have not appeared before, signalling a greater textual shift:

53. <u>It</u> came as a joyous daybreak to end the long night of their captivity.
54. But **one hundred years later**, <u>the Negro</u> is still not free.

We can thus see how marked and unmarked Themes work together to signal the method of development of the clause and, as such, the skills of the speaker as a weaver. In the following section we will look at the function of interpersonal and textual elements within the thematic element as a whole and in Section 5.5 we will explore how shifts in focus are woven into coherent text.

Exercise 5.1

Read the following text and answer the questions that follow:

Text 5.1 Wikipedia's entry for Napoleon

1 Napoleon Bonaparte was a French military and political leader who rose to prominence during the latter stages of the French Revolution and its associated wars in Europe.

2 As Napoleon I, he was Emperor of the French from 1804 to 1815.

3 His legal reform, the Napoleonic Code, has been a major influence on many civil law jurisdictions worldwide,

4 but he is best remembered for his role in the wars led against France by a series of coalitions, the so-called Napoleonic Wars.

5 He established hegemony over most of continental Europe

6 and sought to spread the ideals of the French Revolution, while consolidating an imperial monarchy which restored aspects of the deposed *Ancien Régime*.

7 Due to his success in these wars, often against numerically superior enemies, he is generally regarded as one of the greatest military commanders of all time,

8 and his campaigns are studied at military academies worldwide.

9 Napoleon was born at Ajaccio in Corsica in a family of noble Italian ancestry which had settled Corsica in the 16th century.

10 He trained as an artillery officer in mainland France.

11 He rose to prominence under the French First Republic

12 and led successful campaigns against the First and Second Coalitions arrayed against France.

13 He led a successful invasion of the Italian peninsula.

14 In 1799, he staged a *coup d'état*

15 and installed himself as First Consul;

16 five years later the French Senate proclaimed him emperor, following a plebiscite in his favour.

17 In the first decade of the 19th century, the French Empire under Napoleon engaged in a series of conflicts – the Napoleonic Wars – that involved every major European power.

18 After a streak of victories, France secured a dominant position in continental Europe,

19 and Napoleon maintained the French sphere of influence through the formation of extensive alliances and the appointment of friends and family members to rule other European countries as French client states.

20 The Peninsular War and 1812 French invasion of Russia marked turning points in Napoleon's fortunes.

21 His *Grande Armée* was badly damaged in the campaign

22 and never fully recovered.

23 In 1813, the Sixth Coalition defeated his forces at Leipzig;

24 the following year the Coalition invaded France,

25 forced Napoleon to abdicate

26 and exiled him to the island of Elba.
27 Less than a year later, he escaped Elba
28 and returned to power,
29 but was defeated at the Battle of Waterloo in June 1815.
30 Napoleon spent the last six years of his life in confinement by the British on the island of Saint Helena.
31 An autopsy concluded he died of stomach cancer,
32 but there has been some debate about the cause of his death,
33 as some scholars have speculated
34 that he was a victim of arsenic poisoning.

(Source: http://en.wikipedia.org/wiki/Napoleon)

Questions

1. Identify the Themes in Text 5.1. Where there is a marked Theme also mark the Subject.
    Identify the category of the marked Themes. See answer on p. 201.
2. What are the focuses and shifts in topic signalled by the unmarked Themes and Subjects?
3. What general angle of development/reading is implied?
4. Now read the following text and compare the use of marked and unmarked Themes in terms of shifts, continuity and angle of development. Remember to consider the position of subordinate clauses.

Text 5.2 University regulations

1 6.1.5 Your Address and Contact Details
2 You must keep us informed of your current contact details including Cardiff and home postal addresses, mobile telephone number and email addresses.
3 Should any of this information change during the year
4 you should make the changes via SIMS Online
5 and notify the administrative staff as soon as possible.
6 This is most important.

7 6.1.6 Attendance
8 The University requires all students to be present in Cardiff during the whole of both semesters (including throughout reading weeks, guided study weeks and examination periods).
9 This means that you should plan to be in Cardiff
10 even when you do not have to attend classes or sit examinations.
11 However, if you must miss a lecture or seminar,
12 try to make sure that you collect any handouts which may have been distributed,
13 and find out from others as much as you can about what the session covered.
14 Year 1 students should note that attendance at seminars is compulsory.

15 If you fail to attend any seminar,
16 your seminar tutor will expect an explanation
17 and you must catch up with any work you have missed.
18 If you fail any of your assessments,
19 you must also be available in the summer resit examinations period,
20 which usually falls in the second half of August.
21 Bear this in mind when making plans for the summer vacation.
22 See also Section 10 below and the following website: http://www.cardiff. ac.uk/regis/sfs/regs/index.html.

23 6.1.7 Absence
24 It is important that you inform the School of any period of absence from University.
25 (See 'Failure to Engage with Programme of Study' below)
26 You should do this by contacting the administrative office
27 (see 'School Administration' (1.3) for details).

28 6.1.8 Failure to Engage with Programme of Study/Points of Engagement
29 It is a University requirement that student attendance is monitored at a number of points of engagement throughout the year.
30 Where a student fails to provide evidence of engagement on 2 consecutive points of engagement,
31 the Head of School or nominee will remind the student in writing of their requirement to engage,
32 and will state
33 that continued failure to engage will result in their exclusion from their programme of study.
34 Registry will also be informed of the student's failure to engage.
35 Where a student continues to fail to provide evidence of engagement with their programme of study,
36 or where a student fails to respond to written communication regarding their failure to engage,
37 the Head of School will inform Registry of his/her decision that the student should be excluded from their programme of study.

> (Source: www.cf.ac.uk/encap/degreeprogrammes/courseinformation/ guides/years_1_2_school_ug_handbook_2012.pdf © Cardiff University)

5.4 Interpersonal and textual Themes

As I said above, it is possible to have elements of interpersonal and textual meaning placed at the beginning of the clause, before the experiential Theme. These are referred to as *textual Themes* and *interpersonal Themes*. I said that this increased the thematicity of these elements in that, if we think of the experiential Theme as the starting-off point for the clause as representation, then we can see that textual and interpersonal Themes highlight those ideas that need to be "got out of the way" before we even start the representation.

Textual elements within the thematic element are most generally conjunctives or coordinating elements, words that signal the logical relationship between one clause and the next but which do not add any experiential meaning. We saw two examples of these above, with "but" and "so" appearing before the experiential Theme:

55. **One hundred years later, the Negro** is still languishing in the corners of American society
56. and **[he]** finds himself an exile in his own land.
57. So **we** have come here today to dramatize a shameful condition.

58. **It** came as a joyous daybreak to end the long night of their captivity.
59. But **one hundred years later**, the Negro still is not free.

As stated, "so" and "but" show the logical relationship between one clause and the next, in the first case signalling there is a cause and effect relationship between the two ideas and in the second that there is an element of counterexpectancy. In these examples we have two major clauses linked together to form a clause complex, but in other examples we have a subordinate clause linked to a main clause with a conjunction signalling the relationship as a textual Theme:

60. **This sweltering summer of the Negro's legitimate discontent** will not pass
61. until **there is an invigorating autumn of freedom and equality**.

And remember that the subordinate clause can come before the main clause in marked cases:

62. *When **the architects of our republic** wrote the magnificent words of the Constitution and the Declaration of Independence,*
63. **they** were signing a promissory note to which every American was to fall heir.

A more complex example of a textual Theme occurs in Churchill's *On the Beaches* speech (in italics):

64. **Parliament** has given us the powers to put down Fifth Column activities with a strong hand,
65. and **we** shall use those powers subject to the supervision and correction of the house, without the slightest hesitation
66. until **we** are satisfied, and more than satisfied,
67. that **this malignancy in our midst** has been effectively stamped out.
68. *Turning once again, and this time more generally, to the question of invasion,* I would observe

69. that **there has never been a period** in all these long centuries of which we boast when an absolute guarantee against invasion, still less against serious raids, could have been given to our people.

What Churchill is doing with the phrase "Turning once again, and this time more generally, to the question of invasion" is making an explicit comment to the effect that he is changing focus. While this might look like part of the experiential meaning of the clause, and is connected to it, it is really more of a preamble to the main idea that "there has never been a period … when an absolute guarantee against invasion … could have been given to our people". It doesn't add the how, what, when or why to this idea, as an experiential Circumstance would, but rather explicitly refers to how Churchill is developing his text and so can be analysed as a textual Theme.

If the main idea of clause 69 is the idea that there has never been a guarantee against invasion, as I have said, then what do we make of the phrase "I would observe that" in clause 68, which would also therefore be a part of the preamble? While this phrase certainly can be analysed in experiential terms, I think that in this case it is acting as a means of attribution, with an added modal effect, as verbs of saying and thinking often do (see Chapter 4). This case is interesting in that it is self-attribution, suggesting, perhaps, that Churchill expects his cultural capital as Prime Minister to provide the appropriate symbolic capital to his opinions. By this interpretation the phrase has an interpersonal function in the clause as a whole and, as it appears before any experiential elements, it is an interpersonal Theme.

More common examples of interpersonal Themes are vocatives (70), Modal Adjuncts (71) and Comment Adjuncts (72), double underlined below:

70. <u>Mary</u>, will **you** marry me please?
71. <u>Perhaps</u> **you** don't love me?
72. But <u>bizarrely</u>, **I** think you do!

Let's look at another extract from *I have a Dream* (experiential Theme in **bold**; Subject <u>underlined</u>; interpersonal Themes <u><u>double underlined</u></u>):

73. **Instead of honoring this sacred obligation**, <u>America</u> has given the Negro people a bad check, a check which has come back marked "insufficient funds."
74. But <u><u>we</u></u> <u>refuse to believe</u>
75. that **the bank of justice** is bankrupt.
76. <u><u>We</u></u> <u>refuse to believe</u>
77. that **there are insufficient funds** in the great vaults of opportunity of this nation.
78. So **we** have come to cash this check — a check that will give us upon demand the riches of freedom and the security of justice.
79. **We** have also come to this hallowed spot to remind America of the fierce urgency of now.

As stated above, projecting clauses can often be considered as "metaphorically" providing interpersonal meaning, so I have double underlined the projecting clauses above. But such clauses also have experiential content, which may be more or less salient, so I have also marked the experiential Theme of the projecting clauses (this is a decision which can be made by the analyst on a case-by-case basis, depending on the angle of analysis and the salience of the experiential meaning in the projecting clauses). In the short extract above we can see how King introduces his (shared) beliefs as, on one level, an interpersonal preface to clauses 75 and 77, with the financial metaphor of America's "bank of justice" providing a constant Theme, while, on another level, he uses the thematic "we" of these projected clauses to act as a means of transition to the experiential Themes of clauses 78 and 79, which have "we" as constant Theme. Clever, eh?

When there is more than experiential information in the thematic element of a clause we refer to *complex Themes*. In complex Themes the sequence is always (textual Theme)^(interpersonal Theme)^experiential Theme, as in the following example, where "but" is a textual Theme, the vocative "Mary" is interpersonal Theme, and "you" is experiential Theme:

80. But, Mary, **you** must love me!

There is possibly something confusing you at this point: if Theme is a textual function, how can you have textual, interpersonal and experiential Themes? The answer is that elements of a clause can be multifunctional, so that in the above clause, "Mary" is an interpersonal element as a vocative, but that it is given thematic status by being placed before the experiential Theme; "you" carries experiential meaning, but also textual meaning through its cohesive function as experiential Theme; and "but" carries textual meaning both in signalling the relationship between this clause and what has been said or understood before and in being placed in a thematic position before the experiential Theme. So, all Themes are textual, only textual Themes are doubly so!

Exercise 5.2

Read the following texts and answer the questions that follow.

Text 5.3 University welcome

1 FOREWORD

2 Welcome, or welcome back, to 'ENCAP'.
3 As one of the largest Schools in the University, with more than a thousand students (one hundred of them postgraduates), and over fifty academic staff, we pride ourselves in providing an excellent experience for our students, based in a friendly, personalised and supportive environment.
4 There are several ways in which you as a student can contribute to the community, generally by participating fully in lectures and seminars and by

engaging with your fellow students and staff in the spirit of mutual respect that we seek to promote in all dealings within the School.

5 As you will be aware,
6 students entering their first year and those in the second year each have their own Facebook page
7 – this is a great way of getting to know each other, sharing experiences and information.
8 You can make a particularly useful contribution by joining the Student–Staff panels associated with the Board of Studies that runs your degree and by standing as a student representative to the Board.
9 In our turn, our job is to help you achieve your best.
10 Your Personal Tutor is there for that purpose
11 – take time to catch up with him or her,
12 and do take advantage of the opportunities for Academic Progress Meetings (APMs) we have introduced.
13 You will find more information about APMs, and much else, in this School Undergraduate Student Handbook.
14 It also contains advice on presentation of work and exam preparation, how staff and students contact each other, personal development and careers, student support, extenuating circumstances, regulations regarding examinations and assessed work and progression.
15 For more detailed information relating to your programme of study,
16 please refer to your Course Guide,
17 which details academic staff email addresses and research interests, word limits for essays and dissertations, grading/assessment criteria, referencing systems etc.
18 This Handbook and your Course Guide should be read in conjunction with each other.
19 Of course, no handbook can cover every possible detail;
20 if you have any queries or need clarification on any issue
21 your first point of contact are the staff in the Undergraduate Office
22 – they are always happy to help (Humanities Building, Room 2.67).
23 Each programme also has a Deputy Director whose job it is to deal with queries that cannot be resolved by the Office.
24 And, of course, personal matters should be discussed with your Personal Tutor.
25 I hope
26 you both enjoy
27 and profit from your time in the School.

(Source: www.cf.ac.uk/encap/degreeprogrammes/courseinformation/ guides/years_1_2_school_ug_handbook_2012.pdf © Cardiff University)

Text 5.4 Bush's *Bring them on* moment

1 Q: A posse of small nations, like Ukraine and Poland, are materializing to help keep the peace in Iraq,

2 but with the attacks on U.S. forces and casualty rates rising, what does the administration do to get larger powers like France and Germany and Russia to join in the American (xxxx)?

3 B: Well, first of all, you know, we'll put together a force structure that meets the threats on the ground.

5 And we got a lot of forces there ourselves.

6 And as I said yesterday,

7 anybody who wants to harm American troops will be found and brought to justice.

8 There are some who feel like

9 That if they attack us

10 that we may decide to leave prematurely.

11 They don't understand what they're talking about,

12 if that's the case.

13 Let me finish.

14 There are some who feel like

15 that, you know, the conditions are such that they can attack us there.

16 My answer is bring them on.

17 We got the force necessary to deal with the security situation.

18 Of course we want other countries to help us.

19 Great Britain is there.

20 Poland is there.

21 Ukraine is there,

22 you mentioned.

23 Anybody who wants to help, we'll welcome to help.

24 But we got plenty tough force there right now to make sure the situation is secure.

25 We always welcome help.

26 We're always glad to include others in.

27 But make no mistake about it,

28 and the enemy shouldn't make any mistake about it,

29 we will deal with them harshly

30 if they continue to try to bring harm to the Iraqi people.

31 I also said yesterday an important point,

32 that those who blow up the electricity lines really aren't hurting America,

33 they're hurting the Iraq citizens.

34 Their own fellow citizens are being hurt.

35 But we will deal with them harshly as well.

Questions

1. Identify and discuss the movement of unmarked Themes and Subjects in the two texts.

2. Discuss how marked Themes contribute to the textual meaning of the two texts.
3. Identify and discuss the use of the complex Themes in the two texts.

See p. 204 for an analysis of Themes.

5.5 Thematic progression

In this section we will look at *methods of development* other than constant Theme: *linear Theme* and *derived Theme*.

5.5.1 Linear Theme

In Sections 5.2 and 5.3 we saw some examples of constant Themes and discussed how these interacted with marked Themes in maintaining or shifting the focus of a text. In this section we will look at another way in which the Theme of a clause can pick up on the preceding text. Let's look again at the following section of King's speech. I've marked Themes and Subjects in bold this time and underlined the element of the previous clause which each picks up on (sorry if this is confusing but there are only so many fonts available!). Again it is important to note that continuity is in terms of reference rather than the exact wording:

81. **I** am happy to join with you today in what will go down in history as the greatest demonstration for freedom in <u>the history of our nation</u>.
82. **Five score years ago, a great American**, in whose symbolic shadow we stand today, signed <u>the Emancipation Proclamation</u>.
83. **This momentous decree** came as a great beacon light of hope to millions of Negro slaves who had been seared in the flames of withering injustice.
84. **It** came as a joyous daybreak to end the long night of <u>their</u> captivity.
85. **But one hundred years later, the Negro** still is not free.
86. **One hundred years later, the life of the Negro** is still sadly crippled by the manacles of segregation and the chains of discrimination.
87. **One hundred years later, the Negro** lives on a lonely island of poverty in the midst of a vast ocean of material prosperity.
88. **One hundred years later, the Negro** is still languishing in the corners of American society
89. and **(he)** finds himself an exile in his own land.
90. So **we** have come here today to dramatize a shameful condition.

What we see here is that King opens the speech with himself as Theme, commenting on his role in the events of the day. As we saw with Coe's and Blair's address, with Uncle Henry and Sara's contributions, and as we will see below when we look at the inaugural speeches of Bush and Obama, this is a very common way for important speeches to begin, and can be regarded as a generic convention, a feature of speech that is expected in a given situation. What King does next is to take up an idea from the end of his first clause (the Rheme) within the Theme+Subject of the next clause:

81–82. … the history of our nation>Five score years ago, a great American …

He uses the same strategy to connect the following clauses:

82–83. … the Emancipation Proclamation>This momentous decree …

Clause 84 continues with the same Theme, signalled by the pronoun "it", but then in clause 85 King once again takes elements of the preceding Rheme (time and the black population) for his Theme+Subject:

84. **It** came as a joyous daybreak to end the long night of <u>their</u> captivity.
85. But one hundred years later the Negro still is not free.

King maintains a constant Theme in clauses 85 to 89, and also in clause 90, but this time including himself and his audience within the referential scope of "the Negro":

85. **But one hundred years later, the Negro** still is not free.
86. **One hundred years later, the life of the Negro** is still sadly crippled by the manacles of segregation and the chains of discrimination.
87. **One hundred years later, the Negro** lives on a lonely island of poverty in the midst of a vast ocean of material prosperity.
88. **One hundred years later, the Negro** is still languishing in the corners of American society
89. and **(he)** finds himself an exile in his own land.
90. So **we** have come here today to dramatize a shameful condition.

When we have an element of the Rheme picked up in the following Theme+Subject as in 81–82 and 82–83, we refer to this as *linear Theme* or *linear progression*, as opposed to the constant Theme described above. Whereas a constant Theme allows the speaker to make a succession of points about the same referent (as in clauses 85 to 88), linear Theme allows the speaker to push the Theme on, moving into new areas while maintaining a thread of continuity. In this section of text we therefore see King following *generic expectations* in starting his speech with reference to himself as speaker, but using linear progression to move seamlessly from here to the nation's history and the subjugated position of the Black population. He then moves back to himself, but now no longer as a single speaker (I) in a position of authority in front of his audience, but as a member of the same group (WE), and with all of them identified with the subjugated Black population of the previous one hundred years. The use of "we" in clause 90, therefore, not only unites King with his audience in an act of solidarity, but also marks a shift from the Generalisations of the previous clauses, framed in terms of "the Negro" as a general category, to a personal Commentary (see Chapter 6) that makes the subjugation of the Black people much more immediate. It also brings his audience into the speech as an event, not as a YOU set apart from the speaker as I, but as the WE that is the deictic centre of the speech as an act, the heart of the immediate context.[4]

5.5.2 Derived Theme

As well as constant Theme and linear Theme, there is a further type of thematic progression that is really a combination of both. This is derived Theme, where the Rheme of one clause is picked up in a succession of following clauses, each focusing on one aspect of it. This is commonly found in academic writing in order to describe the different parts or types of general category. I've used a bold underline in the following example in order to show that the phrase "the Outer Hebrides" provides the Theme for the following three clauses:

91. **<u>The Outer Hebrides</u>** comprise seven principal islands.
92. **Lewis** is the northernmost and the largest of these islands.
93. **Harris** is next, heading south,
94. and **North Uist** is a further hop away, skip and jump across the Minch.

Often the Themes deriving from a superordinate category are developed at length and over multiple clauses, with each section exhibiting its own thematic structure, as for example when the opening paragraph of an essay sets out the main topic of discussion and the following sections each pick up on one aspect of this. In this case we are dealing with macroThemes and hyperThemes (see Martin and Rose 2003, Chapter 6). As the relationship between a superordinate and its derived Themes can be distributed at various distances across a text they are often messy and difficult to analyse. There is a relatively clear example in the King speech, where the movement from describing the historic subjugation of the Black people to the need for action today, established in clause 95, provides a superordinate idea that is then picked up in the Themes of the following clauses and developed in the Rhemes:

95. **<u>This</u>** is no time to engage in the luxury of cooling off or to take the tranquilizing drug of gradualism.
96. **Now** is the time to make real the promises of democracy.
97. **Now** is the time to rise from the dark and desolate valley of segregation to the sunlit path of racial justice.
98. **Now** is the time to lift our nation from the quick sands of racial injustice to the solid rock of brotherhood.
99. **Now** is the time to make justice a reality for all of God's children.

Of course, it is also possible for the Rheme of a clause to pick up on ideas from a previous clause as in the following:

100. and we will not be satisfied
101. until <u>justice</u> rolls down like waters and <u>righteousness</u> like a mighty stream.
102. I am not unmindful that some of you have come here out of *great trials and tribulations*.

Here the Rheme of the final clause (in italics) picks up on ideas from the previous clause complex (underlined) through a relationship of antonymy (though in the full text you can see that the previous section was dwelling on injustices, so it is justice and righteousness that are the antonyms in the broader cotext). This is a type of thematic development known as *expansion* and it will be discussed in the following chapter.

Exercise 5.3

Choose any of the texts we have looked at in this chapter and identify and discuss the different types of thematic progression they display.

5.6 Worked text

To finish this chapter I am going to work through a complete text, illustrating and commenting on the ideas that have been introduced so far and also introducing a few twists. The text is once again Tony Blair's address to the press in the wake of the London bombings of 7 July 2005 (see also O'Grady 2010):

1 **I** am just going to make a short statement to you on the terrible events that have happened in London earlier today,
2 and **I hope**
3 **you** <u>understand</u>
4 that **at the present time** <u>we</u> are still trying to establish exactly what has happened,
5 and **there is a limit to what information I can give you**,
6 and **I** will simply try and tell you the information as best I can at the moment.
7 <u>It is reasonably clear that</u> **there have been a series of terrorist attacks in London**.
8 **There are obviously casualties**, both people that have died and people seriously injured,
9 and **our thoughts and prayers** of course are with the victims and their families.
10 **It is my intention** to leave the G8 within the next couple of hours and go down to London and get a report, face-to-face, with the police, and the emergency services and the Ministers that have been dealing with this, and then to return later this evening.
11 **It is the will** of all the leaders at the G8 however that the meeting should

continue in my absence, that we should continue to discuss the issues that we were going to discuss, and reach the conclusions which we were going to reach.

12 **Each of the countries round that table** have some experience of the effects of terrorism

13 and **all the leaders**> < share our complete resolution to defeat this terrorism.

14 >as **they** will indicate a little bit later<

15 <u>It is particularly barbaric</u> that **this** has happened on a day when people are meeting to try to help the problems of poverty in Africa, and the long term problems of climate change and the environment

16 Just as <u>it is reasonably clear</u> that **this** is a terrorist attack, or a series of terrorist attacks,

17 <u>it is also reasonably clear</u> that **it** is designed and aimed to coincide with the opening of the G8.

18 **There will be time to talk later about this**.

19 <u>It is important</u> however that **those engaged in terrorism** realise

20 that **our determination to defend our values and our way of life** is greater than their determination to cause death and destruction to innocent people in a desire to impose extremism on the world.

21 **Whatever** <u>they</u> do,

22 **it is our determination** that they will never succeed in destroying what we hold dear in this country and in other civilised nations throughout the world.

Looking first at clauses 1–6 we can see that, as in *I have a Dream*, above, Blair starts this public statement with himself as speaker as experiential Theme, explaining why he is there. In clauses 2 to 4 we see "I" repeated as experiential Theme (2), with this shifting to "you" as the general public (3) and then an exclusive "we" (that is, the hearers are not included), which includes Blair as speaker but extends to unspecified absent others, possibly the Government. In using first and second person Themes in this way Blair is able to establish the relationship between the himself and Government as information providers and the public as information receivers as the hyperTheme in the immediate context as a whole. As we saw with the King extract above, we can analyse clause 2 as both an interpersonal preface to clauses 3 and 4 and as a clause in its own right. There is an extra twist here as clause 3 itself can be analysed as an interpersonal preface to clause 4 or as a clause in its own right. The use of this double interpersonal Theme enables Blair both to thematise the relationship between himself and the public and to move the text on to a description of the day's events. In clauses 5 to 8, Blair moves towards this description, but only after emphasising that the information will only be partial. He does this in clause 5 through the use of an ***existential Theme***:

there is a limit ...

Here we see that existential constructions, analysed as process types in Chapter 3 can also be analysed as a specific type of Theme, with the Existent as the *enhanced* Theme. It is called an enhanced Theme, as the "dummy construction" *there is* which precedes it allows the Existent to fall at the end of a clause and therefore to receive tonic prominence as "New" information (Halliday and Matthiessen 2004:87–92), that is, to be stressed in tone, signalling the part on which the hearer should focus. In this way the Existent is both Theme and New, an unusual combination, and one that is ideal for introducing a new idea or participant into the text. In clause 6 Blair returns to himself as information-giver in the immediate context as Theme and in Clauses 7 and 8 Blair uses parallel existential structures to introduce the main topic of his announcement: that attacks that took place earlier that day and the ensuing casualties.

Clause 7 is another type of enhanced Theme, this time an ***enhanced evaluative Theme***, with the "dummy" phrase allowing the evaluative word "clear" to be given tonic prominence. In Chapter 4 we analysed such structures as explicit objective modality, in this case with "reasonable clear" as an example of median probability. An added effect of this structure is that Blair's use of modality, a form of *hedging*, is also thematised. In many cases this might not be particularly significant, after all the "enhanced" form Blair uses is less marked than the "more congruent" form "that there have been a series of terrorist attacks in London is reasonably clear". We might therefore simply say that this structure is a means of realising explicit objective modality; however, as we work through the text we will see that there is good reason to consider the textual effect of this construction as Blair repeatedly makes use of structures that thematise both his hedging of his assertions and his evaluation of various events. Clause 8 also hints at this idea, with "obviously", an example of implicit objective modality (high probability) occurring within the existential Theme that stretches as far as the Existent "casualties".

In this opening section, then, Blair has thematised three separate and distinct ideas in different ways: (i) the relationship between himself, the public and other politicians; (ii) the events earlier in the day; and (iii) the various degrees of hedging that qualify his statements. As we will see, all three of these ideas are picked up on in the rest of the text.

In clause 9, which runs on as a coordinated clause from clause 8, Blair thematises his reaction to the events, including the public here as part of the inclusive "our" which is part of the Theme. Similarly, in Clause 10 Blair thematises the reaction to events with "It is my intention". This is an example of a third type of enhanced Theme, an ***enhanced experiential Theme***, in which an element of experiential meaning is given tonic prominence in following the dummy construction "it is". As the phrase "my intention" refers back to "it" I have marked the whole construction as the Theme. Note that Blair could have said "My intention is to leave the city …". But note too that intention is also a feature of modality. I have not analysed it as such here (by marking it as interpersonal Theme) as it is clearly a constituent of experiential structure and, unlike other examples, does not preface a full clause. However, the modal semantics are clear, and what we have is a modal concept being *reified* (turned into a thing) so that it can be discussed as part of the experiential meaning and, as in this case, thematised. An alternative analysis could have "it is my intention" as an interpersonal Theme, with all the following *to* clauses analysed as clauses in their own right. By this analysis, Blair as the implicit Actor in these clauses is thematised and we have a thematic shift from emotional reactions to material action. Both analyses offer insights into the text, as does the fuzziness of the analysis, which allows for a dual thematisation of the modality and the actions. Combining the analyses we have both a constant Theme of modality, shifting from probability (clause 7) to intention (clause 10), and an experiential Theme that moves from Blair's emotions and intentions (clauses 2, 6, 9 and 10) to Blair as Actor – someone who doesn't just react emotionally, but who also acts on these emotions (clause 10). Clause 11 parallels and develops this Theme with another enhanced experiential Theme emphasising the will of those in power to act, but with the Actors now as the leaders of the G8 working together.

Clauses 12 to 14 place the thematic stress more squarely on the leaders of the G8 and the countries they represent, with three unmarked Themes (which would appear to be the marked case in this text!) each with the leaders or their countries as Theme.

Clause 15 is another example of an enhanced evaluative Theme, this time with a non-modal element "barbaric" as the Theme. As we saw in Chapter 4 evaluation and modality are closely linked as elements of interpersonal meaning, and the dividing line between them is often fuzzy. The enhanced evaluative Theme in clause 14 therefore picks up on the earlier enhanced evaluative Themes of modality. As this enhanced Theme prefaces a complete clause, we can analyse it as an interpersonal Theme, which would leave "this", referring to the events of the day, as experiential Theme. So once again we see a distribution of Themes between events, reactions and modality that provides for various shifts in the development of the text as a whole.

This is again the case in clause 16, where we have both an enhanced evaluative Theme of modality (probability:median) acting as an interpersonal Theme to preface the experiential Theme "this", which is constant with the previous clause. This strategy is repeated in clause 17, before clause 18 uses an enhanced existential Theme to introduce a new idea "time to talk about this", which has certain semantic parallels with the heavy hedging that has marked the text this far.

Clause 19 uses another enhanced evaluative Theme as an interpersonal preface and the contrastive textual Theme "however" (a rare occasion where a textual Theme follows an interpersonal one, made possible by the marked structure of the clause) to emphasise that while action will not be immediate (and possibly rash?) it will be strong once it occurs. There is a certain parallelism, therefore, with the earlier thematic shift from Blair as Senser to Blair as Actor. Clause 20 picks up on this idea, with another Theme, "determination", that is another example of a reified modal, this time intention:high in contrast to the intention:median of "will" in clause 11. Note that in clause 20 "determination" can only be analysed as experiential Theme and not as an enhanced interpersonal Theme.

The announcement finishes by contrasting the actions of those engaged in terrorism as the Theme of clause 21 with the nation's response to this, realised through the enhanced experiential Theme (intention:high) "our determination". In this final clause we have the enhanced Theme prefacing a full clause, so its status as either an interpersonal or experiential Theme is debatable – but this seems entirely appropriate given the way in which the text has developed – is it about reified modality or the events of the day? As the *hyperNew* of the whole text, these closing clauses therefore capture both the ambiguity of Theme that runs through the text and, looking back to the analysis of the text from the point of view of evaluative content in Chapter 4, a strong statement of "our" values winning out, despite the determination shown by the enemy. It seems to be saying "We must be prepared for a long battle, and there are many uncertainties ahead, but our determination will in the end win out" – a mixed message made coherent through the many thematic devices Blair has employed in this intricately woven text.

Exercise 5.4

Compare the Blair and Bush speeches and discuss the differences between them in terms of the positioning of the speakers, the storyline of contemporary events (including their relation to each other) and the different audiences. Remember that Bush's response was (largely?) unscripted whereas Blair's response has clearly been very carefully worded.

5.7 Summary

In this chapter we have looked at how various thematic devices are used to indicate continuity and progression across texts. There are eight central points to consider whenever analysing a text for Theme, which are:

1. Identify the experiential Theme
2. Is the Theme marked or unmarked?
3. If marked, also identify the Subject.
4. What is the method of development between Themes (constant, linear or derived)?
5. What topics are thematised and how does the text move between them?
6. What angle(s) of reading is/are provided by the marked Themes?
7. Is the Theme simple or complex?
8. What interpersonal elements are thematised and why?

Once you have dealt with these basic questions (and see Thompson 2007 for an excellent and very readable overview) you can discuss the functions of the textual variables in weaving a text and in providing prominence to certain angles and features before moving on to consider how the textual metafunction plays a role in construing the speaker's position and the function/effect of the text as discourse.

Notes

1 Other authors use the term *topical Theme*, which perhaps captures better the function of this element in textual development. I will use the term *experiential Theme*, however, as this captures the contrast with interpersonal and textual Themes, discussed later in the chapter.

2 This is often referred to as simply the *Theme*; I use *thematic element* to avoid confusion. Several authors within SFL, for good reason, define the extent of the Theme and/or thematic element differently. In order to maintain correspondence with Hallidayan terminology I follow his definition of *experiential Theme*. However, my use of *thematic element* corresponds with what Halliday calls the *Theme*, but I also highlight the cohesive role of the Subject when this does not fall within the thematic element, an approach that mirrors those of Berry (1996), Fawcett (2003) and others.

3 In fact Fawcett (1999, 2003) analyses the subject as a type of Theme, called the Subject Theme, and Berry (1996) analyses the Theme as all elements up to and including the Subject.

4 My thanks to my friend Jane Mulderrig for providing me with this idea.

6

SPACE, TIME AND CHUNKS OF TEXT

6.1 Introduction

In Chapter 2 we saw how sections of texts maintain and shift fields of discourse, often intermingling immediate and displaced contexts, and in the previous chapter we saw how the grammatical resource of Theme served, among other things, to weave these movements together into text. We can say, then, that Theme serves to make texts cohesive in and of themselves, to show how they hang together as pieces of language. In this chapter we will look at a different though related aspects of coherence, how the texts are woven around the speaker and their audience as the *deictic centre* of the text as discourse. The deictic centre means the immediate here and now of the speech act, the *locus*, or site, of its most immediate purpose. As we have seen, however, texts very often focus on the non-immediate, the displaced, and in this chapter we will consider the different degrees to which a (section of) text can be displaced, the grammatical means by which this is signalled, and the *rhetorical function* of the different degrees of displacement. Stretches of text with the same degree of displacement are called **rhetorical units** or RUs (Cloran 2010[1]). We'll then return to look again at Theme to see how these serve to mark how consecutive RUS are functionally related.

In Chapter 2 we considered stretches of text which construed the same subfield. RUs provide an alternative way of sectioning text into consistent stretches; if we then add to these stretches of text construing a consistent tenor we will have three different ways of dividing up the text, one for each metafunction.[2] These different divisions may or may not overlap, and it is the combination of overlap and disalignment that allows a speaker to develop a text through a mixture of continuity and change – exactly the features that make it a text, as you're probably sick of hearing by now. Following Gregory we can call stretches of text that show a continuity across all three metafunctions a **phase**, so that when there is a significant change in any of the three metafunctions we have a new phase.

In a way, phases are the central unit of analysis of this book, what we have been building up to so far. We talked earlier about how changes in field can correspond with changes in tenor because of the different positions that are potentially open to the speaker; we will now extend this idea to talk about how different conjunctions of field, tenor and mode (in terms of RUs) correspond to a speaker's position at that point in the discourse. Hasan (in Halliday and Hasan 1985:55) refers to the conjunction of field, tenor and mode as the ***contextual configuration*** and highlights the importance of treating all three metafunctions together. Changes in phase also correspond very closely to what are known in *interactional sociolinguistics* as changes in *frames* (roughly field, but also mode to some extent) and *footing* (roughly tenor). By looking at different contextual configurations and the movement from one to another we can see how speakers are able to construct, through the combination of different experiential, interpersonal and textual meanings in their discourse acts, complex yet coherent combinations of positions for themselves and how these different positions rely on features of the environment in order to be accepted, or legitimated, by the audience or audiences.

6.2 Types of Rhetorical Unit

In the following section I'll work through the opening 28 clauses of President George Bush's second inaugural address to introduce how to analyse for RUs. Once we have completed the analysis, we will look at similarities and differences between Bush's address and President Obama's first inaugural address.

Text 6.1 Opening of Bush's second inaugural address

President Bush delivers his inauguration speech, 20 January 2005

1 Vice President Cheney, Mr. Chief Justice, President Carter, President Bush, President Clinton, reverend clergy, distinguished guests, fellow citizens: On this day, prescribed by law and marked by ceremony, we celebrate the durable wisdom of our Constitution,

2 and recall the deep commitments that unite our country.

3 I am grateful for the honor of this hour,

4 mindful of the consequential times in which we live,

5 and determined to fulfill the oath that I have sworn and you have witnessed.

6 At this second gathering, our duties are defined not by the words I use, but by the history we have seen together.

7 For a half century, America defended our own freedom by standing watch on distant borders.

8 After the shipwreck of communism came years of relative quiet, years of repose, years of sabbatical

9 – and then there came a day of fire.

10 We have seen our vulnerability

11   – and we have seen its deepest source.
12   For as long as whole regions of the world simmer in resentment and tyranny – prone to ideologies that feed hatred and excuse murder – violence will gather,
13   and multiply in destructive power,
14   and cross the most defended borders,
15   and raise a mortal threat.
16   There is only one force of history that can break the reign of hatred and resentment, and expose the pretensions of tyrants, and reward the hopes of the decent and tolerant,
17   and that is the force of human freedom.
18   We are led, by events and common sense, to one conclusion:
19   The survival of liberty in our land increasingly depends on the success of liberty in other lands.
20   The best hope for peace in our world is the expansion of freedom in all the world.
21   America's vital interests and our deepest beliefs are now one.
22   From the day of our Founding, we have proclaimed that every man and woman on this earth has rights, and dignity, and matchless value, because they bear the image of the Maker of Heaven and earth.
23   Across   the   generations   we   have   proclaimed   the   imperative   of self-government,
24   because no one is fit to be a master,
25   and no one deserves to be a slave.
26   Advancing these ideals is the mission that created our Nation.
27   It is the honorable achievement of our fathers.
28   Now it is the urgent requirement of our nation's security, and the calling of our time.

(Source: The White House)

In analysing for rhetorical units we need to look at the combination of two semantic features: the **central entities** being discussed and the **event orientation** of stretches of text. The first five clauses of Bush's address, much like the openings of the Seb Coe and Uncle Henry texts, are centred on the immediate activity: Bush standing before his audience to make the address. The *central entities* of this section, realised grammatically as the Subjects, are the audience (1–2) and Bush himself (3–5, with ellipsis in 4 and 5). Bush and the audience can be labelled as *interactants* in the discourse, as speaker and addressees. The *event orientation*, signalled grammatically by the tense used, is *concurrent* with the time of speaking (that is, immediate). When we have interactants as the central entities and a concurrent event orientation we label the stretch of text as a *Commentary*, one of the most immediate RUs.

In Clause 6 there is a slight difference. The central entities are still Bush and his (wider) audience, but the "duties" Bush refers to are not quite as immediate as his standing there: they are better described as *habitual*. When we have interactants as the central entities and a habitual event orientation, the RU is labelled a *Reflection*. Notice, then, how Bush has maintained continuity through the central entities but has moved the text on in terms of event orientation.

In clauses 7 to 11 the event orientation is no longer concurrent but *prior* (though the present perfect in clauses 10 and 11 could be seen as uniting past and present). Whenever we have a prior event orientation, no matter who or what the central entities are, we label the RU a *Recount*.

Clauses 12 to 15 shift event orientation again, with the modal "will" signalling a *Prediction*. Predictions can refer to any central entities, though there is also a *Plan* RU which centres on interactants but is more definite (for example, signalled by non-modal WILL or GOING TO).

Lines 16 to 20 provide another type of RU, an *Account*, where the central entity (here variously realised as "human freedom", "liberty" and "peace" – an interesting example of semantic development) is not present in the immediate setting (referred to as the Material Situational Setting, or MSS, by Cloran) and the event orientation is habitual. Note here that Clause 18 is largely interpersonal in meaning and so is not analysed as a separate Commentary.

Clause 21 is another Refection; Clauses 22 to 27 are another Recount; and Clause 28 is a further Reflection.

There are several RU types not present in the text. These are *Actions*, RUs that are involved in controlling the immediate context, generally imperative clauses (as we saw in *I have a Dream*) or indirect commands using modals; *Observations*, the habitual orientation of non-interactants that are nonetheless present in the MSS; *Reports*, which are concurrent or ongoing, rather than habitual, orientations of people or things not in the MSS; *Generalisations*, the habitual orientation of whole classes of people or things; and *Conjectures*, which are more hypothetical than predictions. Some of these types are very close in meaning: had Bush said in Clause 12, for example, that "violence gathers" in such situations, rather than predicting that it "will gather", the RU would have been a Generalisation and not a Prediction; had he said it "might gather" it would have been a Conjecture. It is not always possible, therefore, to be entirely sure when assigning RU labels, and this is an example of the "fuzzy" boundaries of language that can be exploited by speakers!

Table 6.1 provides the full schema for RU types. Underneath there is a continuum roughly suggesting the order in which different RU types range from being most ancillary to other actions in construing contexts to those which are most constitutive of the context themselves. Or, in other words, from those that construe the most immediate contexts to those that construe the most displaced. I say that this is roughly suggestive as Recounts that involve people or things outside the MSS would probably best be considered more displaced than Plans or than Conjectures involving the interactants themselves. For a fuller treatment of RUs see Cloran 2010.

In Table 6.2, I've added columns listing shifts in field and tenor to supplement the development of mode (RUs) described above. Field includes subject matter, potentially including changing lexis for key motifs, and prevalent transitivity types. Tenor includes features of mood, modality and appraisal. Marked Themes could

TABLE 6.1 Types of rhetorical unit

| Central entity | *Event orientation* | | | | | |
| | *Habitual* | *Realis* | | *Irrealis* | *Information exchange* | |
		Concurrent	*Prior*	*Goods/services exchange*	*Forecast*	*Hypothetical*
Within material situational setting (MSS)						
Interactant	Reflection				Plan/Prediction	Conjecture
Other: person/object	Observation	Commentary	Recount	Action	Prediction	
Not within MSS						
Person/object	Account	Report			Prediction	
Class	Generalisation					

Note

Continuum of role of language in social process:

ancillary [e.g. immediate]   constitutive [e.g. displaced]

Action–Commentary Observation–Reflection Report–Recount Account Plan–Prediction Conjecture Generalisation

TABLE 6.2 RUs in Bush's address

Clauses	Phase	Field	Tenor	Mode/RU
1–5	**Positioning of self as leader and servant, one among many Americans recalling the past**	President/oath Verbal, mental, and relational processes of remembrance	I as President as sworn representative of the people	Commentary
6	**Linking common past to present duties.**	Memories defining duties	Presidential role (I) as secondary to shared history (we)	Reflection
7–11	**US as witness to change from peace to troubles.**	We become "America" Behavioural and mental processes of watching as peace turned to trouble	Our shared history as defenders of American dream of freedom	Recount
12–15		"Vulnerability" identified as other nations' tyranny Material processes of evil spreading	International others appraised negatively (-Judgement; –Affect)	Prediction
16–20	**Identification of America's historic mission as the overcoming of evil.**	Freedom as antidote to tyranny.	Contrast of positive and negative appraisal in international context (+/– Judgement); common sense conclusions of 'right' (+Judgement)	Account
21		Freedom identified as simultaneously US ideal and protector of interests i	Dual positive Appraisal (+ security) and (+social sanction)	Reflection
22–27		Verbal processes of America proclaiming liberty becoming clauses identifying America's destiny as the overcoming of evil.	We and founding fathers as one, appraised positively as evaluators (+Judgement)	Recount
28	**Historic and present mission identified**	America destiny again identified as the overcoming of evil.	Strong positive Judgement of positive action.	Reflection

also be included within the mode column as these are generally textual markers of a shift in angle. The table also shows the phasal development of the section of text as a whole: that is, shifts in the contextual configuration. Notice for clauses 7 to 15 and 16 to 27 I've given the phase a single label although there is a change in the contextual configuration within each. This is because I think that the two distinct sections in each work together to achieve the same effect. It would, of course, have been possible to make distinctions here if it seemed useful.

Exercise 6.1

Table 6.3 is my phasal analysis of the opening 17 clauses of President Obama's first inaugural address.

Have a look at this and compare it with Bush's address, then answer the questions that follow.

Text 6.2 Opening of Obama's first inaugural address

1 My fellow citizens: I stand here today humbled by the task before us, grateful for the trust you have bestowed, mindful of the sacrifices borne by our ancestors.

TABLE 6.3 RUs in Obama's address

Clauses	Phase	Field	Tenor	Mode/RU
1–2	Positioning of self as leader and servant	President/oath Verbal/behavioural processes and lexis of speaking. Oath taken in good times and bad.	I as President, entrusted by people = personal authority within context of history. Positive appraisal of fortitude (+Judgement)	Commentary
3–4			I as President and one of line; oath as sign of duty, before God	Recount
5			Duty in hardship; contrastive appraisal of prosperity (+/-Affect)	Account
6–8	Establish theme of vagaries of history and	Americans' endurance in general facing problems.	We the People throughout history; positive appraisal	Recount/ Reflection
9	shared endurance of leaders and populace	Relational processes and lexis of endurance.	of loyalty to founding documents (+Judgement)	Action
10–16	Establish theme of shared present problems	Present hardships.	We the People now; common sense	Reflection
17		Relational processes with America as Carrier and Attributes of crisis. Material processes of deterioration becoming a token of general problems.	understanding; 'our' shared problems; negative evaluation of current domestic situation (-Affect)	Generalisation

2 I thank President Bush for his service to our nation, as well as the generosity and cooperation he has shown throughout this transition.

3 Forty-four Americans have now taken the presidential oath.

4 The words have been spoken during rising tides of prosperity and the still waters of peace.

5 Yet, every so often the oath is taken amidst gathering clouds and raging storms.

6 At these moments, America has carried on not simply because of the skill or vision of those in high office,

7 but because We the People have remained faithful to the ideals of our forbears, and true to our founding documents.

8 So it has been.

9 So it must be with this generation of Americans.

10 That we are in the midst of crisis is now well understood.

11 Our nation is at war, against a far-reaching network of violence and hatred.

12 Our economy is badly weakened, a consequence of greed and irresponsibility on the part of some, but also our collective failure to make hard choices and prepare the nation for a new age.

13 Homes have been lost; jobs shed; businesses shuttered.

14 Our health care is too costly;

15 our schools fail too many;

16 and each day brings further evidence that the ways we use energy strengthen our adversaries and threaten our planet.

17 These are the indicators of crisis, subject to data and statistics.

Questions

1. What similarities do you see between the opening of the two speeches and the development of more specific topics and motifs? How would you account for such similarities?

2. What differences do you see in the way the two texts develop? What linguistic devices are used to maintain continuity on the one hand and to move on the text on the other?

3. In what way do the two texts move between immediate and displaced contexts and what is the effect of this and its relevance to the texts as inaugural addresses?

4. How would you relate these textual differences to the addresses as discourse, given the different speakers and the historical environment in which they were produced?

5. Look at the later section of Obama's address, given below, and describe the position taken up by Obama.

6. What environmental conditions "allow" Obama to take the position he does in this section? Think of the contextual configuration(s) of the extract and the connection between this/these and Obama's personal status (particularly as the

first black President of the US), the various audiences he is addressing and the storyline of recent (and relatively recent) US history.

Text 6.3 Later in Obama's second inaugural address

1 And for those who seek to advance their aims by inducing terror and slaughtering innocents, we say to you now
2 That "Our spirit is stronger and cannot be broken.
3 You cannot outlast us,
4 and we will defeat you."
5 For we know
6 that our patchwork heritage is a strength, not a weakness.
7 We are a nation of Christians and Muslims, Jews and Hindus, and nonbelievers.
8 We are shaped by every language and culture,
9 drawn from every end of this Earth.
10 And because we have tasted the bitter swill of civil war and segregation
11 and emerged from that dark chapter stronger and more united,
12 we cannot help but believe
13 that the old hatreds shall someday pass;
14 that the lines of tribe shall soon dissolve;
15 that as the world grows smaller,
16 our common humanity shall reveal itself;
17 and that America must play its role in ushering in a new era of peace.
18 To the Muslim world, we seek a new way forward, based on mutual interest and mutual respect.
19 To those leaders around the globe who seek to sow conflict or blame their society's ills on the West, know
20 that your people will judge you on what you can build, not what you destroy.
21 To those who cling to power through corruption and deceit and the silencing of dissent, know
22 that you are on the wrong side of history,
23 but that we will extend a hand if you are willing to unclench your fist.
24 To the people of poor nations, we pledge//to work alongside you to make your farms flourish and let clean waters flow; to nourish starved bodies and feed hungry minds.

6.3 Relations between RUs

The above presentation gives the impression that RUs progress in a linear sequence, but this is not the whole story. As I said above, Theme and Rheme, the other main grammatical devices for construing textuality, are involved in RU development. Let's consider first the relationship between constant Theme and linear Theme, which were described in the previous chapter, and the changes in RUs in Bush's address. The following description is quite condensed and it will help if you refer to both Text 6.1 above and Table 6.4 below as you read it.

The first change in RU is between Clauses 5 and 6. Here the Theme of clause 6 is "At the second gathering". As this is a marked Theme (a Circumstance of time/place) we should also consider the Subject, "our duties" when looking at thematic development. Between them the marked Theme and the Subject pick up on the semantics of the "ceremony" of clause 1 and "the oath that I have sworn" of clause 5. When previous ideas are picked up in the Theme of a new RU we say that that RU is **embedded** within the other RU, which is the **matrix** RU. This is because the new RU develops the old one by going deeper into one particular aspect of it. The second RU therefore serves some function within the matrix RU and is considered a part of it. This is signalled, as suggested, by the Theme of the embedded RU not being entirely new. Strictly speaking then, the new RU is not entirely new or separate as it forms part of the matrix RU as well as being an RU in its own right. To show this embedding the RU beginning with Clause 6 is labelled as .1 and is boxed to show it is entirely within its matrix RU.

Embedding can be complex, as shown by the next change of RU, between Clauses 6 and 7. Here we have another Circumstance, "For a half century" and the Subject "America". The use of the term "America" clearly picks up on (and develops) the idea of "we" in the preceding clause (and before), so we have another embedding. This means that the RU starting with Clause 7 is doubly embedded, both within the matrix RU beginning with Clause 6, and the matrix RU of that RU, beginning with Clause 1. In other words, we are still delving deeper into the same topics. To show this double embedding the RU beginning with Clause 7 is labelled as .1.1 and is boxed entirely within the RU numbered as .1. So, we have a box within a box.

The next RU, beginning with Clause 12 is a further embedding, as both the marked Theme and the Subject pick up on and develop the "our vulnerability" as the "violence" that comes of "resentment and tyranny" and the "ideologies" of others. This RU is thus marked as .1.1.1, a triple embedding also represented by the box within a box within a box!

We then have something different in Clause 16, which picks up on the idea of tyranny with "the reign of hatred and resentment ... and the pretensions of tyrants". However, as these ideas are expressed in the Rheme and not the Theme we no longer have a deeper delving into the original idea but an *expansion* of this idea with a new thematic element, "one force in history", which can then be developed. However, as this Theme picks up on the idea of "history" in Clause 6, the RU is embedded within RU .1 and is labelled as .1.2 (as .1.1 has already appeared). So, the RU beginning with Clause 16 is simultaneously an expansion of the previous RU and embedded within the RU beginning with Clause 6. This is represented by the numbering and by the boxing, which is separate from the previous RU but embedded within the RU beginning with Clause 6 (which is embedded in the RU beginning with Clause 1).

The next shift in RU occurs between Clauses 21 and 22. Here the idea of "America's deepest beliefs" from Clause 21 is picked up on with "every man and woman ... Maker of Heaven and Earth". This is the Rheme of Clause 22 and so we have another example of expansion. However, once again the Theme "From the day of our founding" and the Subject "we" pick up on earlier ideas and so this RU is embedded within the RU beginning with Clause 6. This is shown by the numbering and the boxing. It could be argued that the Subject "we" picks up on "America" in the previous clause, but I think that my analysis captures the overall movement a little better. There is often room for discussion when we are dealing with tightly cohesive texts such as this one and analysis often entails making changes until the picture of the whole text hangs together.

Similarly, I have marked the last Change in RUs, between lines 27 and 28, as an expansion as I think the elaboration of the previous ideas in the Rheme is the central development of this Clause. I have marked this RU as one again embedded in the RU beginning with Clause 6 because of the return of time reference in the marked Theme "now" to the earlier mention of "at this second gathering" in Clause 6.

Note that embedding and elaboration are only marked when there is a change of RU. If there is a change of field or tenor without a change in RU, no relationship is marked (though this would represent a different phase).

When a new RU does not pick up on ideas from the previous RU we can analyse this in one of two ways. If the new RU picks up on ideas from an earlier RU we can say that it is *discontinuous*. If there is no continuity, then to all intents and purposes we have a new text, as a text is defined by Halliday and Hasan (1976) as a cohesive stretch of language. However, many texts include a preamble which may not be cohesively linked to what follows but which is clearly part of the text – although, as we see in the two addresses and have seen in other texts, the speaker usually contrives to make a cohesive link between the preamble and what follows. That is part of the art of rhetoric!

All of this might seem very complicated and an analytical nicety rather than a genuine reflection of what the speaker is doing with the text. However, I believe that if you consider what is meant by embedding and expansion when looking at the analysis in Table 6.4 you will get the feeling that yes, this is indeed what is happening; this is how the text coheres and develops.

Exercise 6.2

1. Discuss the relations between RUs as marked up in Table 6.4 and explain how these can shed light on the development of this section of the address as a whole.
2. Look at the marked Themes in Bush's address and discuss how these signal an angle of development for the text and how they interact with the shifts in RUs.
3. Now look at the analysis of RU relations in the opening of Obama's address in Table 6.5 below and discuss the similarities and differences between the two texts and how these correspond to the two texts as historically situated discourse.

TABLE 6.4 Relations between RUs in Bush's address

Vice President Cheney, Mr. Chief Justice, President Carter, President Bush, President Clinton, reverend clergy, distinguished guests, fellow citizens:	Commentary
On this day, prescribed by law and marked by ceremony, we celebrate the durable wisdom of our Constitution, and recall the deep commitments that unite our country. I am grateful for the honor of this hour, mindful of the consequential times in which we live, and determined to fulfill the oath that I have sworn and you have witnessed.	
At this second gathering, our duties are defined not by the words I use, but by the history we have seen together.	.1 Reflection
For a half century, America defended our own freedom by standing .watch on distant borders. After the shipwreck of communism came years of relative quiet, years of repose, years of sabbatical – and then there came a day of fire. We have seen our vulnerability – and we have seen its deepest source.	.1.1 Recount
For as long as whole regions of the world simmer in resentment and tyranny .- prone to ideologies that feed hatred and excuse murder – violence will gather, and multiply in destructive power, and cross the most defended borders, and raise a mortal threat.	.1.1.1 Pred.
There is only one force of history that can break the reign of hatred and resentment and expose the pretensions of tyrants, and reward the hopes of the decent and tolerant, and that is the force of human freedom. We are led, by events and common sense, to one conclusion: The survival of liberty in our land increasingly depends on the success of liberty in other lands. The best hope for peace in our world is the expansion of freedom in all the world. America's vital interests and our deepest beliefs are now one.	.1.2 Account
From the day of our Founding, we have proclaimed that every man and woman .on this earth has rights, and dignity, and matchless value, because they bear the image of the Maker of Heaven and earth. Across the generations we have proclaimed the imperative of self-government, because no one is fit to be a master, and no one deserves to be a slave. Advancing these ideals is the mission that created our Nation. It is the honorable achievement of our fathers.	.1.3 Recount
Now it is the urgent requirement of our nation's security, and the calling of our time.	

6.4 Summary

In this chapter we have looked at Rhetorical Units and the relationship between sections of a text and the deictic centre of speaker and hearer at the time of speaking. This has provided a more finegrained distinction than the notions of immediate and displaced context that were introduced in Chapter 2. We have also seen how RUs are related in ways that build on and expand our analysis of thematic development

TABLE 6.5 Relations between RUs in Obama's address

1	My fellow citizens: I stand here today humbled by the task before us, grateful for the trust you have bestowed, mindful of the sacrifices borne by our ancestors.	Commentary
2	I thank President Bush for his service to our nation, as well as the generosity and cooperation he has shown throughout this transition.	
3	Forty-four Americans have now taken the presidential oath	Recount
4	The words have been spoken during rising tides of prosperity and the still waters of peace.	
5	Yet, every so often the oath is taken amidst gathering clouds and raging storms.	.1 Account
6	At these moments, America has carried on not simply because of the skill or vision of those in high office,	.1.1 Recount
7	but because We the People have remained faithful to the ideals of our forbearers, and true to our founding documents.	
8	So it has been.	
9	So it must be with this generation of Americans.	.1.1.1 Action
10	That we are in the midst of crisis is now well understood.	.1.2 Comm.
11	Our nation is at war, against a far-reaching network of violence and hatred.	
12	Our economy is badly weakened, a consequence of greed and irresponsibility on the part of some, but also our collective failure to make hard choices and prepare the nation for a new age.	
13	Homes have been lost; jobs shed; businesses shuttered.	
14	Our health care is too costly;	
15	our schools fail too many;	
16	and each day brings further evidence that the ways we use energy strengthen our adversaries and threaten our planet.	
17	These are the indicators of crisis, subject to data and statistics.	.1.2.1 Gen.

in Chapter 5. This look at RUs therefore completes our survey of meaning across the three metafunctions and I here set out one way of analysing how these three types of meaning interact in terms of speaker positioning and compared the opening lines of inaugural addresses from Bush and Obama in these terms. In the final chapter of this book we will look at the full analyses of a couple of the texts we have been analysing so far and then consider some of the sociolinguistic and discourse analytical ideas the method of analysis can be used to illustrate and discuss.

Notes

1 Cloran talks about degrees of contextualisation/decontextualisation, but as the text construes the context I prefer to talk of degrees of displacement of the context from the immediate environment.
2 Cloran treats RUs as sections of text that are derived from all three metafunctions, but to my mind they are essentially textual in nature and I shall treat them as representative of textual continuity here.

7

VOICE AND HYBRIDITY

7.1 Introduction

In Chapters 2 to 6 we looked in turn at lexical and grammatical features that are used to construe three different types of meaning: experiential, interpersonal and textual. The purpose of analysing texts in this way was to open them up to a broader questioning in terms of how they operate in real life, what purposes they might serve and the conditions necessary for them to be effective. For ease of presentation we looked at each of these areas of meaning in turn; however, while each area of analysis might be possible in textual terms, it is really the interplay of the different types of meaning at any one point and the sequencing of different phases of combinations that is important when considering how the texts work as discourse. We considered this idea briefly in the previous chapter and in this final chapter we will explore in greater detail how the different types of meaning in a text work together in discourse. The discussion will focus on examples from my Guyanese fieldwork but will open up discussion of some key concepts in social and critical linguistics and their relationship to positioning and power: voice, intertextuality and interdiscursivity, roles and hybridity.

7.2 Key concepts 2

To introduce some of the key concepts discussed in this chapter, let's look again at the Archbishop of Canterbury's Christmas sermon, discussed in Chapter 1 and reproduced below as Text 7.1. This will prepare the way for a more detailed working of the ideas introduced through the analysis of Sara and Uncle Henry's explanation of the SUA process, which we have already looked at in Chapter 2.

Text 7.1 Archbishop of Canterbury's 2011 Christmas sermon

1 The most pressing question we now face, we might well say, is who and where we
2 are as a society.
3 Bonds have been broken,
4 trust abused and lost.
5 Whether it's an urban rioter mindlessly burning down a small shop that serves his
6 community or a speculator turning his back on the question of who bears the ultimate
7 cost for his acquisitive adventures   in the virtual reality of today's financial world,
8 the picture is of atoms spinning apart in the dark. But into that dark, the word of God
9 has entered, in love and judgement,
10 and has not been overcome
11 … in the darkness … the question sounds as clear as ever:
12 to each of us, and to our church and our society: Britain, where are you?

The first point I want to take from Text 7.1 is that it appears to be mixing the language from two different **Discourses**. "Discourses" with a capital D is used to refer to the whole body of talk on a particular subject and the conventions that have arisen regarding the way in which the discussion takes place. We can refer, for example, to the Discourse of Marxism, or Feminism, or Development. Discourse with a capital D is therefore to be distinguished from small-d discourse, which is any talk in context. The two are of course intricately related, as the conventions of Discourse bring with them the constraints and affordances on discourse that I have tried to capture in the Positioning Star of David. Features of established Discourses are generally fairly recognisable and a lot of work in linguistics has been undertaken to pin down the linguistic differences between Discourses and to discuss the function of these differences in sociopolitical terms (Fairclough 1992; Young and Fitzgerald 2006). A more recent current, particularly in Critical Discourse Analysis (CDA), has been to see how the linguistic features of one Discourse have **colonised** other Discourses. For example, when the Discourse of Education takes on the linguistic characteristics of (that is, is colonised by the discourse of) marketing. This is referred to as interdiscursivity, defined by Fairclough (2003:218) as: "the particular mix of genres, of discourses, and of styles upon which [a text] draws, and how different genres, discourses or styles are articulated (or 'worked together') in the text".

The term colonisation suggests a power imbalance in favour of the coloniser, but **interdiscursivity** also allows for a reversal of power relations as features of the dominant Discourse can be **appropriated** by minority groups and put to service for their own ends (see below and Bartlett 2012a). In cases such as these the points of the Positioning Star can be seen as areas for strategic manipulation in perturbing the status quo.

Interdiscursivity, as an array of linguistic features from one Discourse entering another, is to be distinguished from the simple transposing of fragments of language from one text to another, through quoting or paraphrasing. Both have been referred to as intertextuality but, following Fairclough, the approach we'll take in this book is to limit intertextuality to Fairclough's (2003:218) definition: "The intertextuality of a text is the presence within it of elements of other texts ... which may be related to ... in various ways."

In Text 7.1 there is a clear example of *intertextuality* with the words "But into that dark, the word of God has entered, in love and judgement, and has not been overcome", which resonates particularly with Isaiah 9:2, "The people that walked in darkness have seen a great light: they that dwell in the land of the shadow of death, upon them hath the light shined", a text that is often read in Church at Christmas. It also resonates with a whole host of other biblical quotes (see http://bible.cc/isaiah/9-2.htm) which display heightened intertextuality among each other. Such quotation and paraphrase is a staple of Christian preaching and so should hardly surprise us here; what is of greater interest is the opening section of the sermon with its reference to urban rioters and reckless speculators and the economic and social costs of recent events. We would be less surprised to hear such language (in terms of content and expression) in a political speech, and as such its use in a sermon marks it as an example of interdiscursivity. If this were the end of the matter, the concept of interdiscursivity would imply the existence of stable and easily identified Discourses which would allow us to identify when the features of one have entered the domain of another. This would be to ignore the fact that the stable Discourses of today are the product of yesterday's interdiscursivity (Foucault 1972) and what might appear marked usage today will be commonplace tomorrow. So, for example, while Text 7.1 might still be marked as mixing two discourses, it is becoming increasingly less unusual for clerics to enter the political debates of our times and the mix of features of Text 7.1 are on the path to becoming *naturalised* as features of a single Discourse.

The term interdiscursivity is often used in connection with genre theory. The term *genre* refers to the recognised way of performing social acts through language in a given community and much work in linguistics has gone into describing genres, from service encounters (see Chapter 2) to university prospectuses, academic essays and political interviews. The focus of genre is therefore on the stable ways of doing things that already exist and interdiscursivity is a way of accounting for the intrusion of new features from the genres of different Discourses. While many of the tools we have looked at so far in this book can be employed in genre description, the angle I will take in the remainder of this chapter is rather different in that my focus is not on describing the linguistic features of pre-established ways of acting through language, useful as this is, but on seeing what patterns emerge as a result of the social differences people bring with them and their ways of construing these differences linguistically. So, while genre analysis focuses on the visible structural patterns of language as it is put to use for different purposes, our focus is more on the less structured but no less systematic patterning of social relations in language, the different *voices* that are realised.

The sociolinguistic concept of *voice* refers to the way of speaking specific to a particular community and the social functions language fulfils within that community. The following quote is from Dell Hymes (1996:45 in Blommaert 2005:70), one of the principal theorists of voice. In it he compares the concept of fashions of speaking, or the functional organisation of language, with Whorf's notion of linguistic relativity, the idea that differences in language structure reveal different communities' ways of construing the world in physical terms:

> This second type of linguistic relativity, concerned with functions of languages, has more than a critical, cautionary import. As a sociolinguistic approach, it calls attention to the organisation of linguistic features in social interaction. Work has begun to show that descriptions of fashions of speaking can reveal basic cultural values and orientations. The worlds so revealed are not the ontological and epistemological worlds of physical relationships, of concern to Whorf, but worlds of social relationships. What are disclosed are not orientations towards space, time, vibratory phenomena and the like, but orientations towards persons, roles, statuses, rights and duties, deference and demeanour.

Clearly, the way in which language encodes "orientations towards persons, roles, statuses, rights and duties, deference and demeanour" has been the central idea of this book. What is different about Hymes' conception of voice is that in previous chapters we have been looking at individual instances of discourse to see how these orientations have been strategically manipulated, whereas voice suggests that there are ways of acting socially through language that are embedded within the community. As Hymes suggests in the quote above, this raises important issues about social interaction, access to resources and mobility. We'll return to these ideas at the end of the chapter; for now we'll revisit Sara and Uncle Henry's explanations of Sustainable Utilisation Areas to the local community to explore the idea of voice in some detail and to consider what happens when different voices come together in a single discourse, a different way of looking at interdiscursivity.

7.3 Voice, roles and hybridity

We saw in Chapter 2 how, although they were explaining the same concept, SUAs, Sara and Uncle Henry construed very different fields in order to do so. I also suggested in that chapter that the mixing of immediate and displaced contexts was different in the two texts – an idea that was developed in Chapter 8 when the concept of RUs was introduced. We can now take a look at these ideas in more detail, adding interpersonal features to our analysis, to see if the differences in ways of speaking between the two speakers might reveal something about different community voices.

I explained in Chapter 2 how Uncle Henry's contribution followed Sara's (and others') attempts to explain the concept of the SUAs and that, by common assent, Uncle Henry had succeeded where others had failed. That got me wondering about what textual features of Uncle Henry's contribution had made this possible. As I had just discovered Rhetorical Units at the time and was rather excited about them, I decided to do an RU analysis on the two texts. There is not space to reproduce the full analyses (see Bartlett 2012a if you want to see these) but a representative stretch of Uncle Henry's contribution follows:

Text 7.2 NRDDB meeting 4/11/2000

Account

  2 So you have (TAPE TURNS) …
  3 …. (slender) lines,
  4 so that you can observe … changes.
  5 How things changes?
  6 How do they form?
  7 What happen within a year after, within a year, five year, a ten year, a fifteen year period?

> .1.1 Prediction
>
>   8 So, you would get to understand the forest better
>   9 and those things would be left in their normal state.

> .1.2 Reflection
>
> 10 Because there are other important issues which we,
> 11 because we live among them,
> 12 we live inside,
> 13 it's a way of life,
>   we take it for granted.
> 14 We are not (x),
> 15 many of us do not have sense of value,
> 16 don't know how valuable those things are to us,
> 17 and we just discard it, like many of us who pushing fire in the savannah –
> 18 you know how many innocent birds' lives you destroying
> 19 (probably, even though xx xxx)?
> 20 If a snake (xxxxxxx xxxxxx) inside your house?
>
> > .1.2.1 Action
> >
> > 21 So, don't blame the snakes
> > 22 where you can't put fire in the savannah,
> >
> > > .1.2.1.1 Reflection
> > >
> > > 23 it's not good,
> > > 24 it's a very bad habit, like poisoning,
> > > 25 all these things are detrimental.
> > > 26 But because we never study it in depth,
> > > 27 we don't know how disastrous it is.

.1.3 Commentary

28 So these are things which we are now asked to participate in our knowledge (about it), to find certain things.
29 And when we come to sustainability of the forest,
30 it does not confine that to Iwokrama alone,
31 we have to look on the other communities way outside.

.1.3.1 Conjecture

32 Because you might not find
33 (when it–
34 when the plant come,) to assess it:
35 "What do we have?
36 Okay, this piece of thing, yeah yeah,
37 we'll try this for sustainable utilisation."
38 What is there that we can use sustainably?

39 One of the things you have to do is research.

.1.4 Recount

40 A lot has been done with animals, reptiles, birds, and all those things.
41 Bit of a botanical collection was done,
42 there's a lot more to be done.
43 The greenhearts of Iwokrama, that was one of the key elements they (classified).

.1.4.1 Account

44 They want to do (away with them) now.
45 Because no sense putting up all the Wilderness Preserve
46 and then there's no greenheart in there.

.1.4.1.1 Prediction

47 And we leave that for commercial harvesting, sustainable ....
48 in a short while it will disappear.

49 So they have to pinpoint those areas.

.1.5 Commentary

50 Now they have a good idea,
51 but I'm still a bit sceptical about certain areas I notice that are for sustainable –
52 I look at the map,

.1.5.1 Account

53 "Oh oh of course it just ends there",
54 and to have a wilderness preserve,
55 and you have a sustainable portion (xxxxxxx) –

.1.5.1.1 Prediction

56 to my mind it will backfire after you get (x) population,
57 because this wildlife (is our stuff).
58 as soon as applications start here,
59 (we're started … xx).
60 And once they adapt,
61 there are migration uhm migratory routes which they will take
62 and they will find themselves right up in Pakaraimas for the next year.

63 So these are things still to be discussed
64 because there is not –

65 I don't think that that is already confirmed where (x),
66 those are just tentative demarcation (x).

Both Sara's and Uncle Henry's contributions began with descriptions (as Accounts and Recounts) of the meeting they had attended (see Chapter 2 for the text of Sara's contribution), but then something interesting happened: where Sara went on to use heavily decontextualised language (that is language construing displaced contexts) such as Generalisations, Uncle Henry repeatedly contextualised his discourse, bringing the concepts closer to his audience and the community way of life by embedding (see Chapter 6) Commentaries and Reflections in his Recount (as demonstrated in Text 7.2), and also through Actions, that is commands and injunctions. Figure 7.1 demonstrates the most extreme example of this contextualisation through multiple embedding (from elsewhere in Uncle Henry's contribution).

Recount
   Account
      Reflection
         Commentary
            Generalisation
               Action

FIGURE 7.1 RU structure of Text 6.2, ll.113–130

As part of my fieldwork I had produced an ethnographic account of life on the North Rupununi Savannahs and this had revealed that the normal way for the community to pass on information about the environment, farming and hunting was in practice, through providing Commentaries of what they were doing so that their children would learn by observation. In this way, Uncle Henry's use of highly contextualised language was closer to the community's voice, or way of speaking, in terms of textuality.

Something similar was also observable in terms of experiential and interpersonal meanings. As described in Chapter 2, Sara and Uncle Henry construed the SUAs in very different ways: Sara in terms of meetings, groups and organisations, with some reference to marketing; Uncle Henry, on the other hand, construed the SUAs in terms of the resources of the forest and the community's knowledge of these and their daily practices in interacting with the environment. Now, Hymes's concept of voice, above, seems to ignore experiential meaning in favour of inter-personal aspects of voice, relegating an understanding of how the world is captured in language to the Whorfian, structural concept of linguistic relativity. There is an important difference, however, in Whorf's concept and what is happening here: Whorf talks about the way key concepts are encoded differently in the *grammar* of different languages and how this reflects differences in worldviews; what we are dealing with here, I suggest, is understandings of the world that are created through ongoing community discourse, through language as social action. In these terms, the different experiential representation and understanding of the world are just as much aspects of voice as are interpersonal features, and textual features in the case of contextualisation and RUs. This understood, we can say that Uncle Henry's representation of SUAs in terms of the community's understanding of the forest and their interaction with it are also a feature of community voice.

Turning to the interpersonal, a feature of Sara's contribution was that it was largely realised through unmodalised declaratives, relying on her status as a knowledgeable outsider to give it authority. In contrast, Uncle Henry's contribution was peppered with MUSTs and imperatives, which reflect his status as a community elder and his authority to tell the community what to do. Another noticeable interpersonal difference between the two contributions was that for Sara Iwokrama was US while the community was YOU, whereas for Uncle Henry the community was often WE – though this was not always the case, as we'll see below. In this way Uncle Henry was able to combine authority with solidarity, again as befitting his status in the community. In interpersonal terms, then, just as in experiential and textual terms, Uncle Henry's contribution was closer to the community voice than Sara's.

We can thus see how the SFL concept of three types of meaning in language is a useful tool in analysing discourse and voice. If we consider voice as a code, and bear in mind the importance of the speaker's status and the nature of the audience, we see also how this fits in with the Positioning Star of David introduced in Chapter 2. A three-strand (that is, by metafunction) analysis of Text 7.2 appears in Table 7.1.

However, further considerations of Sara's and Uncle Henry's contributions in terms of the Star of David led to a more complex understanding of what was going on here.

TABLE 7.1 Phases and contextual configurations in Uncle Henry's presentation

Lines	Rhetorical function	Field	Tenor	Mode
2–9	**Importance of observation of changes [as transition to call for collaborative research].**	Community Sen and Beh of material processes of change.	Pedagogic [+knowledge/+control]: Dialogic engagement through rhetorical questions.	Account of observation and change leading to Prediction of enhanced understanding.
10–27	**Problematises local familiarity with respect to sustainability**	Community abuse of forest resources (lexis) resulting from familiarity and lack of knowledge (mental and behavioural processes).	WE as community, but becoming YOU for worst errors.Bare imperative [+moral authority] through distance within solidarity. Negative and interrogative mood for processes of knowing. Negative Judgement of processes of Appreciation. Instructional context projecting regulatory.	Multiple embeddings contextualising concept of change in community experience.
28–49	**Research carried out on various natural resources of the forest as necessary complement to traditional knowledge and potential problems.**	Community asked to be Sensers and Actors in processes of participation and research; Iwokrma as Actors in Assigners in processes of research with local ecology as Scope and Identified.	Operates symbolic capital as elder [+solidarity/+control] through WE and direct imitated speech mixed with statement of obligations. Contrast with symbolic capital as external experts [-solidarity/+knowledge] of Iwokrama as THEY carrying out research. Regulatory context with instructional embeddings. Positive appraisal of sustainability [+Appreciation]	Commentary on proposed role in knowledge relations embedding Conjecture of possible problems paralleled with Recount of important but incomplete outside research and Conjecture of potential problems.
50–66	**UF's knowledge used to question imported knowledge.**	UH as Sen and Ca of cognitive Ats concerning Iwokrama's practice of classifying (including relational processes of meronymy). Potential material results of poor classsification and mapping. Mental processes of future discussions	I as sceptic = [+power/knowledge] of communities over Iwokrama and of UH within community. Regulatory projecting interpersonal and instructional. Negative appraisal of actions [-Judgement]	Commentary: Uncle Henry's evaluation of Iwokrama's knowledge embedding Account of Iwokrama's classification and Prediction of further work needed.

First, it became clear that Sara was not in a position to use the same language as Uncle Henry as she did not have the appropriate cultural capital. Describing SUAs in the terms she did was more or less the only option open to her.

Second, Uncle Henry's use of modality and pronouns was not as straightforward as I have suggested. In different phases of his contribution, Uncle Henry very clearly "others himself" from his audience, referring to them as YOU and at times asserting the benefits of outside knowledge over local experience and understanding of the forest. Moreover, these two things tend to happen at the same time. In other words, Uncle Henry is creating two different positions for himself in the same discourse: as local elder and as expert in outside science. He is uniquely able to do this given the combination of his status as local elder and the instrumental role he played in setting up Iwokrama with the government and international experts. This unique position is stressed in lines 50 to 66 of Text 7.2 where Uncle Henry is now the "I" who casts doubt on outside knowledge and weighs up the evidence from both sides of the discussion.

The way in which Uncle Henry does this shows the importance of considering the three metafunctions together, in their contextual configuration, as it is through the combination of these that positions are taken up and different voices realised.

Another important point to notice here is that the different positions taken up by Uncle Henry do not realise a set of **roles** that all belong together because of a single **status**, as with a doctor switching from his role as diagnostician to his role as counsellor (Sarangi 2010, 2011); rather, they are related to the different statuses based in different communities and can therefore be considered an example of *hybrid voice*. In contrast, texts in which speakers take up a number of roles deriving from a single status (a *role set*) have been described as *complex genres* (Sarangi 2010, 2011).

To make things more complicated, I would say that Uncle Henry's success in explaining the SUAs derived in no small part from Sara's failed explanation. In effect, Uncle Henry is able to *piggyback* on Sara's technical explanation and her status as an outside scientist, *subsuming* these into his own discourse in different phases of his contribution, something he is able to do because of his unique hybrid status. The fact that both discourses contributed to the discussion suggests that NRDDB meetings use interdiscursivity and as such the contributions within them can be considered hybrid genres. That is, of course, until such a mixture of ways of speaking become naturalised in this context, when we have not interdiscursivity and hybrid voices, but new discourses and new voices.

This raises one further problem for the notion of voice: how can we say that Sara's and Uncle Henry's very different ways of speaking, deriving from very different backgrounds, are both representative of this new voice? My response to this would be that, rather than see voice as a single concept representative of a whole social group, we say that *a particular voice is in operation when the contextual configuration of a speaker's discourse realises a role that is recognised within a particular community* (and, ideally, to which they have a right owing to their status in that community). This replaces the rather essentialising idea of communities as homogenous groups with a single way of speaking with the idea that there are different ways of speaking for different people within a single community and that the conjunction of all these is the community voice. And just as a single community has multiple inter-related ways of speaking, so a single speaker can belong to many communities and can speak with different voices, as demonstrated by Uncle Henry. Lastly, once recognisable roles, each with their own way of speaking, wherever they derive from, have been integrated into a given community, then we can say that these different ways of speaking are all representative of the voice of that community. In this case it is the voice of the NRDDB rather than the local community per se. To return to an earlier example, the mixing of religious and political voices in Martin Luther King's *I have a Dream* speech should not be considered a hybrid as it had become the naturalised way of making speeches for (some sectors of) the Civil Rights Movement of the time and therefore represented a distinctive voice of that community.

Exercise 7.1

1. Carry out a phasal analysis of Tony Blair's 7/7 address. Mark the first RU with a 1 and any RUs embedded in this as 1.1, etc. Mark expansions with a new number, for example, 2, 3, etc., and embeddings as 3.1 etc., with multiple embeddings as 3.1.1, etc. I've provided my analysis on p. 206. Yours may be a little different, but hopefully not too different!
2. Discuss your phasal analysis and in particular comment on any overlap between the field and the tenor.
3. Identify the different positions Blair construes for himself, the other leaders and the public through his recalibration of the immediate and displaced contexts and his construal of solidarity and authority. How does this relate to the idea of cultural capital?
4. Consider whether this is an example of a complex genre, with the different positions realising different roles from a single role set and a single status, or an example of hybridity, where different discourses and voices are brought together. The answer, of course, may not be straightforward!

7.4 Conclusion

Short though this chapter is, the ideas in it sum up what I have been trying to say and everything in the previous chapters has really just been a way of enabling me to say these things. I hope to have shown how position and voice are crucial concepts in analysing for power in language and that looking at the language alone is not enough when discussing texts as discourse. While, by its nature, this book has focused on textual features, this has always been with an eye to how they might be interpreted within the heuristic model of the Positioning Star. The approach outlined here sprang from my fieldwork in Guyana and ten years of thinking about it once I had finished my PhD. No doubt there is plenty more to think about and the model will have to be revised, so hopefully I should be kept in work for a while yet.

The main social concern behind my PhD was how minority groups can have their voices heard by those who have the power to make decisions that control their lives. The analysis in this chapter touches in some way upon such *intercultural communication*, but is restricted to an example where a relatively small and homogenous group is dealing with a sympathetic gatekeeper. A major new trend in sociolinguistics is to consider much more diversified contexts. Modern migration patterns, coupled with advances in technology, mean that more and more discourse involves people from different linguistic backgrounds, not only in terms of the "languages" they speak but also in terms of their ways of speaking, their voices. This has been called *superdiversity*. Whether the methods outlined in this book and the conception of voice I have put forward will be useful in discussing discourse in a superdiverse world remains to be seen. In such a context Blommaert (2005:255) has suggested that voice amounts to "the capacity to make oneself understood", but I'm not sure that that is enough, at least on a superficial understanding of what it means "to be understood". My own view is that being understood is only the first step to becoming a legitimate participant in the discourses that matter. I hope the approach in this book will contribute to some socially meaningful research in an ever-changing social world.

APPENDIX

Hidden text

Text 1.2

9   But into that dark, the word of God has entered, in love and judgment,
10 and has not been overcome
11 … in the darkness … the question sounds as clear as ever:
12 to each of us, and to our church and our society: Britain, where are you

(Source: www.telegraph.co.uk/news/religion/8977482/Archbishop-of-Canterbury-
laments-Britains-broken-bonds-in-Christmas-sermon.html)

For those of you without Google, the speaker is Rowan Williams, the Archbishop of Canterbury at the time, and the occasion is his 2011 Christmas sermon.

Suggested answers to questions 6–15

6. The sermon was given at a time of unrest in Britain, just after there had been rioting in the streets of major cities and in the wake of popular discontent with the banks who had been bailed out by the government after their investments had failed but who had continued to pay large bonuses to their top executives and healthy dividends to their shareholders.

7. (i) The Archbishop portrays contemporary society in negative terms as, among other things, greedy, mindlessly violent and lacking in social cohesion;
(ii) The Archbishop generally orients himself to his listeners as part of the same social group – through the use of the pronoun 'we', the common nouns 'community' and 'society' and the proper noun 'Britain'. While the rioters and bankers are not referred to as 'we', they are included within the ideas of community, society and Britain, and so there is possibly an idea that, even if we are not directly responsible for the behaviour of these groups, we are in some way responsible as a society.

8. In criticising the behaviour of both bankers and rioters the Archbishop includes both those perceived of as rich and as disadvantaged, the targets of both the left-wing and right-wing press, in his criticism.

9. The pomp and ceremony of the occasion serve to emphasise the Archbishop's socially sanctioned status as the head of the Church of England.

10. The Archbishop's status imbue his words with a degree of authority (at least to some people …) that they would not have if uttered by someone else.

11. In this particular text the Archbishop would seem to be taking on the role of social commentator rather than that of spiritual advisor, though there are, of course, elements of both.

12. Social issues have not always been considered within the authority of religious leaders in Britain and for some within the Church of England this is still a matter of some debate. Rowan Williams, in particular, is well known for becoming involved in social issues. We can thus distinguish between the position of 'Archbishop of Canterbury' in general and 'Rowan Williams as Archbishop' more specifically.

13. I would say that the Archbishop is addressing at least three different audiences. Most directly, but not necessarily primarily in this case, he is addressing the assembled congregation. Beyond that he will be aware that his sermon will be broadcast on national television and also that it is likely to cause debate in the daily papers and other media (including YouTube and, though I'm sure he did not consider this, students of discourse analysis). I suppose he may also have God in mind as an audience. It therefore is an interesting question how his sermon was worded to appeal to these different audiences simultaneously.

14. I would think that his sermon and the Archbishop's status will attract different responses from regular churchgoers, religious people in general, non-religious people and staunch atheists (to put it a little simply), as well as politicians. However, these are questions for discussion and research and not facts that we can glean from the text alone.

15. My own personal feeling (and therefore an idea needing further research) is that the Archbishop is not only suggesting a religious solution to a particular problem, but also trying to show that the Church of England is socially involved and a relevant institution in the modern world.

16. The two extracts are held together by the theme of light and darkness (at least) with the social problems of the day characterised by the metaphor of 'darkness' which is then contrasted with the traditional Christmas theme of the Nativity as the coming of light into darkness. The way in which speakers and writers create a continuity in their texts while developing different themes is an important point we will consider later, in particular inasmuch as it serves to make their message appear, on the surface at least, to be logical and consistent.

GLOSSARY

An **Adjunct** is a non-essential element of the clause. *Cf.* **nucleus**.

Agnate clauses differ in specific features of meaning, usually only one. They are useful in testing for **cryptogrammar** and so distinguishing between process types, for example, I always eat steak/Right now I'm eating steak (material) *cf.*I always think I'm going to fail/Right now I think I'm going to fail (mental).

Anaphoric reference is when a pronoun, etc. refers to something that has previously been mentioned.

Ancillary language works alongside material action (or pictures, etc.) to **construe** a **context**. *Cf.* **constitutive**.

The **angle of development** of a **text** is the basic organising principle, such as moving from one time or place to another or setting out conditions for regulations. The angle of development can often be identified by looking at the **marked Themes** across a text.

Appraisal analysis is a means of identifying and categorising different forms of evaluation in a text.

Appropriation of a dominant discourse is its use by more marginalised groups. *Cf.* **colonisation**.

Attribution of an idea is when you cite someone else as the source.

Attributive.A subtype of **relational** processes, see Chapter 3.

The **audience** or **audiences** of a text are the people who are intended to hear it. See **marketplace**.

Behavioural processes. See Chapter 3.

Capital. See **cultural capital** and **symbolic capital**.

Cataphoric reference is when a pronoun, etc. refers to something that appears later in the clause.

The **central entity** is a concept used in analysing **rhetorical units**. It refers to the person or thing that the clause is primarily talking about and is usually realised in the **lexicogrammar** by the **Subject**.

Circumstances are elements of the **clause** that tell you how, where, when and why (etc.) an event happened.

A **clause complex** is the main clause plus any **subordinate clauses**. Clause complexes realise a single **discourse function**.

A **code** is the way a specific social group uses language.

A text is **coherent** if it is all makes sense together. *Cf.* **cohesion**.

Cohesion refers to the way the **lexicogrammar** signals how parts of a **text** are joined together. It generally helps **coherence** but does not guarantee it.

Colonisation of a **discourse** is when key features of another, usually more powerful, **discourse** begin to become the norm within it. *Cf.* **appropriation**.

A **Comment Adjunct** is an adverb-like word or phrase, such as "hopefully" or "bizarrely", that realises non-modal speaker evaluation of a **proposal** or **proposition**. *Cf.* **Modal Adjunct**.

The **Complement** of a clause is any participant, apart from the **Subject**, that must be included for the clause to be fully "grammatical".

A **complex genre** is one in which participants play a variety of **roles** which are all part of the same **role set** appropriate to single **statuses**. *Cf.* **hybrid**.

Congruence is when the **lexicogrammar** and the **semantics** are in alignment and follow the usual relationship, for example, when an **interrogative** is used to ask a question.

Constitutive language construes a context entirely on its own. *Cf.* **ancillary**.

Speakers **construe** a **context** through language. This captures the ideas that a context does not exist prior to language and that different speakers may construe similar situations differently.

Context refers to the situation that is **construed** through language. Other authors use this term to refer to either what is called **environment** or what is called the **cotext** in this book. See also the definition in Chapter 1 under Key Concepts.

The **contextual configuration** of a **phase** of text is the combination of **experiential**, **interpersonal** and **textual** meanings it realises.

A **contextualisation cue** is a verbal or non-verbal signal that a situation should be understood in a particular way.

Cotext refers to other parts of the same **text**.

Cultural capital is the prestige a speaker has because of their education, experise or social position. See Chapter 1. *Cf.* **symbolic capital**.

A clause is in the **declarative mood** when the **Subject** precedes the **Finite**. *Cf.* **interrogative** and **imperative**.

The **deictic centre** is the immediate here and now: the speaker and the audience at the time of speaking.

Delicacy refers to the level of detail in a linguistic description; for example, relational:attributive is a more delicate description of a process than relational. Note the use of colons in the labels.

Deontic modality is used when a speaker signals how much they want an event to come about or how necessary it is, for example, "You must be home by eleven". *Cf.* **epistemic**.

With a small letter, **discourse** refers to text as a real-time, socially situated event. A **Discourse**, with a capital letter, refers to the accepted ways of talking about an idea, for example, "the Discourse of development". *Cf.* **text**.

The **discourse function** of an utterance refers to its **semantics** in terms of whether it is making a statement, asking a question, asking someone to do something or making an offer. *Cf.* **mood**.

A **displaced** field or context refers to a **field** or **context** that is not part of the immediate event. See Chapter 2. *Cf.* **immediate**.

Ellipsis is when a word or words are missed out but are understood and which would be necessary to make a clause fully "grammatical".

An **embedded** rhetorical unit (RU) is one that takes up and develops the matrix RU through the Theme of its first clause. *Cf.* **expansion**.

Endophoric reference is when a pronoun, etc. refers to something anywhere within the same text. *Cf.* **exophoric, homophoric**.

Enhanced themes are when a clause begins with "it is" followed by an adjective of evaluation (**enhanced evaluative theme**, for example, "It's strange that you should say that") or an element of experiential meaning (**enhanced experiential Theme**, for example, "It's you that I want"). See Chapter 5.

The **environment** of a text refers to all the non-linguistic features of the situation as well as to previous discourse that may be relevant to what the text means. Other authors use **context** in this way.

Epistemic modality is used when a speaker signals how likely they think it is that an event will come about, for example, "He must be home by now". *Cf.* **deontic**.

Event orientation is used in analysing **rhetorical units**. It refers to the temporal relation of the utterance to the deictic centre and is realised grammatically by the **Finite**.

Evidentiality is a semantic area concerning why or how we think something is true, as in "She looks like an interesting woman".

Evoked evaluation is extra evaluative meaning we can get from a word or phrase according to the situation or cotext. It would not be an essential part of a dictionary definition. *Cf.* **inscribed**.

Existential process. See Chapter 3.

An **existential Theme** is one introduced by the Subject "there" as in "There's a man with a bill at the door".

Exophoric reference is when a pronoun etc. refers to something in the immediate environment rather than the text itself. *Cf.* **endophoric, homophoric**.

Expansion is when a rhetorical unit (RU) takes up and develops the previous RU through the Rheme of its first clause. *Cf.* **embedded**.

The **experiential metafunction** refers to a speaker's representation of events. *Cf.* **interpersonal** and **textual**.

Explicit modality is marked by the lexicogrammar as being either **subjective**

(usually through the word "I", as in "I think it will rain") or **objective**, (usually through the word "it", as in "It's likely that it will rain"). *Cf.* **implicit**.

The **field** of discourse is that part of the **context** that relates to the activity taking place and the subject matter. It is **congruently realised** by the **experiential metafunction**. *Cf.* **tenor** and **mode**.

The **Finite** verb in a clause realises tense or **modality**.

A **genre** is the way a particular social group carries out an activity through language and possibly other means. See also Chapter 7.

Hedging is downplaying the force of an utterance. *Cf.* **intensifier**.

Homophoric reference is when we need shared background information to identify the referent, for example, "the Prime Minister". *Cf.* **endophoric**, **exophoric**.

A **hybrid genre** or **voice** is one that draws on the norms of different social groups or which involves different **role sets**. *Cf.* **complex**.

Identifying processes are a subset of **relational** processes. See Chapter 3. *Cf.* **attributive**.

The **immediate context** is what is happening here and now, the present activity. *Cf.* **displaced**. See Chapter 2.

A clause is in the **imperative mood** when the **Subject** and **Finite** are not realised or can be omitted without change in discourse function. *Cf.* **declarative** and **interrogative**.

Implicit modality is when the **subjective** or **objective orientation** is not overtly marked, for example, "You must be home by now" (implicit:subjective) and "He's surely home by now" (implicit:objective). *Cf.* **explicit**.

Inscribed evaluation is when a word or phrase carries a positive or negative meaning according to its dictionary definition. *Cf.* **evoked**.

An **intensifier** heightens the evaluation of a word or clause. *Cf.* **hedge**.

Interdiscursivity is the mixing of different discourses or ways of speaking in the same text. See Chapter 7. *Cf.* **intertextuality**.

The **interpersonal metafunction** is concerned with how speakers' opinions and judgements and the relations between speakers are construed through language. *Cf.* **experiential** and **textual**.

A clause is in the **interrogative mood** when the **Finite** precedes the **Subject**. *Cf.* **declarative** and **imperative**.

Intertextuality is when a text, or a paraphrase of it, appears in a different text. Some authors include interdiscursivity within intertextuality. See Chapter 7. *Cf.* **interdiscursivity**.

Investment refers to whether **modality** is either **explicit** or **implicit**.

The **lexicogrammar** of a language is how the words and grammar of that language make meanings.

Locally contingent meanings and relations depend upon the particular text or environment.

A **macrophenomenon** is a whole event seen as a Phenomenon, as in "I saw them crossing the road". See chapter 3. *Cf.* **metaphenomenon**.

A **marked Theme** is when a **Circumstance**, or occasionally a **Complement** is the **Theme** of a clause. See Chapter 5. *Cf.* **unmarked Theme** and **enhanced Theme**.

Marketplace refers in this book to the set of speakers and the different audiences within a discourse, each with their own linguistic **codes**, social values and expectations.

Material process. See Chapter 3.

Meaning potential is a functional way of referring to the lexicogrammar as a resource for meaning making rather than as a set of rules. See Chapter 1.

Mental process. See Chapter 3.

The **metafunctions** are the groupings of the **semantic** and **lexicogrammatical** resources of a language in terms of their **experiential**, **interpersonal** and **textual** functions.

A **metaphenomenon** is a fact, act, idea or quote (locution) **realised** as a **Phenomenon** or a **projection**. *Cf.* **macrophenomenon**.

The **method of development** of a text is how it progresses in terms of the **Themes** used.

A **Modal Adjunct** is an adverb-like word or phrase, such as "possibly" or "usually", that realises an option in **implicit objective** modality. *Cf.* **Comment Adjunct**.

The **modal auxiliaries** or **modal verbs** are verbs like "must", "may" and "should" that are the **Finite** element in a clause and realise an option in **implicit subjective modality**.

Modality refers to the means a speaker has of evaluating a **proposition** or **proposal** in terms of how usual or probable an event is, how necessary it is, or how willing they or others are to carry it out.

Mode is that aspect of a **context** that relates to its **cohesion**, its **textuality** and, in this book, its relation to the **deictic centre**. *Cf.* **field** and **tenor**.

Mood is a **grammatical** system with the options **declarative**, **interrogative**, and **imperative**. *Cf.* **discourse function**.

The **mood element** of a clause comprises the **Finite** and **Subject** and any intervening **modal Adjuncts**.

A **motif** is a topic or theme developed by a speaker or writer. These terms are not used as they have specific meanings in linguistics.

Naturalisation of a **genre**, **voice** or way of speaking is when it becomes accepted as the norm within a particular social group. *Cf.* **hybridity**.

A **nominal group** is a group of words referring to a single thing, usually a noun plus any article and adjectives.

The **nucleus** of a clause comprises the **Subject**, the **process** and any **Complements**. *Cf.* **Adjunct**.

Objective modality is when a speaker does not take personal responsibility for their evaluation. *Cf.* **subjective**.

Orientation refers to whether **modality** is **objective** or **subjective**.

A **participant** is a person, thing, quality or role that is realised as the **Subject** or **Complement** of a clause, or as part of a **Circumstance**.

A **participant role** is the relation of one **participant** to another in terms of **transitivity** and **process types**, for example, Actor or Attribute.

A **phase** is a stretch of text with a constant **contextual configuration**.

A speaker's **position** is the set of rights and responsibilities they take up in discourse. See Chapter 1.

A **probe** is a grammatical means of testing a clause (usually) to see what process type is involved, usually through re-expressing it. *Cf.* **agnate**.

The **process** in a clause refers to the type of event being **construed** in terms of the **transitivity** relations between **participants**. It is usually realised by the man verb.

A **process type** refers to how **transitivity relations** between the **participants** are **construed** in a clause. There are six main types: material, mental, verbal, behavioural, relational and existential. See Chapter 3.

A **proposal** is a request for or offer of goods and services, as in "You must be home by 11" or "I'll do that for you". *Cf.* **proposition**.

A **proposition** is the giving or requesting of information, as in "He'll be home by now!" or "Are you a ninny?" *Cf.* **proposal**.

A **pseudomodal** is when a process of thinking or hoping, etc. acts as a way of expressing modality, as in "I think it'll rain tomorrow".

A **rankshifted** clause is a clause or part-clause that plays a function *within* a group or another clause (as in "the man who came to dinner").

Realisation refers to the way abstract levels of language are made more concrete, for example, **context** is realised through **semantics** and **semantics** is realised though **lexicogrammar**.

If you **recalibrate** a **storyline** or a **position** you change it in real time through your **discourse**.

Relational process. See Chapter 3.

A **rhetorical unit** (RU) is a stretch of text, such as a Recount, that has a constant relation in time and space to the **deictic centre**. See Chapter 6.

A **role** is a way of acting within an activity, for example, as counsellor. See Chapter 7. *Cf.* **status**.

A **role set** is a group of **roles** that are all part of the same job or are connected with the same **status** relations, for example, when a doctor is both counsellor and diagnostician.

A **semantic domain** is a range of ideas with interconnected meaning.

Semantic prosody is when a text or stretch of texts contains many similar forms of evaluation.

Semantics are the meanings that can be or are made. The semantics realise the context and the **lexicogrammar** realises the semantics.

A **semimodal** is a verb like "have to" which has some properties of modality but not all. See Chapter 4.

Semiotic means related to meaning-making.

A speaker's **speech role** refers to whether they are making a statement, asking a question, asking someone to do something or making an offer.

A speaker's **status** in a discourse is their social position in relation to other speakers, for example, doctor or patient. *Cf.* **role**.

The **storyline(s)** of a discourse are the continuing social activities and histories to which the discourse contributes.

The **Subject** of a clause is the **participant** that the truth or otherwise of the clause is based on and negotiated around. See Chapter 4. *Cf.* **Complement.**

Subjective modality is when a speaker takes personal responsibility for their evaluation. *Cf.* **objective**.

A **subordinate clause** is introduced by a conjunction and cannot stand alone; it acts as a kind of **Circumstance** to the main clause.

Symbolic capital refers to the value that a speaker's language takes on because of the **cultural capital** of that speaker within a specific **marketplace**.

A **system** is a set of options, a choice in meaning with minimal difference.

Tenor is that aspect of a **context** that relates to the interpersonal relations between speakers. *Cf.* **field** and **mode**.

A **text** is any stretch of language that forms a unified whole, without consideration of any non-linguistic features of its use. *Cf.* **discourse**

The **textual metafunction** refers to the semantic and lexicogrammatical resources for creating textuality and cohesion. *Cf.* **experiential** and **interpersonal**.

Textuality is the property of a stretch of language as being a unified whole.

The **thematic element** of a clause is made up of the experiential Theme and any textual or interpersonal Themes that precede it. See Chapter 5.

The **Theme** of a clause usually refers to the first element with **experiential** meaning, though this is properly called the experiential Theme as **interpersonal** and **textual** Themes are also possible. See Chapter 5.

Transitivity refers to the relations between **participants** in terms of their involvement within the **process** construed. See Chapter 3.

An **unmarked Theme** is the **Subject** of a **declarative** clause, the **Subject** or wh-word in an **interrogative** clause and usually the main verb in an **imperative** clause. Cf. **marked Theme** and **enhanced Theme**.

Value in **modality** is high, median or low.

Verbal process. See Chapter 3.

Voice refers to the way the social organisation of a particular group is realised through their ways of speaking. See Chapter 7.

ANSWERS

Exercise 2.2

Cases where the identity of the referent is to be recovered from text or outside are all highlighted:

1 I stand here today because of the inspiration of the Olympic Movement.
2 When I was 12, about the same age as Amber,
3 I was marched into a large school hall with my classmates.
4 We sat in front of an ancient, black and white TV
5 and watched grainy pictures from the Mexico Olympic Games.
6 Two athletes from our home town were competing.
7 John Sherwood won a bronze medal in the 400m hurdles.
8 His wife Sheila just narrowly missed gold in the long jump.
9 That day a window to a new world opened for me.
10 By the time I was back in my classroom,
11 I knew
12 what I wanted to do
13 and what I wanted to be.
14 The following week I stood in line for hours at my local track just to catch a glimpse of the medals the Sherwoods had brought home.
15 It didn't stop there.
16 Two days later I joined their club.
17 Two years later Sheila gave me my first pair of racing spikes.
18 35 years on, I stand before you with those memories still fresh. Still inspired by this great Movement.
19 My journey here to Singapore started in that school hall
20 and continues today in wonder and in gratitude. Gratitude that those flickering images of the Sherwoods, and Wolde, Gammoudi, Doubell and Hines

drew me to a life in that most potent celebration of humanity Olympic sport.

21 And that gratitude drives me and my team to do whatever we can to inspire young people to choose sport.

22 Whoever they are,

23 wherever they live

24 and whatever they believe.

25 Today that task is so much harder.

26 Today's children live in a world of conflicting messages and competing distractions.

27 Their landscape is cluttered.

28 Their path to Olympic sport is often obscured.

29 But it's a world we must understand and must respond to.

30 My heroes were Olympians.

31 My children's heroes change by the month.

32 And they are the lucky ones.

33 Millions more face the obstacle of limited resources and the resulting lack of guiding role models.

34 In my travels over the last two years, speaking with many of you, I've had many conversations about how we meet this challenge.

35 And I've been reassured

36 and I've been uplifted

37 we share a common goal for the future of sport.

38 No group of leaders does more than you to engage the hearts and minds of young people.

39 But every year the challenge of bringing them to Olympic sport becomes tougher.

40 The choice of Host City is the most powerful means you have to meet this challenge.

41 But it takes more than 17 days of superb Olympic competition.

42 It takes a broader vision. And the global voice to communicate that vision over the full four years of the Olympiad.

43 Today in Britain's fourth bid in recent years we offer London's vision of inspiration and legacy.

44 Choose London today

45 and you send a clear message to the youth of the world:

46 more than ever, the Olympic Games are for you.

47 Mr President, Members of the IOC: Some might say

48 that your decision today is between five similar bids.

49 That would be to undervalue the opportunity before you.

50 In the past, you have made bold decisions: decisions which have taken the Movement forward in new and exciting directions.

51 Your decision today is critical.

52 It is a decision about which bid offers the vision and sporting legacy to best promote the Olympic cause.

53 It is a decision about which city will help us show a new generation why sport matters. In a world of many distractions, why Olympic sport matters. And in the 21st century why the Olympic Ideals still matter so much.

54 On behalf of the youth of today, the athletes of tomorrow and the Olympians of the future, we humbly submit the bid of London 2012.

55 Mr President, that concludes our presentation.

56 Thank you.

Exercise 3.1

N.B. Participants are in bold.

1 **I** [α] am happy to [α Ac] <u>join</u> with you today in **what** (Ac) will <u>go down</u> in history as the greatest demonstration for freedom in the history of our nation.

2 Five score years ago, **a great American** (Ac), >< <u>signed</u> **the Emancipation Proclamation** (Go).

3 >in whose symbolic shadow we stand today,<

4 **This momentous decree** (Ac) <u>came</u> as a great beacon light of hope to millions of Negro slaves **who** (Go) had been <u>seared</u> in the flames of withering injustice.

5 **It** (Ac α) <u>came</u> as a joyous daybreak to [α <u>Ac</u>] <u>end</u> **the long night of their captivity** (Go).

6 But one hundred years later, the Negro still is not free.

7 One hundred years later, **the life of the Negro** (Go) is still sadly <u>crippled</u> by **the manacles of segregation and the chains of discrimination** (Ac).

8 One hundred years later, **the Negro** (Ac) <u>lives</u> on a lonely island of poverty in the midst of a vast ocean of material prosperity.

9 One hundred years later, **the Negro** (Ac) is still <u>languishing</u> in the corners of American society

10 and finds himself an exile in his own land.

11 So **we** (Ac α) have <u>come</u> here today to [α Ac] <u>dramatize</u> **a shameful condition** (Go).

12 In a sense **we** (Ac α) have <u>come</u> to our nation's capital to (α Ac) <u>cash</u> **a check** (Go).

13 When **the architects of our republic** (Ac) <u>wrote</u> **the magnificent words of the Constitution and the Declaration of Independence** (Go:cre),

14 **they** (Ac) were <u>signing</u> **a promissory note to which every American was to fall heir** (Go).

15 This note was a promise that all men, yes, black men as well as white men, would be guaranteed the unalienable rights of life, liberty, and the pursuit of happiness.

16 It is obvious today that **America** (Ac) has <u>defaulted</u> on this promissory note

17 insofar as her citizens of color are concerned.
18 Instead of [α Ac] <u>honoring</u> **this sacred obligation** (Go), **America** (Ac α) has <u>given</u> **the Negro people** (Rct) **a bad check** (Go), a check **which** (Ac α) has <u>come back</u> [α Go] <u>marked</u> **"insufficient funds."** (At)
19 But we refuse to believe
20 that the bank of justice is bankrupt.
21 We refuse to believe
22 that there are insufficient funds in the great vaults of opportunity of this nation.
23 So **we** (Ac α) have <u>come</u> to [α Ac] <u>cash</u> **this check** (Go) — a check **that** (Ac) will <u>give</u> **us** (Rect) upon demand **the riches of freedom and the security of justice** (Go).
24 **We** (Ac) have also <u>come</u> to this hallowed spot to remind America of the fierce urgency of now.

Exercise 3.2

Note: " signals a projection

1 **I** (Sayer) am just going to <u>make</u> **a short statement** (Vb) to **you** (Recr) on **the terrible events** (Ac) that have <u>happened</u> in London earlier today
2 and **I** (Sen:cog[1]) <u>hope</u>
3 "**you** (Sen:cog) <u>understand</u>
4 "that at the present time **we** (Sen:cog) are still trying to <u>establish</u> exactly **what** (Ac) **has happened** (Phen),
5 and there is a limit to **what information** (Go) **I** (Ac) can **give** **you** (Rect),[2]
6 and **I** (Sayer) will simply try and <u>tell</u> **you** (Rect) **the information** (Vb) as best I can at the moment.
7 It is reasonably clear that there have been a series of terrorist attacks in London.
8 There are obviously casualties, both **people** (Ac) that have <u>died</u> and **people** (Go) seriously <u>injured,</u>
9 and our thoughts and prayers of course are with the victims and their families.
10 It is my intention to [Blair Ac] <u>leave</u> the G8 within the next couple of hours and [Blair] <u>go down</u> to London and [Blair Ac] <u>get</u> **a report** (Go), face-to-face, with the police, and the emergency services and the Ministers **that** (Ac) have been <u>dealing with</u> **this** (Go), and then to [Blair Ac] <u>return</u> later this evening.
11 It is the will of all the leaders at the G8 however that **the meeting** (Ac) should <u>continue</u> in my absence, that **we** (Sayer α) should continue to <u>discuss</u> **the issues that we were going to <u>discuss</u>** (Tg[3]), and [α Sen:cog] <u>reach</u> **the conclusions** (Sc) **which** (Sc) we (Sen:cog) were going to <u>reach</u>.
12 Each of the countries round that table have some experience of the effects of terrorism

13 and **all the leaders** [α]> < share our complete resolution to (α Ac) <u>defeat</u> **this terrorism** (Go).
14 >as **they** (Sayer[4]) will <u>indicate</u> a little bit later<
15 It is particularly barbaric that **this** (Ac) has <u>happened</u> on a day when **people** (Ac α) are <u>meeting</u> to (α Ac) try to <u>help</u> **the problems of poverty in Africa, and the long term problems of climate change and the environment** (Go)
16 Just as it is reasonably clear that this is a terrorist attack, or a series of terrorist attacks,
17 it is also reasonably clear that it is designed and aimed to coincide with the opening of the G8.
18 There will be time to [leaders? Beh] **talk** later about this.
19 It is important however that **those engaged in terrorism** (Sen:cog) <u>realise</u>
20 "that our determination to [us Ac) <u>defend</u> **our values and our way of life** (Go) is greater than their determination to [they Ac] <u>cause</u> **death and destruction** (Sc) to innocent people in a desire to [they Ac] <u>impose</u> **extremism** (Go[5])on the world.
21 **Whatever** (Go) **they** (Ac) <u>do,</u>
22 it is our determination that **they** (Ac) will never succeed in <u>destroying</u> **what we hold dear in this country and in other civilised nations throughout the world** (Go).

Notes to Exercise 3.2

1   This certainly looks desiderative from a notional perspective, but it's clearly cognitive grammatically – interesting!
2   There aren't enough typefaces to do justice to the complexity of this sentence – I hope you get all the relations!
3   This is debatable, but seems to be the best grammatical fit.
4   It might be possible to analyse "as" as the projected speech here.

Exercise 3.3

1   I am just going to make a short statement to you on the terrible events that have happened in London earlier today,
2   and I hope
3   you understand
4   that at the present time we are still trying to establish exactly what has happened,
5   and there <u>is</u> **a limit to what information I can give you** (Ex),
6   and I will simply try and tell you the information as best I can at the moment.
7   It is reasonably clear that there have <u>been</u> **a series of terrorist attacks in London** (Ex).
8   There <u>are</u> obviously **casualties** (Ex), both people that have died and people seriously injured,

9 and **our thoughts and prayers** (Ca) of course <u>are</u> **with the victims and their families** (At:circ).

10 It <u>is</u> **my intention** (Val[1]) **to leave the G8 within the next couple of hours and go down to London and get a report, face-to-face, with the police, and the emergency services and the Ministers that have been dealing with this, and then to return later this evening** (Tkl).

11 It <u>is</u> **the will of all the leaders at the G8** (Val) however **that the meeting should continue in my absence, that we should continue to discuss the issues that we were going to discuss, and reach the conclusions which we were going to reach** (Tk).

12 **Each of the countries round that table** (Ca) <u>have</u> **some experience of the effects of terrorism** (At:pos)

13 and **all the leaders** (Tk[2])> < <u>share</u> **our complete resolution to defeat this terrorism** (Val).

14 >as they will indicate a little bit later<

15 It <u>is</u> **particularly barbaric** (At) **that this has happened on a day when people are meeting to try to help the problems of poverty in Africa, and the long term problems of climate change and the environment** (Ca)

16 Just as it <u>is</u> **reasonably clear** (At) **that this (Ca)** <u>is</u> **a terrorist attack, or a series of terrorist attacks (At)** (Ca),[3]

17 it <u>is</u> also **reasonably clear** (At) **that it (Ca)** <u>is</u> **designed and aimed to coincide with the opening of the G8 (At)** (Ca).[4]

18 There will <u>be</u> **time to talk later about this** (Ex).

19 It <u>is</u> **important** (At) however **that those engaged in terrorism realise**

20 **that our determination to defend our values and our way of life (Ca)** <u>is</u> **greater than their determination to cause death and destruction to innocent people in a desire to impose extremism on the world (At)** (Ca).[5]

21 Whatever they do,

22 it <u>is</u> **our determination** (Val) **that they will never succeed in destroying what we hold dear in this country and in other civilised nations throughout the world** (Tk).

Notes to Exercise 3.3

1 This is a marked thematic structure – see Chapter 5.

2 This is an odd one – but it is a reversible relational process.

3 Confusing I know. Paraphrases of the relations analysed are: " **this (Ca)** <u>is</u> **a terrorist attack, or a series of terrorist attacks (At)**" and " **that this is a terrorist attack, or a series of terrorist attacks (Ca)** <u>is</u> **reasonably clear (Ca)**".

4 Difficult again! I've analysed this as " **that it is designed and aimed to coincide with the opening of the G8 (Ca)** <u>is</u> also **reasonably clear (At)**" and " **it (Ca)** <u>is</u> **designed and aimed to coincide with the opening of**

the G8 (At)". The second example could have been analysed as a passive material process.

5   Tricky yet again. You can work out the two sets of relations yourselves this time!

Exercise 4.1

1	S:	Okay, so … so the activity … is … to do what? **WH INT Q**¹
2		>To get a reservoir … set up … in the village?< Right? **ANSWER + CHECK**
3		That's the activity? **DEC Q**
4	N?:	Yeah. **ANSWER**
5	S:	Right. **CONFIRM**
6		And then … how does that fit with … with all these other things in terms of
7		of agricultu:re, health, and all of those … is the next thing you're talking
8		about? **WH-INT Q**
9		Makes it more accessible, makes it easier … maybe healthier, those kind of
10		stuff, right? **DEC Q**
11		So … so, let's just back up. **1PLIMP SUGGESTION**
12		So, you wanna ↑ do … ↓ three.
13		(15s)
14		And remember this from yesterday … the various points we've built, right?
15		**IMP REQ +CHECK**
16		(5s)
17		Right? **CHECK**
18		And re … re … and so … that's one, it is "How does it ↑ fit with other things
19		in the
20		village?",
21		and you're saying it makes it more accessible an' easier.
22		So …
23		(6s)
24		Any other … things [to go with] **INT Q**
25	N:	[Safer], it was safer.
26	S:	Sa:fer. ((writing it down?)) **ECHO**
27	W:	(xxx) safer (xxx). **ECHO**
28	S:	(xxx).
29		(9s)
30	S:	Because drinking water is such a straightforward thing, these two collapse into
31		one basically.
32		I mean 'cause it's not like you're talking about lo:gging or … or cutting
33		down trees to do agriculture, right? **DEC STATEMENT + CHECK**
34		So 1 and 2 would …
35	N:	Less time taken to … t= =for your water. **SUGGESTED ITEM**
36	S:	Yeah. 1 and 2. Less time taken to acquire (our) water. **CONFIRM AND**
37		**ECHO**

38   So, less labour, right? SUGGESTED ITEM + CHECK
39 ?:   ((grunt of assent))
40   (14s)
41 S: Mm-hmm. Anything else? INT^2 Q
42   (6s)
43 W: Encourage agr … kitchen gardens. SUGGESTED ITEM
44 S: Encourage agriculture, right? CHECK ITEM
45   (20s)
46   Anything else? INT Q
47 W: Is it okay that hoping they erm … a flush toilet system (xxxxx)? INT Q
48 S: In the future? CHECK ELEMENT
49 W: Mm-hmm.
50 S: But that's not meant to be activity right now? DECL Q
51   (Eh,) the activity right now is to find somebody to fund … the reservoir. .and
52   the pipes … to
53   certain points, right? DEC STATEMENT + CHECK
54   So, potential future … so that's potential. ITEM
55 N: I think maybe we should put that part. DEC SUGGESTION
56   ((W and N mutter a while)) (12s)
57 S: We have … you talked about this yesterday, activity (xx), how it's going to each
58   home and … and …
59 N: We could have taken it from under … easier access, (xxx).
60   (12s)
61 S: (What about other) sanitation, Walter? WH INT Q
62   Flush toilet system, (?sanitary towel) system. (This is to put under) positive=
63 N: =We don't see water in the home as something that should be automatic.
64   ((mumbling from floor)) (16s)
65 S: They would get what? WH INT Q
66   ((further mumbling, with N's voice suddenly becoming prominent.)) (6s)
67 N: … not a necessity,
68   you could collect (more than) water from outside).
69   I mean, which can happen,
70 S: [Could everyone] INT REQUEST
71 W: [When we] talked about the flush toilet, it was the … around the nearby
72   well … (xxxxx). Nearby homes to the wells, because of er … (away then
73   from) the shit-
74   juice bringing into the wells and the water stream.
75 S: Right. CONFIRM
76   So it links (xxxx).
77   Sanitation, right? ITEM + CHECK
78 W: Right. CONFIRM
79 S: We also talked yesterday about ecotourist things … having better water supply.
80   So that if we collapse … in here we could do one and two together, kind of
81   collapse it

82   in … okay? DEC SUGGESTION
83   So …
84   ((mumbling leading to laughing, especially from N)) (23s)

Notes to Exercise 4.1

1   This is a very marked form of wh–interrogative which suggests the asker possible knows the answer or has a good idea.
2   This really depends on whether you think anything has been ellipted or it's just an item check as in other cases.

Exercise 4.3

Modality

1 I am just going to make a short statement to you on the terrible events that have happened in London earlier today,
2 and I hope *(explicit; subjective; inclination; median)*
3 you understand
4 that at the present time we are still trying to establish exactly what has happened,
5 and there is a limit to what information I can give you,
6 and I will *(?implicit; subjective; inclination; median)* simply try and tell you the information as best I can at the moment.
7 It is reasonably clear *(explicit; objective; probability; median)* that there have been a series of terrorist attacks in London.
8 There are obviously *(implicit; objective; probability; high)* casualties, both people that have died and people seriously injured,
9 and our thoughts and prayers of course *(implicit; objective; probability; high)* are with the victims and their families.
10 It is my intention *(explicit; objective; inclination; median)* to leave the G8 within the next couple of hours and go down to London and get a report, face-to-face, with the police, and the emergency services and the Ministers that have been dealing with this, and then to return later this evening.
11 It is the will *(explicit; objective; inclination; median)* of all the leaders at the G8 however that the meeting should continue in my absence, that we should continue to discuss the issues that we were going to discuss, and reach the conclusions which we were going to reach.
12 Each of the countries round that table have some experience of the effects of terrorism
13 and all the leaders>< share our complete resolution to defeat this terrorism.
14 >as they will *(?implicit; subjective; probability; high)* indicate a little bit later<
15 It is particularly barbaric that this has happened on a day when people are meeting to try to help the problems of poverty in Africa, and the long term problems of climate change and the environment.

16 Just as it is reasonably clear *(explicit; objective; probability;median)* that this is a terrorist attack, or a series of terrorist attacks,

17 it is also reasonably clear *(explicit; objective; probability; median)* that it is designed and aimed to coincide with the opening of the G8.

18 There will *(?implicit; subjective; probability; high)* be time to talk later about this.

19 It is important however that those engaged in terrorism realise

20 that our determination to defend our values and our way of life is greater than their determination to cause death and destruction to innocent people in a desire to impose extremism on the world.

21 Whatever they do,

22 it is our determination *(explicit; objective; inclination; high)* that they will never succeed in destroying what we hold dear in this country and in other civilised nations throughout the world.

Appraisal

1 I am just going to make a short statement to you on the terrible *(inscribed; judgement:social sanction:-propriety)* events that have happened in London earlier today,

2 and I hope

3 you understand

4 that at the present time we are still trying to establish exactly what has happened,

5 and there is a limit to what information I can give you*(inscribed; judgement:social esteem:-capacity),*

6 and I will simply try and tell you the information as best I can *(inscribed; judgement:social esteem:+capacity)* at the moment.

7 It is reasonably clear that there have been a series of terrorist *(inscribed; judgement:social sanction:-propriety)* attacks *(incribed; affect:-security)* in London.

8 There are obviously casualties*(evoked; affect:-happiness),* both people that have died *(evoked; affect:-happiness)* and people seriously injured*(evoked; affect:-happiness),*

9 and our thoughts and prayers *(inscribed; affect:inclination)* of course are with the victims *(evoked; affect:-happiness)* and their families.

10 It is my intention *(inscribed; affect:inclination)* to leave the G8 within the next couple of hours and go down to London and get a report, face-to-face, with the police*(incribed;affect:+security),* and the emergency *(incribed;affect:-security)* services and the Ministers that have been dealing with *(inscribed; judgement: social esteem:+capacity)* this, and then to return later this evening.

11 It is the will *(inscribed; affect:inclination)* of all the leaders *(inscribed; judgement: social esteem:+capacity)* at the G8 however that the meeting should continue *(inscribed; judgement:social esteem:+tenacity)* in my absence, that we should continue *(inscribed; judgement:social esteem:+tenacity)* to discuss the issues that we were going to discuss, and reach *(inscribed; judgement:social esteem:+tenacity)* the conclusions which we were going to reach.

12 Each of the countries round that table have some experience of the effects of terrorism *(inscribed; judgement:social sanction:-propriety)*

13 and all the leaders *(inscribed; judgement:social esteem:+capacity)>*< share our complete resolution *(inscribed; judgement:social esteem:+tenacity)* to defeat *(inscribed; judgement:social esteem:+tenacity)* this terrorism*(inscribed; judgement:social sanction:-propriety)*.

14 >as they will indicate a little bit later<

15 It is particularly barbaric *(inscribed; judgement:social sanction:-propriety)* that this has happened on a day when people are meeting to try to help *(inscribed; judgement:social sanction:+propriety)* the problems of poverty *(inscribed; judgement:social esteem; -capacity)* in Africa, and the long term problems of climate change and the environment *(incribed;affect:-security)*

16 Just as it is reasonably clear that this is a terrorist *(inscribed; judgement:social sanction:-propriety)* attack *(incribed;affect:-security)*, or a series of terrorist *(inscribed; judgement:social sanction:-propriety)* attacks *(incribed;affect:-security)*,

17 it is also reasonably clear that it is designed and aimed *(inscribed; affect:+inclination)* to coincide with the opening of the G8.

18 There will be time to talk later about this.

19 It is important *(inscribed; appreciation:+valuation)*: however that those engaged *(inscribed; affect:+inclination)* in terrorism *(inscribed; judgement:social sanction:-propriety)* realise

20 that our determination *(inscribed; judgement:social esteem:+tenacity)* to defend *(inscribed; judgement:social esteem:+tenacity)* our values and our way of life *(inscribed; judgement: social sanction:+propriety)* is greater than their determination *(inscribed; judgement:social esteem:+tenacity)* to cause death and destruction *(inscribed; judgement: social sanction: - propriety)* to innocent *(inscribed; judgement: social sanction: +propriety)* people in a desire *(inscribed; affect:inclination)* to impose *(inscribed; judgement:social esteem:+tenacity)* extremism *(inscribed; judgement:social sanction: +propriety)* on the world.

21 Whatever they do,

22 it is our determination *(inscribed; judgement:social esteem:+tenacity)* that they will never succeed in destroying *(inscribed; judgement:social sanction:-propriety)* what we hold dear *(inscribed; judgement:social sanction:+propriety)* in this country and in other civilised *(inscribed; judgement:social sanction:+propriety)* nations throughout the world.

Exercise 5.1

Themes in **bold**; non-Theme Subjects <u>underlined</u>; category of marked Theme in brackets; ellipted material in square brackets.

1 **Napoleon Bonaparte** was a French military and political leader who rose to prominence during the latter stages of the French Revolution and its associated wars in Europe.

2 **As Napoleon I** (Circ:guise), <u>he</u> was Emperor of the French from 1804 to 1815.

3 **His legal reform**, the Napoleonic Code, has been a major influence on many civil law jurisdictions worldwide,

4 but **he** is best remembered for his role in the wars led against France by a series of coalitions, the so-called Napoleonic Wars.

5 **He** established hegemony over most of continental Europe

6 and **[he]**sought to spread the ideals of the French Revolution, while consolidating an imperial monarchy which restored aspects of the deposed *Ancien Régime*.

7 **Due to his success in these wars** (Circ:reason), **often against numerically superior enemies** (Circ:manner), <u>he</u> is generally regarded as one of the greatest military commanders of all time,

8 and **his campaigns** are studied at military academies worldwide.

9 **Napoleon** was born at Ajaccio in Corsica in a family of noble Italian ancestry which had settled Corsica in the 16th century.

10 **He** trained as an artillery officer in mainland France.

11 **He** rose to prominence under the French First Republic

12 and **[he]** led successful campaigns against the First and Second Coalitions arrayed against France.

13 **He** led a successful invasion of the Italian peninsula.

14 **In 1799** (Circ:temp), <u>he</u> staged a *coup d'état*

15 and **[he]** installed himself as First Consul;

16 **five years later** (Circ:temp) **the French Senate** proclaimed him emperor, following a plebiscite in his favour.

17 **In the first decade of the 19th century** (Circ:temp), <u>the French Empire under Napoleon</u> engaged in a series of conflicts—the Napoleonic Wars—that involved every major European power.

18 **After a streak of victories** (Circ:temp), <u>France</u> secured a dominant position in continental Europe,

19 and **Napoleon** maintained the French sphere of influence through the formation of extensive alliances and the appointment of friends and family members to rule other European countries as French client states.

20 **The Peninsular War and 1812 French invasion of Russia** marked turning points in Napoleon's fortunes.

21 **His** Grande Armée was badly damaged in the campaign

22 and **[it]**never fully recovered.

23 **In 1813** (Circ:temp), <u>the Sixth Coalition</u> defeated his forces at Leipzig;

24 **the following year** (Circ:temp) <u>the Coalition</u> invaded France,

25 **[it]** forced Napoleon to abdicate

26 and **[it]** exiled him to the island of Elba.

27 **Less than a year later** (Circ:loc), **he** escaped Elba

28 and [**he**] returned to power,
29 but [**he**]was defeated at the Battle of Waterloo in June 1815.
30 **Napoleon** spent the last six years of his life in confinement by the British on the island of Saint Helena.
31 **An autopsy** concluded he died of stomach cancer,
32 but **there has been some debate about the cause of his death,**[1]
33 as **some scholars** have speculated
34 that **he** was a victim of arsenic poisoning.

Note to Exercise 5.1

1   This is an existential Theme, covered later.

Exercise 5.2

Experiential Themes in **bold**; non–Theme Subjects <u>underlined</u>; category of marked Theme in brackets; interpersonal Themes <u><u>double underlined</u></u>; subordinate clause Themes in *italics*; ellipted material in square brackets. Textual themes are not marked, so any unmarked elements before the experiential Theme are textual Themes.

Text 5.3 University welcome

1   FOREWORD

2   <u>Welcome, or welcome back, to 'ENCAP'.</u>
3   **As one of the largest Schools in the University, with more than a thousand students (one hundred of them postgraduates), and over fifty academic staff** (Circ:guise), <u>we</u> pride ourselves in providing an excellent experience for our students, based in a friendly, personalised and supportive environment.
4   **There are several ways in which you as a student can contribute to the community,**[1] generally by participating fully in lectures and seminars and by engaging with your fellow students and staff in the spirit of mutual respect that we seek to promote in all dealings within the School.
5   *As you will be aware*,
6   **students entering their first year and those in the second year** each have their own Facebook page
7   – **this** is a great way of getting to know each other, sharing experiences and information.
8   **You** can make a particularly useful contribution by joining the Student–Staff panels associated with the Board of Studies that runs your degree and by standing as a student representative to the Board.

9 **In our turn** (Circ:manner), <u>our job</u> is to help you achieve your best.

10 **Your Personal Tutor** is there for that purpose

11 – **take time** to catch up with him or her,

12 and **do take advantage** of the opportunities for Academic Progress Meetings (APMs) we have introduced.

13 **You** will find more information about APMs, and much else, in this School Undergraduate Student Handbook.

14 **It** also contains advice on presentation of work and exam preparation, how staff and students contact each other, personal development and careers, student support, extenuating circumstances, regulations regarding examinations and assessed work and progression.

15 **For more detailed information relating to your programme of study** (Circ:reason),

16 <u>please</u> **refer** to your Course Guide,

17 **which** details academic staff email addresses and research interests, word limits for essays and dissertations, grading/assessment criteria, referencing systems etc.

18 **This Handbook and your Course Guide** should be read in conjunction with each other.

19 <u>Of course</u>, **no handbook** can cover every possible detail;

20 if you have any queries or need clarification on any issue (Clause:condition)

21 **your first point of contact** are the staff in the Undergraduate Office

22 – **they** are always happy to help (Humanities Building, Room 2.67).

23 **Each programme** also has a Deputy Director whose job it is to deal with queries that cannot be resolved by the Office.

24 And, <u>of course</u>, **personal matters** should be discussed with your Personal Tutor.

25 <u>I hope</u>

26 **you** both enjoy

27 and [**you**] profit from your time in the School.

Text 5.4 Bush's *Bring them on* moment

1 Q: **A posse of small nations, like Ukraine and Poland,** are materializing to help keep the peace in Iraq,

2 but **with the attacks on U.S. forces and casualty rates rising** (Circ: reason), <u>what</u> does the administration do to get larger powers like France and Germany and Russia to join in the American (xxxx)?

3 B: Well, first of all, <u>you know</u>, **we'll** put together a force structure that meets the threats on the ground.

5 And **we** got a lot of forces there ourselves.

6 <u>And as I said yesterday</u>,[2]

7 **anybody who wants to harm American troops** will be found and brought to justice.

8	**There are some**[3]who feel like
9	That if they attack us (clause:condition)
10	that **we** may decide to leave prematurely.
11	**They** don't understand what they're talking about,
12	if that's the case.
13	**Let** me finish.
14	**There are some** [4] who feel like
15	that, <u>you know</u>, **the conditions** are such that they can attack us there.
16	**My answer** is bring them on.
17	**We** got the force necessary to deal with the security situation.
18	<u>Of course</u> **we** want other countries to help us.
19	**Great Britain** is there.
20	**Poland** is there.
21	**Ukraine** is there,
22	you mentioned.[5]
23	**Anybody who wants to help** (Complement), <u>we</u>'ll welcome to help.
24	But **we** got plenty tough force there right now to make sure the situation is secure.
25	**We** always welcome help.
26	**We** 're always glad to include others in.
27	But **make** no mistake about it,
28	and **the enemy** shouldn't make any mistake about it,
29	**we** will deal with them harshly
30	if they continue to try to bring harm to the Iraqi people.
31	<u>I also said yesterday an important point,</u>[6]
32	that **those who blow up the electricity lines** really aren't hurting America,
33	**they** 're hurting the Iraq citizens.
34	**Their own fellow citizens** are being hurt.
35	But **we** will deal with them harshly as well.

Notes to Exercise 5.2

1   This is another existential Theme.
2   This is a mix of textual and interpersonal information.
3   This is an experiential Theme and really stretches as far as "prematurely".
4   Another existential Theme stretching as far as "attack us there".
5   I'm analysing this as non-thematic interpersonal information.
6   This is a mix of textual and interpersonal information.

Exercise 7.1

TABLE 7.2 Answers to Exercise 7.1

Clause nos.	phase	field	tenor	Mode (RU)
1–6	Blair establishing his role as a spokesman	Blair as Sayer, public as Recipients and Sensers	Information as plain declaratives; Blair's hope for understanding from audience construes tenor of authority and solidarity	1 Commentary
7	Introduction to events of the day	attacks	-judgement:social sanction	1.1 Recount
8	Establishing details	Casualties and victims	-Affect: happiness	1.1.1 Report
9	Creating empathy		-Affect: happiness; +Affect:inclination; empathy Blair and public	1 Commentary
10–11	Establishing determined response of leaders	Plans of the leaders.	+Affect:inclination and +judgement:social esteem:tenacity of leaders in response to-judgement:social sanction of terrorists. Leaders as responding on behalf of people.	2 Plan
12–13	Establishing joint cause with other leaders.	Shared experiences and determination of other leaders.	Solidarity of leaders of other countries with UK and joint +judgement:social esteem:tenacity.	2.1 Report
14				2.1.1 Plan
15–17	Barbarism of attack in contrast with good intentions of leaders.	Aims of the attack	-judgement:social sanction of terrorists	3 Report t[1]
18	Establishing response as considered.	Leaders and public as joint talkers.	Establishing solidarity in response.	3.1 Prediction
19	Establishing response a strong.	Superior determination of leaders and public.	Solidarity of +judgement:social esteem:tenacity between leaders and public	4 Actio n[2]
20–22	Triumphal coda.	Strength of tenacity of leaders and people.	Greater +judgement:social esteem:tenacity of leaders and public; solidarity in shared values of leaders and people; triumph of good over evil.	4.1 Pla n[3]

Notes

1 The present perfect can be analysed as primarily concerned with the present or the past and I've analysed this as a Report of the present situation, though the evaluation is obviously the central idea here.

2 I've analysed this as a call for the terrorists to recognise Blair and the other leaders' position.

3 I've analysed these projected clauses as embedded in the projecting clause.

REFERENCES

Austin, J. J. (1962) *How to do Things with Words: The William James Lectures delivered at Harvard University in 1955.* Edited by J. O. Urmson and Marina Sbisà. Oxford: Clarendon Press.

Banks, D. (forthcoming) 'On the (non)necessity of the hybrid category behavioural process'.

Bartlett, Tom (2008) 'Wheels within wheels or triangles within triangles: time and context in positioning theory'. In M. Fathali, Rom Harré Moghaddam and Naomi Lee (eds) *Global Conflict Resolution through Positioning Analysis.* New York: Springer.

Bartlett, Tom (2009) 'Legitimacy, comprehension and empathy: the importance of recontextualisation in intercultural negotiations'. *European Journal of English Studies* 13(2). Special Edition on Intercultural Negotiation.

Bartlett, Tom (2012a) *Hybrid Voices and Collaborative Change: Contextualising Positive Discourse Analysis.* London and New York: Routledge.

Bartlett, Tom (2012b) 'Lay metalanguage on grammatical variation and neutrality in Wikipedia's entry for Che Guevara'. *Text and Talk* 32(6).

Bauman, Richard and Briggs, Charles L. (1990) 'Poetics and performance as critical perspectives on language and social life'. *Annual Review of Anthropology* 19: 59–88.

Bednarek, Monika (2006) 'Epistemological positioning and evidentiality in English news discourse: a text-driven approach'. *Text and Talk* 26(6): 635–60.

Bernstein, Basil (1971) *Class, Codes and Control, Volume 1: Theoretical Studies towards a Sociology of Language Learning.* London and Boston: Routledge and Kegan Paul.

Bernstein, Basil (2000) (Revised Edition [1996]) *Pedagogy, Symbolic Control and Identity: Theory, Research, Critique.* Lanham, Boulder, CO, New York and Oxford: Rowman and Littlefield Publishers Inc.

Berry, Margaret (1996) 'What is theme? A(nother) personal view'. In M. Berry, C. Butler, R. P. Fawcett and Guowen Huang (eds) *Meaning and Form: Systemic Functional Interpretations.* New Jersey: Ablex.

Blommaert, J. (2005) *Discourse: A Critical Introduction.* Cambridge: Cambridge University Press.

Bourdieu, Pierre (1977) 'The economics of linguistic exchanges'. In *Social Science Information* 16 (6): 645–68.

Bourdieu, Pierre (1991) *Language and Symbolic Power*. Cambridge: Polity Press.

Brazil, David (1995) *A Grammar of Speech*. Oxford: Oxford University Press.

Brown, Penelope and Levinson, Stephen C. (1987) *Politeness*. Cambridge: Cambridge University Press.

Cloran, C. (2010) 'Rhetorical unit analysis and Bakhtin's chronotope'. *Functions of Language* 17(1): 29–70.

Coffin, C. and O'Halloran, K. A. (2006) 'The role of APPRAISAL and corpora in detecting covert evaluation'. *Functions of Language* 13(1): 77–110.

Fairclough, Norman (1992) *Language and Social Change*. Cambridge: Polity Press.

Fairclough, Norman (2001) (2nd edn) *Language and Power*. London: Longman.

Fairclough, Norman (2003) *Analysing Discourse: Textual Analysis for Social Research*. London and New York: Routledge.

Fawcett, R. P. (1999) 'On the subject of the Subject in English: two positions on its meaning (and on how to test for it)'. In *Functions of Language* 6(2): 243–73.

Fawcett, R. P. (2003) 'The many types of "theme" in English: their semantic systems and their functional syntax' (115 pp.). Available from the Systemic Paper Archive at micko@wagsoft.com.

Fawcett, R. P. (2007) 'Auxiliary extensions: six new elements for describing English'. In R. Hasan, C. Matthiessen and J. J. Webster (eds) *Continuing Discourse on Language: A Functional Perspective*. London and Oakville, CA: Equinox.

Foucault, M. (1972) *The Archaeology of Knowledge*. New York: Pantheon.

Halliday, M. A. K. (1978) *Language as Social Semiotic: The Social Interpretation of Language and Meaning*. Baltimore, MD: University Park Press.

Halliday, M. A. K. (2002) *On Grammar: Volume 1 of the Collected Works of Michael Halliday*. London and New York: Continuum.

Halliday, M. A. K. and Greaves, W. S. (2008) *Intonation in the Grammar of English*. London: Equinox.

Halliday, M. A. K. and Hasan, R. (1976) *Cohesion in English*. London and New York: Longman.

Halliday, M. A. K. and Hasan, R. (1985) *Language, Context and Text: Language in a Social-Semiotic Perspective*. Victoria: Deakin University Press.

Halliday, M. A. K. and Matthiessen, C. M. I. M. (2004) (3rd edn) *An Introduction to Functional Grammar*. London: Hodder Arnold.

Harré, Rom and Van Langenhove, Luk (eds) (1999) *Positioning Theory*. Oxford and Malden, MA: Blackwell.

Hasan, R. (1995) 'The conception of context in text'. In P. Fries and M. Gregory (eds) *Discourse in Society: Systemic Functional Perspectives. Meaning and Choice in Language: Studies for Michael Halliday*. Westport, CT and London: Ablex.

Hasan, R. (1996) 'Semantic networks: a tool for the analysis of meaning'. In C. Cloran, D. Butt and G. Williams (eds) *Ways of Saying, Ways of Meaning: Selected Papers of Ruqaiya Hasan* (pp. 104–131). London: Cassell.

Hasan, R. (2009) 'The place of context in a Systemic Functional Model'. In M. A. K. Halliday and J. J. Webster (eds) *The Continuum Companion to Systemic Functional Linguistics*. London and New York: Continuum.

Hasan, R. (in press) 'Choice taken in the context of realization'. In L. Fontaine, T. Bartlett and G. O'Grady (eds) *Systemic Functional Linguistics: Exploring Choice*. Cambridge: Cambridge University Press.

Hasan, R. and Cloran, C. (1990) 'A sociolinguistic interpretation of everyday talk between mothers and children'. In M. A. K. Halliday, J. Gibbons and H. Nichols (eds) *Learning, Keeping and Using Language: Volume 1* (pp. 67–100). Amsterdam: John Benjamins.

Hasan, R., Matthiessen, C. and Webster, J. J. (eds) (2007) *Continuing Discourse on Language: A Functional Perspective: Volume 2* (pp. 921–52). London and Oakville, CA: Equinox.

Hymes, D. (1996) *Ethnography, Linguistics, Narrative Inequality: Towards an Understanding of Voice*. London: Taylor and Francis.

Jones, Owen (2012) *Chavs: The Demonization of the Working Class*. London: Verso.

Kress, G. and Van Leeuwen, T. (2001) *Multimodal Discourse: The Modes and Media of Contemporary Communication*. Arnold: London.

McCarthy, M. (2000) 'Mutually captive audiences'. In J. Coupland (ed.) *Small Talk* (pp. 84–109). Harlow: Longman.

Martin, J. R. (1992) *English Text: System and Structure*. Philadelphia, PA and Amsterdam: John Benjamins.

Martin, J. R. and Rose, David (2003) *Working with Discourse: Meaning above the Clause*. London and New York: Continuum.

Martin, J. R. and White, P. R. R. (2005) *The Language of Evaluation: Appraisal in English*. Basingstoke: Palgrave Macmillan.

Martin, J. R., Matthiessen, C. M. I. M. and Painter, Clare (1997) *Working with Functional Grammar*. London, New York, Sydney and Auckland: Arnold.

O'Grady, Gerard (2010) *A Grammar of Spoken English Discourse: The Intonation of Increments*. London and New York: Continuum.

O'Halloran, K. A. and Coffin, C. (2004) 'Checking overinterpretation and underinterpretation: help from corpora in Critical Linguistics'. In C. Coffin, A. Hewings and K. A. O'Halloran (eds) *Applying English Grammar: Functional and Corpus Approaches*. London: Hodder-Arnold.

Sarangi, S. (2010) 'Reconfiguring self/identity/status/role: the case of professional role performance in healthcare encounters'. *Journal of Applied Linguistics and Professional Practice* 7(1): 75–95.

Sarangi, S. (2011) 'Role hybridity in professional practice'. In S. Sarangi, V. Polese, G. Caliendo (eds) *Genre(s) on the Move: Hybridization and Discourse Change in Specialized Communication*. Naples: Edizioni Scientifiche Italiane.

Tench, Paul (1996) *The Intonation Systems of English*. London: Cassell.

Thompson, G. (2007) 'Unfolding theme: the development of clausal and textual perspectives on theme'. In R. Hasan, C. Matthiessen and J. J. Webster (eds) *Continuing Discourse on Language: A Functional Perspective* (pp. 671–96). London and Oakville, CA: Equinox.

Ventola, E. (1983) 'Contrasting schematic structures in service encounters'. *Applied Linguistics* 4(3): 242–58.

Watts, R. (2003) *Politeness*. Cambridge: Cambridge University Press.

Widdowson, H. G. (2004) *Text, Context, Pretext*. Blackwell: Oxford, Malden MA and Carlton, Australia.

Young, Lynne and Fitzgerald, Brigid (2006) *The Power of Language: How Discourse Influences Society*. London and Oakville, CA: Equinox.

INDEX